Corporate Finance
DeMYSTiFieD®

DeMYSTiFieD® Series

Accounting Demystified
Advanced Statistics Demystified
Algebra Demystified
Alternative Energy Demystified
ASP.NET 2.0 Demystified
Biology Demystified
Biotechnology Demystified
Business Calculus Demystified
Business Math Demystified
Business Statistics Demystified
C++ Demystified
Calculus Demystified
Chemistry Demystified
Commodities Demystified
Corporate Finance Demystified, 2e
Data Structures Demystified
Databases Demystified, 2e
Differential Equations Demystified
Digital Electronics Demystified
Electricity Demystified
Electronics Demystified
Environmental Science Demystified
Everyday Math Demystified
Financial Accounting Demystified
Financial Planning Demystified
Financial Statements Demystified
Forensics Demystified
Genetics Demystified
Grant Writing Demystified
Hedge Funds Demystified
Human Resource Management Demystified
Intermediate Accounting Demystified
Investing Demystified, 2e
Java Demystified
JavaScript Demystified
Lean Six Sigma Demystified
Linear Algebra Demystified

Macroeconomics Demystified
Management Accounting Demystified
Marketing Demystified
Math Proofs Demystified
Math Word Problems Demystified
Mathematica Demystified
Matlab Demystified
Microbiology Demystified
Microeconomics Demystified
Nanotechnology Demystified
OOP Demystified
Operating Systems Demystified
Options Demystified
Organic Chemistry Demystified
Pharmacology Demystified
Physics Demystified
Physiology Demystified
Pre-Algebra Demystified
Precalculus Demystified
Probability Demystified
Project Management Demystified
Public Speaking and Presentations Demystified
Quality Management Demystified
Real Estate Math Demystified
Robotics Demystified
Sales Management Demystified
Six Sigma Demystified, 2e
SQL Demystified
Statistical Process Control Demystified
Statistics Demystified
Technical Analysis Demystified
Technical Math Demystified
Trigonometry Demystified
UML Demystified
Visual Basic 2005 Demystified
Visual C# 2005 Demystified
XML Demystified

The Demystified Series publishes over 125 titles in all areas of academic study. For a complete list of titles, please visit www.mhprofessional.com.

Corporate
Finance
DeMYSTiFieD®

Troy A. Adair, Jr.

New York   Chicago   San Francisco   Lisbon   London   Madrid   Mexico City
Milan   New Delhi   San Juan   Seoul   Singapore   Sydney   Toronto

3 4 5 6 7 8 9 10   QFR/QFR   1 9 8 7 6 5 4 3

ISBN   978-0-07-174907-7
MHID   0-07-174907-1

This publication is designed to provide accurate and authoritative information in regard to
the subject matter covered. It is sold with the understanding that the publisher is not
engaged in rendering legal, accounting, securities trading, or other professional services. If
legal advice or other expert assistance is required, the services of a competent professional
person should be sought.

*—From a Declaration of Principles Jointly Adopted by a Committee of the American Bar
Association and a Committee of Publishers and Associations*

Library of Congress Cataloging-in-Publication Data

Adair, Troy A. (Troy Alton), 1964-
    Corporate finance demystified / by Troy Adair. — 2nd ed.
      p.   cm.
    Includes index.
    ISBN 978-0-07-174907-7 (alk. paper)
    1. Corporations—Finance—Textbooks. I. Title.
    HG4026.A32   2011
    658.15—dc22   2010029979

McGraw-Hill books are available at special quantity discounts to use as premiums and sales
promotions or for use in corporate training programs. To contact a representative, please
e-mail us at bulksales@mcgraw-hill.com.

This book is printed on acid-free paper.

To my wife, Kieran, the love of my life, for her understanding and support throughout the writing of this book.

About the Author

Troy A. Adair, Jr., Ph.D., is the Director of Educational Initiatives for the Jay S. Sidhu School of Business and Leadership at Wilkes University in Wilkes-Barre, Pennsylvania. He has taught the introductory corporate finance course at Wilkes University, the University of Michigan, Alma College, Hofstra University, and Indiana University. He received his B.S. degree in Computers/Information Science from the University of Alabama at Birmingham, his M.B.A. from the University of North Dakota, and his Ph.D. in Finance from Indiana University. Dr. Adair has written articles on bank regulator self-interest, analyst earnings per share forecasting, and capital budgeting in continuous time, and is the author of *Excel Applications in Corporate Finance* and *Excel Applications in Investments*, and a coauthor of *Finance: Applications and Theory*.

Contents

Acknowledgments

The successful completion of this book is due mostly to the assistance of the very capable folks at McGraw-Hill, with special thanks going to Margie McAneny and Agatha Kim. Any errors, of course, are solely my responsibility.

Introduction

If you've just bought (or are thinking about buying) this book, then you're probably looking for help with a finance class you've already started, or else you're a practitioner who wants to study up on the subject on your own. I think you'll like this book, and I think you'll find it very helpful in explaining the concepts that give most students trouble. However, there are a couple of things you should realize as you start using it.

First, finance isn't easy, and it isn't the kind of topic that you can get just by reading. I've tried to make all the explanations and examples in this book as straightforward as possible, and I think I've made it a lot more user-friendly than just about any other book out there, but to get the most out of this book, you're going to *have* to work some problems. I'll be glad to help you do so (please see below), but you need to accept that just *reading* this book isn't going to be enough; you're going to have to *do* this stuff in order to get it down.

Second, please understand that this book isn't meant to be a comprehensive introduction to everything you ever wanted to know about corporate finance; instead, it's intended to be a concise, understandable introduction to the basic concepts of corporate finance that are the most widely applicable and most crucial to our intended audience. As such, it tends to "cut to the chase" fairly quickly, explaining things in an almost blunt manner that often ignores some of the extra "stuff" that other finance textbooks will cover. Practitioners will appreciate that, and students in corporate finance classes who are already being asked to read far too much background material will love it, but, if you don't fall into one of those two classes, please be aware that this book offers an intentionally designed bare-bones approach to corporate finance.

How to Use This Book

When you first start a finance class, you get the impression that finance is all about the math. Well, it is and it isn't: you *do* need to know how to do the math, and, for a lot of students, that can seem pretty overwhelming. This book tries to make learning the necessary math as straightforward as possible by giving you lots of tips and techniques, but they will be less than useless *if you don't practice them.*

To help you get that necessary practice, this book contains a quiz at the end of each chapter and a comprehensive, 100-question final exam at the end of the book. All of these are multiple-choice, and the questions are similar to the sorts of questions used in standardized tests. The best way to use each chapter quiz is to study the chapter until you're comfortable with the material and then take the entire quiz, rather than trying to solve selected problems as you study. The answers are listed in the back of the book, and you should stick with a chapter until you get most of the answers right.

However, as mentioned above, finance is also about *more* than the math. You may not believe that, particularly if you've just started a finance course, because most professors spend the first one-third to one-half of the course dwelling on the mathematical formulas, but the *real* focus of finance is on the problems and decisions that can be solved with the math.

Along those lines, there is one important point that needs to be made about this book: it *does not* contain recipes for solving *every* possible type of financial problem. It can't; no book can, because there is an almost infinite number of types of such problems. What it *does* do is try to give you the necessary insight into the relevant formulas and concepts so that you can figure out how to solve a problem from basic principles.

To get the most out of this approach, after you've gone through the in-chapter examples and solved the end-of-chapter quiz, sit back and ask yourself, "Now, what *other* types of problems can be solved using the math and concepts discussed in this chapter? How would the attributes of the variables/formulas/techniques we talked about affect those types of problems?"

This book is divided into five major sections. Depending upon the outline for your class, you may not need to cover some of the chapters in the last section, "Advanced Topics in Corporate Finance," and that's OK. However, you may also be tempted to skip some of the earlier material, particularly if you've had Time Value of Money in another class, or you have just finished accounting. ***Don't do it!*** The material in this book builds on a common body of knowledge as you go through it, and if you skip some of the seemingly simple stuff, you may find yourself floundering in the later chapters.

Note that I'm assuming that you've bought (or are considering buying) this book for a class in finance. If so, I recommend that you read each chapter in this text *after* you've read the relevant chapter in your course's textbook. This will help to clarify the concepts covered in your "main" textbook. And it will provide you with a second, complementary point of view on the concepts and techniques involved.

Now, I said above that I'd be glad to help you, and I will. If you have any questions or comments while working through this book, please e-mail me at asktroy@fin101.com, and I'll get back to you as soon as I can.

Part I

Introduction

chapter 1

What Is Corporate Finance?

CHAPTER OBJECTIVES

At the end of this chapter, the reader should be able to:

- Explain and illustrate the primary cash flows of finance
- Detail and explain the four major subfields of finance
- Compare and contrast the capital structure decision, the capital budgeting decision, and the dividend decision

When people first start studying finance, they usually have an idealized view (driven mainly by the movies they've seen and stories in the news about tycoons wheeling and dealing on Wall Street) of just what finance and financial markets are. They come to the class eager to start trading stocks, pricing options, transacting in the currency forwards, or simply cornering the market on orange juice futures. Even if they're lucky enough to have an introduction to finance which presents them with the correct "big picture," they're left feeling a little put out when they realize that the corporate finance they'll be studying is (in their initial opinion, at least) the least sexy subfield of finance.

To prove this to yourself, wait until we've covered the four different subfields of finance below, then make a list of every movie involving finance that you've ever seen and divide the list up by the subfield most closely associated with each movie: corporate finance films are few and far between.

In this chapter, we'll start out with the big picture first, making sure we know what finance is in the context of a diagram describing investment cash flows in our economy. Next, we'll use this same diagram to describe the different subfields of finance along with the major problems and decisions faced by each subfield. Then we'll focus more specifically on the problems and decisions of corporate finance, wrapping up with a discussion of why corporate finance is arguably the most important subtopic, and the one that you *should* study first.

What Is Finance?

To understand what finance is, let's envision the economy as being composed of four types of people, where the types are defined based upon whether the people have "extra" money to invest in speculative ventures and/or whether they have potentially lucrative ideas of their own (or the time to implement them):

1. People with no extra money and no ideas
2. People with extra money but no ideas (or no time to implement any ideas)
3. People with ideas but not enough money
4. People with both ideas and extra money

Of these four types, Type 1 doesn't really play a direct part in finance. These people have just enough money to cover their own needs, and they have no ideas or time for investing in potential projects even if they did.

We also won't normally talk much about Type 4. These people are interesting enough, but the problems and decisions that they face tend to be only a subset of those seen in the interaction between Type 2 and Type 3, where we will focus our attention.

In such an economy, Type 2 and Type 3 can enter into a mutually beneficial agreement, in which those of Type 2 lend their extra money to those of Type 3, who will in turn invest that money in ventures or "projects," using the potential proceeds from those projects to repay those of Type 2.

In our economy, those in Type 2 will often be individual investors, but they may also include such entities as venture capital funds, retirement funds, or insurance companies, all of which will typically have an excess of cash that they need to invest. To simplify our discussion, we will use the term *investors* to refer to any of these Type 2 entities.

Similarly, although Type 3 may include individual entrepreneurs or government organizations formed to foster economic growth, we typically tend to think of it as being primarily composed of companies, many of which have employees or divisions whose primary job is to think up new money-making products or services; in large corporations, such divisions are usually referred to as the research and development, or R&D, division. Again, so as to further simplify our discussion, we will use the specific term *companies* to refer to any Type 3 entities.

This mutually beneficial agreement between investors and companies is shown in Figure 1-1.

Now, in the real world, the repayment of the investors is complicated by the presence of taxes and by the fact that the company may need to reinvest some of the proceeds of the projects to continue operations, so actual cash flows tend to more closely resemble those shown in Figure 1-2.

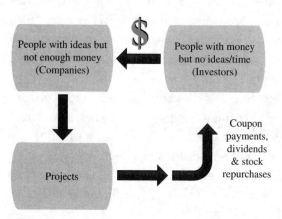

FIGURE 1-1 · The primary cash flows of finance.

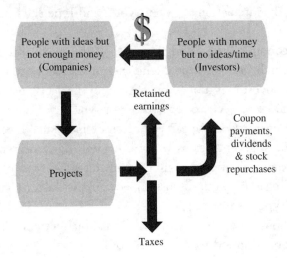

FIGURE 1-2 · The complete cash flows of finance.

The study of this resulting system of cash flows is what finance is all about.

The arrows in Figure 1-2 correspond to decisions or choices that the various participants in this system must make, and we can visualize the various subfields of finance by considering the perspectives from which those decisions must be made.

The Subfields of Finance

For example, consider the decisions faced by one of the investors whose perspective is indicated by the box shown in Figure 1-3. They have to decide which company or companies to invest in, what form (for example, buying stocks, bonds, and the like) that investment will take, and in what manner they wish to be repaid. Looking at these decisions from this perspective is called the study of investments.

Companies face decisions concerning how to raise capital, what projects to invest in, and how to go about paying investors back. Looking at these decisions from their perspective, as shown in Figure 1-4, is called the study of corporate finance (or, sometimes, "financial management").

There are two other perspectives that one can take when examining this system of cash flows: one is that of the financial institutions and markets

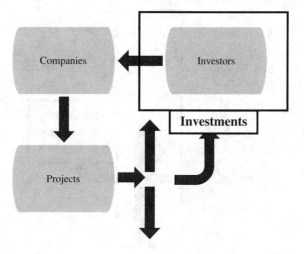

FIGURE 1-3 • Investments.

(see Figure 1-5), which exist for the sole purpose of facilitating this flow of funds between the investors and the companies.

The final subtopic of finance is one that considers the entire system of cash flows, but in a setting where the investors, companies, and/or projects involved are in different countries, as shown in Figure 1-6.

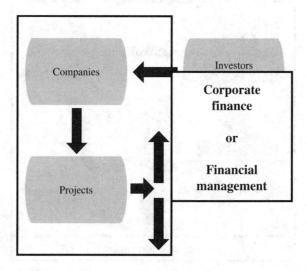

FIGURE 1-4 • Corporate finance.

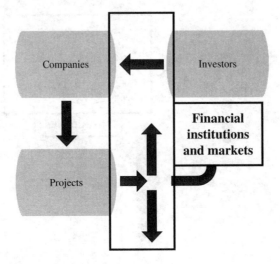

FIGURE 1-5 · Financial institutions and markets.

Technically speaking, this study of international finance probably shouldn't be considered a separate subfield, but rather a group of situations best considered as part of the other three subfields. However, it's been a relatively recent addition to both the major financial textbooks and to curriculums in

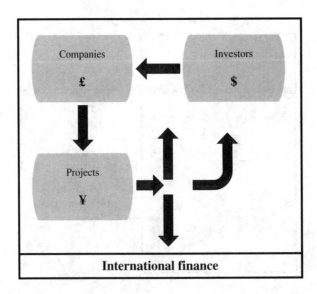

FIGURE 1-6 · International finance.

finance departments around the country; in both cases, the easiest approach to covering this was to treat it as a separate subfield of finance, and so it remains today.

The Parts of Corporate Finance

This approach of visualizing the parts of finance by taking different perspectives on this diagram can even be further extended to the areas within each subfield. For example, there are three arrows or a group of arrows within or interacting with the corporate finance perspective shown in Figure 1-4. These correspond to the three major types of decisions faced by companies' financial managers, which are shown in Figure 1-7.

Now, we can't just call these decisions by these names, of course—that would make it too simple and would drastically reduce the consulting fees that we can charge. So, instead, we have to give them the more impressive-sounding names shown in Figure 1-8.

See, aren't these terms much more impressive (even though they do mean exactly the same things)?

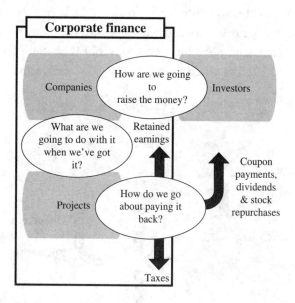

FIGURE 1-7 · Major decisions of corporate finance.

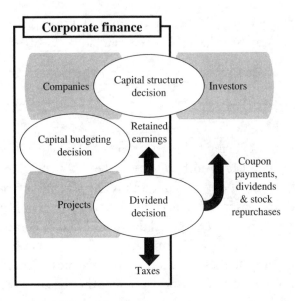

FIGURE 1-8 · Formal names of corporate finance decisions.

So, Why Is This So Complicated?

The story underlying the system of cash flows is a little more complicated than we've made it sound so far. In particular, investors know exactly how much they're going to pay for a stock or a bond in a company, but they don't know how much they're going to get back or when they'll receive it, as shown in Figure 1-9.

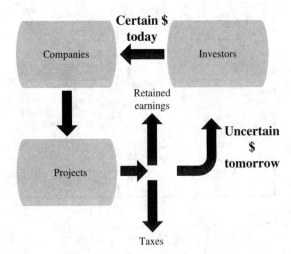

FIGURE 1-9 · Comparison of risks and timing of inflows and outflows for investors.

Why Are We Studying Corporate Finance?

Later on in this book, we'll be covering the formulas for valuing stock and bonds, but simple versions of these would look like:

$$\text{Price}_{\text{bond}} = \sum_{t=1}^{n} \frac{\text{coupon}}{(1+r_{\text{bond}})^t} + \frac{\text{face value}}{(1+r_{\text{bond}})^n}$$

$$\text{Price}_{\text{Stock}} = \sum_{t=1}^{\infty} \frac{\text{dividend}_t}{(1+r_{\text{stock}})^t}$$

Don't worry about the variables or the math; just notice that each of these equations contains an "=" sign, as will all of the other equations that we will discuss for valuing these and other *financial assets*, such as options, futures contracts, and so on.

These are the formulas that are used most heavily in the studies of investments and financial institutions and markets; what the "=" sign indicates is that, in the financial markets, where these financial assets trade, "what you get is (on average, and taking compensation for risk into account) exactly equal to what you paid for it."

On the other hand, in the capital budgeting area of corporate finance, we'll be using decision rules that look like this:

Accept the project if:
NPV > 0
MIRR > 0
Discounted Payback < Maximum Allowable Disc. Payback

Note that these equations have < or > signs. Why? Because that area of corporate finance deals with *nonfinancial assets*, assets that trade in physical markets and that have properties of uniqueness that result in potential monopoly power.

That's right—while the goal in investments and the other more photogenic subfields of finance is to more or less break even, the goal in corporate finance is to ensure that "what you get is (on average, and taking compensation for risk into account) equal to MORE THAN what you paid for it."

QUIZ

1. In finance, people with more money than they need for current consumption, but no time to undertake additional money-making projects, would be considered to be:

    A. Type 1
    B. Type 2
    C. Type 3
    D. Type 4

2. What is the more formal name used for describing the corporate finance decision concerning how to raise the money?

    A. The capital structure decision
    B. The capital budgeting decision
    C. The dividend decision
    D. The retained earnings decision

3. Which of the following statements concerning the cash flows of finance best describes why the study of corporate finance is so difficult?

    A. Both the cash flows to the firm and those from the firm are uncertain
    B. The cash flows from the firm back to investors occur at the same time as the cash flows from investors to the firm
    C. All the cash flows from the firm must be converted to domestic currency amounts using currency exchange rates
    D. The cash flows from the firm to investors are both uncertain and delayed, relative to their purchase of securities in the firm

4. The goal of corporate finance is to ensure that:

    A. What you get is what you pay for
    B. What you get is more than what you pay for
    C. What you get is less than what you pay for
    D. Stocks and bonds for the same firm will have equal values

5. What is the more formal name used for describing the corporate finance decision concerning how the firm should pay back investors?

    A. The capital structure decision
    B. The capital budgeting decision
    C. The dividend decision
    D. The retained earnings decision

6. The decision concerning which firms to buy stock or bonds in is part of the study of:

    A. Investments
    B. Corporate finance
    C. Financial institutions and markets
    D. International finance

7. **A movie about a stockbroker who aided investors in picking which firms to invest in would most likely involve which subfield of finance?**

    A. Investments

    B. Financial institutions and markets

    C. Corporate finance

    D. International finance

8. **A movie about a dashing young corporate manager choosing the best way to pay back the investors in his firm would most likely involve which subfield of finance?**

    A. Investments

    B. Financial institutions and markets

    C. Corporate finance

    D. International finance

9. **Investors are best thought of as:**

    A. People with ideas but not enough money

    B. People with both ideas and extra money

    C. People with no extra money and no ideas

    D. People with extra money but no ideas (or no time to implement any ideas)

10. **Capital budgeting decision rules in corporate finance are expected to choose projects that are worth more than they cost because capital budgeting projects:**

    A. Involve assets with potential monopoly power

    B. Are not subject to the same oversight as the sale of stocks and bonds to the public

    C. Take place in competitive markets

    D. Will always have both economies of scale and economies of scope

chapter 2

Setting the Stage

CHAPTER OBJECTIVES

At the end of this chapter, the reader should be able to:

- Identify the basic forms of business organization and list the major advantages and disadvantages of each

- Discriminate between appropriate and inappropriate goals for financial managers

- Explain how agency relationships can potentially lead to agency conflicts

In every corporate finance text, there's some background information that needs to be covered before you get into the body of the material. The topics in this chapter provide critical background information for understanding the context in which financial decisions are made.

Basic Forms of Business Organization

There are two basic forms of business organization: those that are considered to be inseparable from the owners, such as *sole proprietorships* and *general partnerships*, and those that are considered to be entities in their own right, such as *corporations*. There are also some forms of businesses that are *hybrids*, exhibiting some characteristics in common with both major types, and we'll discuss those after we've detailed the significant differences between the two major types.

For financial purposes, there are two major attributes on which the basic forms differ: the personal liability of a business's owner(s) for the obligations of the firm, and the degree of taxation.

Sole proprietorships and partnerships require the owners to bear unlimited personal liability for the company's obligations, but have the advantage of having all earnings taxed only once, at the same level as the owners' other sources of income. This is usually referred to as *single taxation* to differentiate it from the tax situation of corporate shareholders.

Shareholders in corporations have limited liability for the obligations of the corporation; in most cases, the most that the shareholders can lose is the money that they paid for their shares to start with. However, the earnings of the corporation are subject to *double taxation*—being taxed once at the corporate level and again at the owners' personal level.

In fact, the degree of taxation can sometimes be more than double for the owners of a corporation. If shares in one corporation are owned by another, then earnings will be taxed in the first corporation, the second corporation, and again at the owners' personal tax level. In the United States, the government has taken steps to mitigate this triple taxation, requiring the second corporation to pay taxes on only 30 percent of the dividends it receives from the first corporation, but each dollar of the first corporation's earnings is still taxed approximately 2.3 times before the owners get to spend it. (Note that this problem does not apply to entities such as mutual funds, which are allowed to "pass through" all income to their shareholders.)

There are also several forms of business organizations that allow owners the benefit of single taxation while simultaneously providing limited liability. The most common of these are *Limited Liability Corporations/Partnerships* (LLCs/LLPs) and S Corporations, which are corporations that have elected single taxation by applying to be taxed under Chapter S of the Internal Revenue Code.

In both cases, there are effective limitations that prevent these organizations from being "too big." S Corporations are explicitly limited to no more than 100 shareholders and only certain individuals and entities are allowed to be shareholders, while LLCs face implicit size constraints due to their inability to be publicly traded.

These explicit and implicit restrictions on the size of such hybrid organizations are due to the government's reason for allowing them to exist in the first place: the government wants to encourage the creation and sustainability of small businesses.

Due to their size and complexity, corporations tend to have the most complicated problems and decisions of all the types of business organizations. In this text, as in most other corporate finance books, we will take the approach that, if you learn how to handle the most complicated problems, then other situations involving less complexity will be relatively simple to handle. Accordingly, we will usually assume in our discussions throughout the rest of this text that we are dealing with a corporation.

Goal of the Financial Manager

The major goal of a corporation's financial manager should be to *maximize the value per share of existing stock*, though "maximizing shareholder wealth" or "maximizing stock price" are other common ways to state this same goal.

As we'll see, this goal also motivates the capital-budgeting decision rules that we discussed briefly in the last chapter—firms will only accept projects if they add value to the firm.

There are several inappropriate goals that students often confuse with this goal. Though finance texts typically list these inappropriate goals, they seldom give any detail on exactly *why* they're not appropriate. Let's see if we can shed some light on the inappropriate goals that tend to confuse students the most:

- *Maximize profits,* or the equivalent *maximize net income,* is an inappropriate goal for a couple of different reasons. First, as we will see later in this text, "net income" is an accounting measure that really doesn't do a good job of measuring how much money the firm is actually making. Second, since net income is calculated for lots of different periods, when you say that you want to maximize profits, which profit(s) are you talking about? Next quarter's? Next year's? The profits five years from now? Sure, you could cheat and say that you want to maximize all of them, but that isn't usually a reasonable choice; instead, you usually face a trade-off, where maximizing profits in the short term often involves less-than-optimal long-term profits, and vice versa.

- *Minimize costs* is an inappropriate goal because there is an obviously bad way to accomplish this—if you stop doing business, then costs will be zero.

- *Maximize market share* is an inappropriate goal because there is also an obviously bad way to accomplish this—if you give your product away for free, you will get all the market you can supply (until you go out of business).

Agency Relationships and Conflicts

Whenever one party hires another to act on its behalf, you have an *agency relationship*, where the hired party is acting as the agent for the hiring party, usually referred to as the *principal*. There are several such agency relationships in finance.

The first, and most obvious, is the relationship between the shareholders and the managers of a corporation. In the last chapter, we used a system of cash flows to illustrate the ideas underlying finance and its subfields; if you'll remember, we started our discussion of that system by assuming that investors were a group of people who had some extra money but no ideas or time to implement those ideas. Well, if they don't have ideas of their own or time to act on such ideas, then they're obviously not going to be able to take a very active role in the management of the business that they're investing in, so they'll need to hire managers to act on their behalf.

In this agency relationship, the firm's managers are agents acting on the behalf of their principals, the firm's owners. However, there are other, simultaneous agency relationships in a firm that may involve either of these parties as principal or the agent.

For example, when a firm borrows money, the shareholders—who ultimately control the firm and have the final say with regard to firm decisions—are contractually obligated to act as agents on behalf of the lender, who is the principal in this relationship.

Likewise, the relationship between the managers and their workers is one in which the managers are usually seen as the principals relative to the workers' role as agents.

The reason that these agency relationships are so important is because they often lead to *agency conflicts*—situations where the personal goals of the agent are in conflict with the goals of their principal. For example, suppose that it's time for the manager of your corner coffee shop to get a new company car; the owners of the firm are expecting her to get an economical minivan, but she's really got her mind set on a BMW 760Li. While the BMW may make her a happier and more productive worker, is the improvement in her productivity really worth it to the firm's owners?

If she manages only a single coffee shop, the answer is probably no. But what if she's the district manager in charge of a number of coffee shops, or if she's the CEO of the entire chain? Then the answer may very well change. This line of reasoning also helps explain why some firms buy or lease corporate jets for their executives, or provide company cell phones for their sales force, or have free cappuccino bars for their employees, and so forth.

There are two primary methods used to try to mitigate the impact of these agency conflicts, which we can equate to the carrot and the stick in the old fable.

The "carrot" usually takes the form of managerial stock or option ownership, which serves to directly align the goals of manager with those of the owners. The manager discussed earlier is probably less likely to buy the BMW if part of the purchase price will come out of her own pocket.

The "stick" usually involves the threat of some punitive action, which may either be direct or indirect. Considering our example again, the manager might be fired if she spent the extra $100,000 or so to buy the BMW.

In the corporate environment, even if the shareholders themselves don't take direct actions to stop management from taking too many such extravagant "perks," market forces will generally act to discourage management from overindulging. For example, if a firm's management is taking so many perks that it substantially reduces the firm's bottom line, then the firm will be a prime target for takeover attempts because the acquirer would be able to improve the firm's profitability simply by replacing the management or by stripping it of its perks.

QUIZ

1. Owners of which of the following forms of business organization will be subject to more than single taxation?
    A. Sole proprietorships
    B. General partnerships
    C. Limited liability partnerships
    D. Corporations

2. Suppose that a friend approaches you for advice on what form of business to start, and that she is asking you to help her choose between starting a sole proprietorship or forming a corporation. She also indicates that she is more concerned about personal liability than about double taxation. Which form of business organization would you recommend to her, and why?
    A. A corporation, because it would have double taxation and unlimited personal liability
    B. A sole propietorship, because it would have double taxation and unlimited personal liability
    C. A corporation, because it would have double taxation but no personal liability
    D. A sole proprietorship, because it would have double taxation but no personal liability

3. Assume that 100 of your closest friends want to start a new business. The business is expected to be quite profitable, but it does have a good deal of risk involved. If all of the 100 friends would like to minimize their personal liability while reducing taxes as much as possible, which of the following forms of business organization would you recommend to them?
    A. A partnership
    B. A corporation
    C. An S corporation
    D. A sole proprietorship

4. The primary goal of the financial manager should be to:
    A. Maximize profits
    B. Minimize costs
    C. Maximize the stock price
    D. Maximize market share

5. In the agency relationship between the shareholders and the managers of a corporation:
    A. Managers and shareholders are both principals
    B. Managers and shareholders are both agents
    C. Managers are the principals, and shareholders are the agents
    D. Managers are the agents, and shareholders are the principals

6. **Stock options help to mitigate agency problems between shareholders and managers by:**
   A. Aligning the interest of managers with those of shareholders
   B. Offering managers a stable, constant reward for a job well done
   C. Allowing shareholders to fire underperforming managers
   D. Diluting the ownership structure of the company

7. **Which of the following is an appropriate primary goal for a corporation's financial manager?**
   A. Maximize shareholder wealth
   B. Minimize the stock price
   C. Maximize the number of shares of stock
   D. Maximize the net income of the firm

8. **Shareholders act as:**
   A. Principals in their agency relationship with managers, but as agents in their agency relationship with lenders
   B. Agents in both their agency relationship with managers and their agency relationship with lenders
   C. Agents in their agency relationship with managers, but as principals in their agency relationship with lenders
   D. Principals in both their agency relationship with managers and their agency relationship with lenders

9. **The term "2.3 taxation," when used to refer to selected forms of business organizations, refers to a situation where:**
   A. Corporations collect sales tax from customers and pay taxes on corporate earnings
   B. Corporations pay taxes on corporate earnings, and investors pay taxes on the earnings paid out to them
   C. Corporations own shares in other corporations
   D. Taxes are paid by a corporation both on the interest it pays and on earnings

10. **The two major attributes on which the basic forms of business organization differ are:**
   A. Owners' personal liability and protection of the owners from litigation
   B. The degree of taxation and protection of the firm from product liability suits
   C. The size of the firm and the degree of taxation
   D. Owners' personal liability and the degree of taxation

chapter **3**

Accounting Statements and Cash Flows

CHAPTER OBJECTIVES

At the end of this chapter, the reader should be able to:

- Compare and contrast the intuition behind assets and liabilities in accounting versus the intuition in finance
- Explain the differences between current and fixed assets in terms of liquidity and profitability
- Calculate corporate tax bills and average corporate tax rates

In this chapter, we're going to go over the basic accounting statements, giving particular attention to the parts that are important to us as financial professionals, and taking great care to make sure that we know how those parts are constructed.

The Balance Sheet: Assets versus Liabilities

If you've had an introductory accounting class, you're familiar with the basic structure of the balance sheet, a sample of which is shown in Figure 3-1.

As we've come to expect, the assets are arrayed on the left side of the sheet, and the liabilities and equity accounts are shown on the right-hand side. This division between the two halves of the balance sheet is critical in both accounting and finance, but for very different reasons.

In most accounting classes, students are programmed to view the asset accounts as the "good things" and the liability accounts as the "bad things." Viewed one way, this mentality makes perfect sense: assets have value, and that value, if realized by either selling the assets or by running them to produce a product or service, can be used to pay off the debts represented by the liability accounts.

However, there's another way to view these two parts of the balance sheet, one that's more appropriate for someone making those value-maximizing decisions that we discussed in the previous chapter. Think of assets, not as potential

TMA INC.
Balance Sheets as of December 31, 2010 and 2011
($ in millions)

	2010	2011		2010	2011
Assets			**Liabilities and owners' equity**		
Current assets			Current liabilities		
Cash	$ 104	$ 160	Accounts payable	$ 232	$ 26
Accounts receivable	455	688	Notes payable	196	196
Inventory	553	555	Total	$ 428	$ 222
Total	$ 1112	$ 1403			
Fixed assets			Long-term debt	408	620
Net fixed assets	$ 1644	$ 1709	Owners' equity		
			Common stock and		
			paid-in surplus	600	600
			Retained earnings	1320	1670
			Total	$ 1920	$ 2270
			Total liabilities and		
Total assets	$ 2756	$ 3112	owners' equity	$ 2756	$ 3112

FIGURE 3-1 · Sample balance sheet.

sources of money as accountants do, but as something we have to buy in the first place; that is, as a sort of "sponge" that soaks up or *uses* the available cash of the firm. Likewise, don't think of a liability as something to be paid off, but instead think of how it came to exist on the books in the first place: *somebody lent you money or resources*, which meant that you didn't have to "foot the bill" for at least some of the assets.

Sort of a backward way of thinking about things, isn't it? But, if you realize that "maximizing value per share" is equivalent to using the owners' invested capital as efficiently as possible, it starts to make sense.

So, for the rest of this book, if we want to put ourselves in the mindset necessary to make optimal financial decisions, we have to get used to thinking in terms of assets being necessary evils, and of liabilities being the "good" part of the balance sheet.

The Balance Sheet: Short-Term versus Long-Term Accounts

Referring back to the balance sheet in Figure 3-1, we see that the next level of differentiation, after we divide its parts between assets and liabilities/owners' equity accounts, is between the short-term and long-term parts of each. For the assets side, it's best to think of this differentiation as pertaining to *liquidity*—the ability to convert an asset into cash quickly while still retaining a good deal of its value. *Current assets* tend to be more liquid, while long-term, or *fixed assets*, tend to be less liquid.

But there's a flip side to this issue of liquidity, too, one that we can think of in terms of profitability or productivity. Current assets are extremely liquid, but they don't usually yield a very high rate of return; fixed assets, on the other hand, tend to be relatively illiquid but typically offer a much higher rate of return. Because of this, well-run firms tend to keep as little capital tied up in current assets as possible. However, all firms have to keep at least *some* liquid assets, if for no other reason than that their creditors will eventually want to be paid back.

How much current assets is necessary? Well, it depends upon several factors, the chief one being how many liabilities have to be paid off in the near term—that is, the amount of *current* liabilities owed by the firm. Like current assets, current liabilities are obligations of the firm that need to be "turned into cash" (i.e., paid off) within the course of the next year, and one of the common approaches to determining whether a firm has enough current assets is to compare its level to that of current liabilities.

One of the simplest ways to make this comparison is to calculate the firm's *Net Working Capital* (NWC):

$$NWC = CA - CL$$

where CA = current assets
    CL = current liabilities

Intuitively, NWC measures the amount of excess current assets above and beyond the amount needed to repay current liabilities as they come due. Usually, we would expect NWC to be greater than zero for most healthy firms.

Why "greater than"? We just said that a well-run firm should keep as little assets as possible in the form of current assets, so shouldn't we have said "equal to"? No, for a couple of reasons:

- First, firms need to keep current assets such as inventory and accounts receivable both to attract customers and to pay back current liabilities; if the need to attract customers is great enough, then even a well-run firm may have more current assets than current liabilities.

- Second, though a firm usually knows exactly which current liabilities have to be paid off in the short term, there isn't any such certainty regarding which of the current assets are going to "turn into" cash in the same time span. You can't *make* customers buy your product, so any finished-goods inventory can't really be considered a "cash equivalent," and even some of your customers in your accounts receivable aren't going to pay you on time.

Of course, how much excess current assets are necessary for a firm will be a function of the types of products/services the firm offers, how popular they are, the production process used to produce them, the customers' attributes, and so on. For example, it seems reasonable to assume that Apple probably has proportionately much less capital invested in finished goods inventories for their iPod division than General Motors does for their *Sport Utility Vehicle* (SUV) division.

The Income Statement

The income statement purports to measure how much money a firm makes during a particular period of time. However, there are a couple of reasons that it doesn't actually do a good job of measuring this:

- First, the income statement is constructed using *Generally Accepted Accounting Principles* (GAAP), which dictate that revenues will be recognized at the time of the sale and that expenses will be "matched up" with sales, with the possible end result being that the accounting net income calculated in one period may include expenses that occurred in prior periods.

  To see why this is a problem, consider the income statement shown in Figure 3-2. Suppose that this firm actually produced all the goods that are sold during 2011 back in 2010, and that it didn't sell any items in 2011 until the last part of the year, when it sold them all on credit. This firm won't have actually received any money yet, even though it is going to be expected to pay taxes on those sales. Furthermore, the cost of goods sold is reducing the amount of 2011 taxable income, even though those expenses were actually incurred in 2010.

- Second, the income statement includes *noncash items* such as depreciation; these expenses, though counted against taxable income in this period, were probably actually incurred sometime prior to this year.

TMA INC.
2011 Income Statement
($ in millions)

Net sales	$	1602
Cost of goods sold		750
Depreciation		65
Earnings before interest and taxes	$	787
Interest paid		90
Taxable income	$	697
Taxes (35%)		244
Net income	$	453
Dividends	$ 103	
Addition to retained earnings	350	

FIGURE 3-2 · Sample income statement.

Taxes

Most finance textbooks will have a chart of corporate-tax rates as shown in Figure 3-3. Using this chart is fairly straightforward.

For example, if we take TMA's taxable income of $697,000,000 shown in Figure 3-2, we can calculate the year's tax bill as shown below:

$$
\begin{aligned}
\text{Tax} = \ &\$50,000 \times 15\% + (\$75,000 - \$50,000) \times 25\% \\
&+ (\$100,000 - \$75,000) \times 34\% \\
&+ (\$335,000 - \$100,000) \times 39\% \\
&+ (\$10,000,000 - \$335,000) \times 34\% \\
&+ (\$15,000,000 - \$10,000,000) \times 35\% \\
&+ (\$18,333,333 - \$15,000,000) \times 38\% \\
&+ (\$697,000,000 - \$18,333,333) \times 35\% \\
= \ &\$243,949,997.94
\end{aligned}
$$

However, if you know that you are going to be using this tax table frequently, you can save yourself some time by precalculating the cumulative tax bill at the top of each tax "bracket," as shown in Figure 3-4.

Once this is done, calculating a firm's tax bill will require a lot less math. For example, if we once again take TMA's taxable income of $697,000,000 and then note that it falls into the highest tax bracket, then we can use the fact that we already know the cumulative tax on all the lower brackets to calculate the tax bill as:

$$
\begin{aligned}
\text{Tax} &= \$6,416,664.49 + (\$697,000,000 - \$18,333,333) \times 35\% \\
&= \$243,949,997.94
\end{aligned}
$$

Taxable income			Tax rate
$	- -	50,000	15%
50,001	-	75,000	25%
75,001	-	100,000	34%
100,001	-	335,000	39%
335,001	-	10,000,000	34%
10,000,001	-	15,000,000	35%
15,000,001	-	18,333,333	38%
18,333,334	+		35%

FIGURE 3-3 · Corporate tax brackets in the United States.

Taxable income			Tax rate	Tax in bracket	Cumulative tax
$ -	-	50,000	0.15	$ 7,500.00	$ 7,500.00
50,001	-	75,000	0.25	$ 6,250.00	$ 13,750.00
75,001	-	100,000	0.34	$ 8,500.00	$ 22,250.00
100,001	-	335,000	0.39	$ 91,650.00	$ 113,900.00
335,001	-	10,000,000	0.34	$ 3,286,100.00	$ 3,400,000.00
10,000,001	-	15,000,000	0.35	$ 1,750,000.00	$ 5,150,000.00
15,000,001	-	18,333,333	0.38	$ 1,266,666.54	$ 6,416,666.54
18,333,334	+		0.35		

FIGURE 3-4 · Cumulative tax amounts.

We can also use this number, along with the amount of taxable income of the firm, to calculate the firm's *average tax rate*:

$$\text{Average tax rate} = \frac{\text{tax bill}}{\text{taxable income}}$$
$$= \frac{\$243,949,997.94}{\$697,000,000}$$
$$= 0.35, \text{ or } 35\%$$

Cash Flow From Assets

Most finance textbooks will define *Cash Flow From Assets* (CFFA) in two ways:

$$\text{CFFA} = \text{operating cash flow}$$
$$- \text{net capital spending}$$
$$- \text{changes in NWC}$$

and

$$\text{CFFA} = \text{cash flow to creditors}$$
$$+ \text{cash flow to stockholders}$$

The best way to view these two definitions is to think of the first as defining where cash flow *comes from*, and the second as detailing where it *goes to*.

When calculating CFFA from the first definition, there are several supporting calculations:

OCF = EBIT + depreciation − taxes

NCS = ending net fixed assets − beginning net fixed assets + depreciation

Changes in NWC = ending NWC − beginning NWC

Returning to our TMA example, these would be equal to:

OCF = $787 + $65 − $244 = $608 million

NCS = $1,709 − $1,644 + $65 = $130 million

Changes in NWC = ($1,403 − $222) − ($1,112 − $428) = $497 million

Giving us CFFA of:

CFFA = $608 − $130 − $497 = −$19 million

So this firm actually used more cash flow than it produced. Where did the $19 million in needed cash come from? Turning to the second equation for CFFA, and defining its parts as:

CF to creditors = interest paid − net new borrowing

CF to stockholders = dividends paid − net new equity raised

We see that

CF to creditors = $90 − ($620 − $408) = −$122 million

CF to stockholders = $103 − ($600 − $600) = $103 million

Giving us CFFA of:

CFFA = −$122 + $103 = −$19 million

That is, the $19 million cash flow was raised by selling more bonds; in fact, a total of $122 million worth of new bonds were sold, with the money raised from the sale of excess bonds ($122 − $19 = $103 million) being used to pay the dividend to shareholders.

QUIZ

1. **From a financial cash flow perspective, and assuming everything else held constant, which of the following changes to a firm's balance sheet would be a "good" thing, and why?**
   A. A firm *increasing assets*, because doing so frees up cash flow
   B. A firm *decreasing assets*, because doing so frees up cash flow
   C. A firm *increasing liabilities*, because doing so ties up cash flow
   D. A firm *decreasing liabilities*, because doing so ties up cash flow

2. **A firm with Net Working Capital less than zero has:**
   A. More capital invested in current assets than it has provided by current liabilities
   B. More fixed assets than current assets
   C. Less capital invested in current assets than it has provided by current liabilities
   D. Less fixed assets than current assets

3. **One of the criticisms of the income statement mentioned in this chapter is that it includes noncash items such as depreciation. Everything else held constant, what will be the effect of including depreciation when calculating the income statement versus just ignoring it?**
   A. Including depreciation will cause both the amount of taxes paid and the firm's net income to be higher than if depreciation were left out.
   B. Including depreciation will cause both the amount of taxes paid and the firm's net income to be lower than if depreciation were left out.
   C. Including depreciation will cause the amount of taxes paid to be higher and the firm's net income to be lower than if depreciation were left out.
   D. Including depreciation will cause the amount of taxes paid to be lower and the firm's net income to be higher than if depreciation were left out.

4. **Your company has taxable income this year of $7,500,000 and faces the corporate tax schedule provided earlier in this chapter. What will be your company's tax bill?**
   A. $2,550,000
   B. $2,850,000
   C. $3,250,000
   D. $3,850,000

5. **Your company has taxable income this year of $7,500,000 and faces the corporate tax schedule provided earlier in this chapter. What will be your company's average tax rate?**
   A. 34.00%
   B. 34.45%
   C. 24.43%
   D. 28.19%

AHS INC.
2011 Income Statement
($ in millions)

Net sales	$	9625
Cost of goods sold		5225
Depreciation		1890
Earnings before interest and taxes	$	2510
Interest paid		850
Taxable income	$	1660
Taxes (35%)		581
Net income	$	1079
Dividends	$	679
Addition to retained earnings		400

FIGURE 3-5 · AHS income statement

Please use the income statement and balance sheets for AHS shown in Figures 3-5 and 3-6 to answer the next three questions:

6. **What was this firm's net capital spending for 2011?**

    A. –$1,890
    B. $2,420
    C. $3,215
    D. $4,310

7. **What was this firm's change in net working capital for 2011?**

    A. –$941
    B. –$200
    C. $366
    D. $719

AHS INC.
Balance Sheets as of December 31, 2010 and 2011
($ in millions)

Assets		2010		2011	Liabilities and owners' equity		2010		2011
Current assets					Current liabilities				
Cash	$	1455	$	260	Accounts payable	$	1150	$	2863
Accounts receivable		2460		3975	Notes payable		2600		1628
Inventory		1405		885	Total	$	3750	$	4491
Total	$	5320	$	5120					
Fixed assets					Long-term debt		7000		7600
Net fixed assets	$	19,300	$	21,720	Owners' equity				
					Common stock and				
					paid-in surplus		5500		5700
					Retained earnings		8370		9049
					Total	$	13,870	$	14,749
					Total liabilities and				
Total assets	$	24,620	$	26,840	owners' equity	$	24,620	$	26,840

FIGURE 3-6 · AHS balance sheets

8. **What was this firm's cash flow to creditors for 2011?**
   A. -$50
   B. $50
   C. $150
   D. $250

9. **Your company has taxable income this year of $15,500,000 and faces the corporate tax schedule provided earlier in this chapter. What will be your company's marginal tax rate?**
   A. 34.00%
   B. 34.45%
   C. 24.43%
   D. 38.00%

10. **Under Generally Accepted Accounting Principles (GAAP), a firm that made a product in 2011 and then sold it in 2012 would:**
    A. Show both the revenues and the expenses in 2011
    B. Show both the revenues and the expenses in 2012
    C. Show the revenues in 2011 and the expenses in 2012
    D. Show the revenues in 2012 and the expenses in 2011

chapter 4

Common-Size, Common-Base Year, and Ratio Analysis

CHAPTER OBJECTIVES

At the end of this chapter, the reader should be able to:

- Explain how ratio analysis involves both summarization and standardization
- Construct common-size financial statements
- Construct common-base year financial statements
- Construct and interpret commonly used financial ratios

Though they're not usually presented as such in most finance texts, all of the topics covered in this chapter arguably fall into the category of *ratio analysis*, as all involve dividing one or more financial variables by another. Accordingly, the first thing we'll cover in this chapter will be the intuition concerning why ratios in general are useful for financial analysis, after which we'll first discuss how this intuition extends to the fairly specific types of ratio analysis represented by common-size and common-base year analyses. Finally, we'll wrap up this chapter with discussions of each of the common categories that are typically used to classify the more general types of ratios.

The General Goal of Ratio Analysis: Summarization

Ratios, by dividing one value by another, *summarize* the relationship between their numerator and denominator. This summarization intentionally loses some information concerning the *absolute* magnitudes of the numerator and denominator in order to provide a value that measures the difference in *relative* magnitudes of each.

This measurement of relative difference in the sizes of the two components of the ratios is often more important, or more insightful, than the values of the components themselves. However, the value of the ratio by itself is often not enough; we also need an expected, or *benchmark*, value to compare it with.

For example, suppose that we were examining firms in an industry where sales figures generally fall into the range of $100,000 to $1,000,000 per year, and that those same firms usually have from $25,000 to $250,000 invested in fixed assets. Assuming that these two variables are unrelated (which is unreasonable, but we'll correct that in just a moment), we could conceivably expect to see values for the *fixed asset turnover ratios* (sales/net fixed assets, covered in more depth later in this chapter in the section on asset utilization ratios) ranging from $100,000/$250,000 = 0.4 to $1,000,000/$25,000 = 40.

However, common sense would seem to suggest that these two variables should be pretty highly correlated with one another, particularly for firms within the same industry like this, so that we would normally expect to see the firms with $100,000 in sales also being the ones with $25,000 in fixed assets, and those with $1,000,000 in sales being the ones with $250,000 in fixed assets. In both cases, this would result in fixed asset turnover ratio values of 4 ($100,000/$25,000 = $1,000,000/$250,000 = 4).

Let's assume that we double-checked our intuition and found that, in this industry, the average fixed asset turnover was, sure enough, very close to 4.

The underlying expectation for this industry would therefore be that each $1 of fixed assets should typically be expected to support or generate $4 in sales per year. If we then observed a firm in this industry that *did* have a fixed asset turnover ratio of 40, we would be pretty surprised and would probably want to investigate further.

"Good" and "Bad" Values for Ratios

When we do compute a ratio value for a firm that is significantly different from the benchmark value, it will usually be tempting to immediately classify that value as "good" or "bad"; for a couple of very good reasons, you'll want to try to avoid this temptation until you've had a chance to investigate the reasons underlying the difference.

First of all, a firm's ratio that is higher than the benchmark is not always going to be a "good" thing; in the example we just covered using the fixed asset turnover ratio, it probably was, but for other ratios such as days' sales in receivables (see later), a relatively high value will be a bad thing.

Second, even if the firm's ratio value is in the range normally viewed as "good," we'll see that this can be due to both "good" and "bad" reasons. For a particular ratio, figuring out what the possible "good" and "bad" reasons might be is usually as simple as reminding ourselves that, "The ratio might be big because the top is big, or it might be big because the bottom is little."

For example, let's return again to the firm with a fixed asset turnover ratio of 40 in an industry where the average value is around 4. The possible reasons for this firm having such an atypical ratio value can be boiled down into two general categories: either (1) this firm spends about as much as its competitors do on fixed assets and just gets more use out of them, or else (2) the firm doesn't spend anywhere near as much as its competitors do on fixed assets.

Obviously, case (1) here is the "good" reason for this firm having a relatively high fixed asset turnover value and case (2) is the "bad" reason.

So, once we identify an atypical ratio value, how do we tell the difference between cases (1) and (2)? Well, usually by looking to see if comparison of additional, associated ratio values for the firm to their benchmarks can give us enough information to figure out which case holds true. For example, if the firm with a high fixed asset turnover value *also* had a value for "fixed assets/total assets" close to the industry average, we would probably lean more toward case (1) holding true.

An Additional Effect of Ratio Analysis: Standardization

In both of the previous sections, note that we've been implicitly assuming that the relationship measured by a ratio, the relative difference in the sizes of the top and bottom of the ratio, is comparable across firms. This assumption doesn't hold *perfectly* true in the real world, but empirical evidence seems to indicate that it does hold at least *approximately* most of the time; it certainly seems to make more sense to use a firm's fixed asset coverage ratio as a basis for comparison to the prevailing industry norms than it would to use either the firm's sales figures or fixed asset balances by themselves.

In effect, when we do compare ratio values across firms like this, we're basically assuming that the largest source of any differences in the "parts" of the ratios being compared is due to differences in the firms' respective sizes: a large firm will obviously be expected to have more sales *and* more fixed assets than a small firm, and so forth. Therefore, when we construct a ratio for the large firm, the "bigness" of the numbers in the numerator will cancel out the "bigness" of the numbers in the denominator; the same will also hold true for ratios computed for small firms, allowing us to compare ratio value across firms of different sizes.

Common-Size Statement Analysis

To constrict common-size financial statements, we simply divide each item in a financial statement by what we expect to be the largest number in that statement in order to get a percentage value. For balance sheets, the largest number is usually the total assets entry, so we use that as the divisor; for income statements, we use net sales.

The balance sheets for TMA that we discussed in the last chapter are shown in Figure 4-1. Converting these balance sheets to common-size statements yield the statements shown in Figure 4-2.

TMA's income statement and a common-size income statement are also shown in Figure 4-3 and Figure 4-4, respectively.

As you can see, the common-size statements would be especially handy for comparing TMA's financials to those of another company, and can even come in

TMA INC.							
Balance Sheets as of December 31, 2010 and 2011							
($ in millions)							
	2010	**2011**			**2010**	**2011**	
Assets				**Liabilities and owners' equity**			
Current assets				Current liabilities			
Cash	$ 104	$ 160		Accounts payable	$ 232	$ 26	
Accounts receivable	455	688		Notes payable	196	196	
Inventory	553	555		Total	$ 428	$ 222	
Total	$ 1112	$ 1403					
Fixed assets				Long-term debt	408	620	
Net fixed assets	$ 1644	$ 1709		Owners' equity			
				Common stock and paid-in surplus	600	600	
				Retained earnings	1320	1670	
				Total	$ 1920	$ 2270	
Total assets	$ 2756	$ 3112		Total liabilities and owners' equity	$ 2756	$ 3112	

FIGURE 4-1 • TMA balance sheets.

handy for tracking TMA's position across time: for example, comparing the values in the common-size asset sheets across the two years shown can help to highlight some of the subtleties of TMA's position that we might not have noticed using the "dollar" statement, such as the fact that, though TMA's notes-payable account

TMA INC.							
Common-Size Balance Sheets as of December 31, 2010 and 2011							
($ in millions)							
	2010	**2011**			**2010**	**2011**	
Assets				**Liabilities and owners' equity**			
Current assets				Current liabilities			
Cash	3.77%	5.14%		Accounts payable	8.42%	0.84%	
Accounts receivable	16.51%	22.11%		Notes payable	7.11%	6.30%	
Inventory	20.07%	17.83%		Total	15.53%	7.13%	
Total	40.35%	45.08%					
Fixed assets				Long-term debt	14.80%	19.92%	
Net fixed assets	59.65%	54.92%		Owners' equity			
				Common stock and paid-in surplus	21.77%	19.28%	
				Retained earnings	47.90%	53.66%	
				Total	69.67%	72.94%	
Total assets	100.00%	100.00%		Total liabilities and owners' equity	100.00%	100.00%	

FIGURE 4-2 • TMA common-size balance sheets.

TMA INC.		
2011 Income Statement		
($ in millions)		
Net sales		$ 1602
Cost of goods sold		750
Depreciation		65
Earnings before interest and taxes		$ 787
Interest paid		90
Taxable income		$ 697
Taxes (35%)		244
Net income		$ 453
Dividends	$ 103	
Addition to retained earnings	350	

FIGURE 4-3 · TMA income statement.

stayed constant at $196 million across both years, this represented a drop from 7.11 percent of total funding (i.e., total capital in the firm) in 2010 to only 6.30 percent of total funding in 2011. In many industries, such a drop might be of significant interest.

TMA INC.		
2011 Common-Size Income Statement		
($ in millions)		
Net sales		100.00%
Cost of goods sold		46.82%
Depreciation		4.06%
Earnings before interest and taxes		49.13%
Interest paid		5.62%
Taxable income		43.51%
Taxes (35%)		15.23%
Net income		28.28%
Dividends	6.43%	
Addition to retained earnings	21.85%	

FIGURE 4-4 · TMA common-size income statement.

Common-Base Year Analysis

Another handy tool for analyzing changes in a firm's position over time is the common-base year analysis, which involves choosing a base year and then expressing other years in terms of how large each item is relative to its value during the base year. Choosing 2010 as the base year for an analysis of TMA, we get the results shown in Figure 4-5.

The common-base year figures shown in Figure 4-5 represent the relative size of the corresponding year 2011 item compared to the same item for 2010: a value of 1 means that the figures for the two years were the same, a value greater than 1 indicates that the year 2011 figure was larger, and a value less than 1 indicates that the year 2011 figure was smaller than the year 2010 figure. The amount by which the common-base year figures deviate from 1 can be thought of as the percentage change from 2010 to 2011 for that item.

For example, the common-base year figure of 1.52 for long-term debt indicates that debt grew by 52 percent, and the figure of 0.52 for total current liabilities indicates that current liabilities shrunk by 48 percent (because the deviation from 1 for that item is equal to $1 - 0.52 = 0.48$).

It is also possible to use both the common-size and common-base year techniques in conjunction with one another. Figure 4-6 shows the computation of just such a set of values; the common-base year amounts in this figure are different from those in Figure 4-5 because they're calculated using the 2010 and 2011 common-size statements instead of the 2010 and 2011 dollar amounts.

TMA INC.								
Common-Base Year Balance Sheets for December 31, 2011								
($ in millions)								
	2010	2011	Common Base-Year 2011			2010	2011	Common Base-Year 2011
	Assets				Liabilities and owners' equity			
Current assets					Current liabilities			
Cash	$ 104	$ 160	1.54		Accounts payable	$ 232	$ 26	0.11
Accounts receivable	455	688	1.51		Notes payable	196	196	1.00
Inventory	553	555	1.00		Total	$ 428	$ 222	0.52
Total	$ 1112	$ 1403	1.26					
Fixed assets					Long-term debt	408	620	1.52
Net fixed assets	$ 1644	$ 1709	1.04		Owners' equity			
					Common stock and paid-in surplus	600	600	1.00
					Retained earnings	1320	1670	1.27
					Total	$ 1920	$ 2270	1.18
Total assets	$ 2756	$ 3112	1.13		Total liabilities and owners' equity	$ 2756	$ 3112	1.13

FIGURE 4-5 • TMA common-base year analysis.

				TMA INC.							
				Combined Common-Size and Common-Base Year Balance Sheets for December 31, 2011							
				($ in Millions)							
			Common-Size		**Common Base-Year**				**Common-Size**		**Common Base-Year**
	2010	**2011**	**2010**	**2011**	**2011**		**2010**	**2011**	**2010**	**2011**	**2011**
Assets						**Liabilities and Owners' Equity**					
Current assets						Current liabilities					
Cash	$ 104	$ 160	3.77%	5.14%	1.36	Accounts payable	$ 232	$ 26	8.42%	0.84%	0.10
Accounts receivable	455	688	16.51%	22.11%	1.34	Notes payable	196	196	7.11%	6.30%	0.89
Inventory	553	555	20.07%	17.83%	0.89	Total	$ 428	$ 222	15.53%	7.13%	0.46
Total	$ 1,112	$ 1,403	40.35%	45.08%	1.12						
Fixed assets						Long-term debt	408	620	14.80%	19.92%	1.35
Net fixed assets	$ 1,644	$ 1,709	59.65%	54.92%	0.92	Owners' equity					
						Common stock and paid-in surplus	600	600	21.77%	19.28%	0.89
						Retained earnings	1,320	1,670	47.90%	53.66%	1.12
						Total	$ 1,920	$ 2,270	69.67%	72.94%	1.05
Total assets	$ 2,756	$ 3,112	100.00%	100.00%	1.00	Total liabilities and owners' equity	$ 2,756	$ 3,112	100.00%	100.00%	1.00

FIGURE 4-6 • TMA combined common-size and common-base year balance sheets.

The values produced by this combined approach provide us with estimates for relative sizes of the 2011 balance sheet items *after they've already been adjusted for an increase in the size of the firm by converting the balance sheets to common-size statements*. This will allow us to better identify which items changed at a rate different from the average rate of change caused by the overall growth in assets. For example, the common-base year figure for cash in Figure 4-5 is 1.54, indicating that cash grew by 54 percent between 2010 and 2011, while the corresponding common-base year figure of 1.36 for cash in Figure 4-6 tells us that *cash grew 36 percent faster than the rate of increase in total assets*.

Liquidity Ratios

Liquidity refers to the ability of a firm to convert assets to cash while getting as much of the value of the asset as possible. As discussed earlier, current assets tend to be more liquid than fixed assets, so it's no surprise that all of the ratios in this category use either all or part of the current asset value or net working capital, which can basically be thought of as "net current assets above and beyond current liabilities."

Most liquidity ratios will focus on contrasting this measure of current assets with some estimate of money owed in the short term, usually current liabilities or expenses. For example, looking at the list of commonly used liquidity ratios

Liquidity Ratios

$$\text{Current ratio} = \frac{\text{current assets}}{\text{current liabilities}}$$

$$\text{Quick ratio} = \frac{\text{current assets } - \text{ inventory}}{\text{current liabilities}}$$

$$\text{Net working capital to total assets} = \frac{\text{net working capital}}{\text{total assets}}$$

$$\text{Interval measure} = \frac{\text{current assets}}{\text{average daily operating costs}}$$

shown above, we see that calculating the *current ratio* involves simply dividing current assets by current liabilities. For TMA in 2011, this ratio will be equal to $1,403/$222 = 6.32, a rather dramatic increase from the value of $1,112/$428 = 2.60 in 2010.

Assuming that the 2011 value of 6.32 is higher than average, is this good or bad? Well, it depends: if you're looking at this company from the viewpoint of a lender to whom part of the current liabilities are owed, it's probably a good value, because it means that TMA has approximately $6.32 in assets set to sort of "spontaneously convert" to cash for every $1.00 of short-term liabilities that they owe, so you've probably got a good chance of being paid the money you're owed.

On the other hand, if you're asking this question from the viewpoint of an equity investor, such a relatively high value probably isn't such a good thing, as it indicates that you might have too much capital tied up in relatively (compared to fixed assets) poorly performing current assets.

By the way, this answer of "it depends" is going to crop up fairly often when we're talking about whether a particular range or value for a ratio is good or bad; what's going to be hard to determine is *what* it depends on.

Sometimes, however, we *can* state that a particular range for a value is likely to be either good or bad. Such is the case here with the current ratio: by and large, firms should usually have a current ratio greater than 1 if they hope to pay their current liabilities. Depending upon how likely the various types of current assets are to actually turn into cash (remember that not all accounts receivable will be paid, not all inventory will be purchased, and so on), different industries or firms may actually need to consistently have a current ratio that is significantly higher than 1 in order for the firms involved to be confident about paying back their current liabilities, but they'll all usually need to have a current ratio of at least 1.

Notice that we said "usually," but not "definitely." It is possible that a firm may be able to meet current liabilities with a planned liquidation of some fixed assets or something of the sort, so you might occasionally see a perfectly healthy, profitable firm with an occasional current ratio of less than 1; but such circumstances certainly shouldn't be expected to recur period after period unless the firm is in a very unique situation.

The *quick ratio* is a little harder to pin down concerning a reasonable range to expect: if a firm has a pretty good certainty that their current inventories will be sold, then their quick ratio may be significantly less than 1 and they can still have a reasonable expectation of meeting the current liability obligations.

Note that the quick ratio for a given period will always be less than the current ratio for the same period if the firm has any inventory; for TMA, the quick ratios for 2011 and 2010 are ($1,403 − $555)/$222 = 3.82 and ($1,112 − $553)/$428 = 1.31, respectively, as compared to the current ratio values of 6.32 and 2.60 discussed earlier. Mathematically, this makes sense, as both the current and quick ratios have the same denominators, but the quick ratio numerator is a subset of that of the current ratio.

Intuitively, you should think of the quick ratio as a slightly more "paranoid" version of the current ratio. To see why, think about what current assets are included in the current ratio: primarily cash, accounts receivable, and inventory. Of these three types, which is *least* likely to turn into cash in the short term? Inventory, because cash is already cash, and accounts receivable represent obligations of your customers to pay you cash, but most firms usually can't *force* customers to buy your inventory. So, when we subtract out inventory in the computation of the quick ratio, we're basically computing a new version of the current ratio, one where we're reducing the money we expect to have coming in by the part that we're least sure about.

The net working capital to total assets ratio, on the other hand, takes a different approach to addressing the question of whether the firm has an appropriate amount of current assets. By using net working capital as the numerator, this ratio is focusing on the amount of current assets above and beyond current liabilities; that is, the amount of current assets that the firm has to fund. This ratio will normally be greater than 0 for most firms, but there are several situations where it might even be negative. For example, if a firm was in a strong enough market position to force its suppliers to give it very good credit terms (for example, a very long time to pay) while at the same time being able to ask its customers to pay cash-on-the-barrel, current liabilities could actually be greater than current assets.

Finally, the *interval measure* takes yet another approach to measuring how capable a firm is of meeting its short-term obligations. By dividing the firm's current assets by average daily operating costs, this ratio is explicitly measuring how many days the firm could continue operations if it were forced to use just the assets expected to turn into cash sometime soon (i.e., the current assets).

One notable thing about this asset: it's the first one we've discussed that is *not* a pure number. Computing the current, quick, and net working capital to total assets ratios all involve dividing a dollar figure by another dollar figure, and *denominations*, such as the currency symbol, cancel out in algebraic equations just like everything else does, so "$X/$Y" becomes "X/Y," a pure number.

For the interval measure, however, we're dividing a dollar figure by one that's expressed in terms of "$ per day." "$X/($Y per day)" is the same as "$X/($Y/day)," which simplifies to "X/Y × (1/1/day)," which further simplifies to "X/Y days."

The point here is that, if you keep careful track of exactly which units of measurement cancel out in the computation of a ratio, and of which ones don't, you may be able to get at least a small hint concerning what a particular ratio is supposed to be conveying.

Leverage Ratios

As we'll see in later chapters, a firm's debt is often referred to as *leverage* because, like Archimedes' famous lever, debt *magnifies* something: in this case, both the earning power of equity as well as its risk.

The leverage ratios listed below are actually trying to express relationships very similar to those that the liquidity ratios measured; it's just that, while the liquidity ratios dealt with cash coming in versus cash going out *in the short term*, the leverage ratios focus on *all* the cash flows coming in and obligated to go out (i.e., to be repaid to debt holders) in both the short and long terms.

The first two ratios listed, the total debt ratio and the debt-equity ratio, are fairly simple to both calculate and interpret, so we won't dwell on them too long. However, you will find that finance texts often give you one of these when you need the other, so, before we go on to the other ratios, let's talk a little about how they're related and about some shortcuts for converting back and forth between the two.

Leverage Ratios

$$\text{Total debt ratio} = \frac{\text{total assets} - \text{total equity}}{\text{total assets}}$$

$$\text{Debt-equity ratio} = \frac{\text{total debt}}{\text{total equity}}$$

$$\text{Equity multiplier} = \frac{\text{total assets}}{\text{total equity}}$$

$$\text{Long-term debt ratio} = \frac{\textit{long-term debt}}{\textit{long-term debt} + \textit{total equity}}$$

$$\text{Times interest earned ratio} = \frac{\text{EBIT}}{\text{interest}}$$

First, realize that the total debt ratio is theoretically equal to D/A, and the debt-equity ratio can be written as D/E. Now, we can use the basic accounting identity, $A = D + E$, to construct an algebraic formula for converting back and forth between these two ratios:

$A = D + E$

$D = A - E$

$D/E = A/E - E/E$

$D/E = A/E - 1$

$D/E = 1/(E/A) - 1$

$D/E = 1/(1-D/A) - 1$

So, for example, if a firm has a D/A ratio of 1/3, it will have a D/E ratio of 1/2:

$$D/E = 1/(1 - 1/3) - 1 = 1/(2/3) - 1 = 3/2 - 1 = 1/2$$

We can also create an analogous equation for converting back the other way (i.e., from D/E to D/A). However, there is an easier way.

This easier way depends upon a slightly reworked version of the accounting identity. If $A = D + E$, then we can also rewrite this by dividing everything by A:

$$A/A = D/A + E/A$$

But A/A is, of course, 1, so this becomes:

$$1 = D/A + E/A$$

This version is handy in two ways: first, it tells us that, given either D/A or E/A, we can always solve for the other by subtracting the one we know from 1:

$$D/A = 1 - E/A \quad \text{and} \quad E/A = 1 - D/A$$

So, for example, if we're told that $D/A = 0.25$, then

$$E/A = 1 - 0.25 = 0.75$$

The second way that this version helps us is based on simple algebra: once we know both D/A and E/A, then D/E is simply equal to $D/A \div E/A$ (note that the A's will cancel out). For example, if D/A is 0.25, then $E/A = 1 - 0.25 = 0.75$, and $D/E = 0.25/0.75 = 1/3$.

A modification of this approach can also be used to go the other way, solving for D/A if we know D/E. To use this other approach, first make sure that D/E is expressed as a fraction. For example, if you're told that D/E is equal to 0.5, first convert that to 1/2. Now, this fraction doesn't tell us how big D, E, and A are in absolute terms, but it tells how big they are *relative* to each other, and we can use that to solve for D/A and E/A.

For example, if $D/E = 1/2$, then think of A as being the sum of the numerator and the denominator, $1 + 2 = 3$. Then you can express D/A as the numerator over the sum of the numerator plus denominator, or 1/3, and E/A as the denominator over the sum of the numerator plus denominator, or 2/3.

So, to summarize:

a To go from D/A to D/E, calculate E/A as $1 - D/A$, then divide D/A by E/A to get D/E.

b To go from E/A to D/E, calculate D/A as $1 - E/A$, then divide D/A by E/A to get D/E.

c To go from D/E to D/A, convert D/E to a fraction, then take the top of the D/E fraction and divide it by "bottom + top."

d To go from D/E to E/A, convert D/E to a fraction, then take the bottom of the D/E fraction and divide it by "bottom + top."

The *equity multiplier* is simply the inverse of the equity ratio, E/A. If you use one of the techniques listed above to get the total debt ratio, you can just calculate the equity ratio as $E/A = 1 - D/A$, and then take the inverse of the result. For example, if you know (or calculate) that the total debt ratio is 0.60, then the equity ratio will be $1 - 0.60 = 0.40$, and the equity multiplier will be $1/0.4 = 2.5$.

Why is it called the equity "multiplier"? Notice that, even though there's no "D" explicitly listed in the equity multiplier ratio, there is an implicit one, because A/E will get bigger as D/A gets bigger. As discussed above, we'll see later that debt will act as a type of financial leverage; at that time, we'll also see that the multiplier in the name of this ratio refers to how much the earnings and risk of equity will be magnified because of the amount of debt in the company.

The last ratio in this category, the *times interest earned ratio*, is often referred to simply by its acronym as the TIE ratio. Intuitively, the TIE ratio is simply measuring how big the before-interest earnings of the firm, EBIT, is compared to the amount of interest paid by the firm. Obviously, the firm will have a negative net income figure if the TIE is less than 1 (because TIE < 1 implies less before-interest income earned than interest paid).

Asset Utilization Ratios

To the extent that *any* capital tied up in assets is a necessary evil from the viewpoint of the corporation, the asset utilization ratios listed here are measuring how efficiently the firm is using that invested capital.

These ratios have one special attribute that none of the ratios we've covered so far share: while all the previous ratios we've discussed have involved either dividing income statement items by other income statement items, or dividing balance sheet items by other balance sheet items, these ratios each involve dividing an income statement item by a balance sheet item.

Asset Utilization Ratios

$$\text{Inventory turnover} = \frac{\text{cost of goods sold}}{\text{inventory}}$$

$$\text{Days' sales in inventory} = \frac{365 \text{ days}}{\text{inventory turnover}}$$

$$\text{Receivables turnover} = \frac{\text{sales}}{\text{accounts receivable}}$$

$$\text{Days' sales in receivables} = \frac{365 \text{ days}}{\text{receivables turnover}}$$

$$\text{NWC turnover} = \frac{\text{sales}}{\text{NWC}}$$

$$\text{Fixed asset turnover} = \frac{\text{sales}}{\text{net fixed assets}}$$

$$\text{Total asset turnover} = \frac{\text{sales}}{\text{total assets}}$$

Why is that a big deal? Because income statements contain items that measure the *flow* of cash *throughout* a time period, whereas balance sheets contain items that capture a *snapshot* of the amount in an account *at* a particular point in time. This idea of what length of time a measurement is for carries the same weight as a number's denomination, and dividing a flow variable by a snapshot is like comparing apples to oranges.

So, what do we do? We try to simulate a flow variable using multiple snapshots; that is, we take multiple measurements of the same balance sheet item, but taken first from the balance sheet that was constructed at the point in time where the income statement started measuring flows, and again from the point in time where the income statement stopped. By taking the average of these two snapshots, we get a measurement of what the "typical" amount was in that particular balance sheet account during the entire time frame spanned by the income statement.

For example, using TMA's 2011 income statement and its 2010 and 2011 balance sheet from Figure 4-1 and Figure 4-3, we would compute TMA's receivables turnover ratio as $1602/[($455 + $688)/2] = 2.8031$.

All of the "turnover" ratios in this category, such as the one we just computed, are measured in terms of pure numbers and technically measure how much of a particular type of asset supported sales (or another income sheet item) during the year. However, they can also be thought of as representing how many times during the period (in this case, during the year) something happened. The receivables turnover measures how many times, on average, TMA collected on its accounts receivable and then turned around and sold more product on credit; the inventory turnover ratio would measure how many times TMA might have sold out of its inventory and then restocked; and so forth.

The other type of ratio that we see in this category, those whose names start with "Days' sales...," are simply restatements of the respective turnover ratios, and can be thought of either as stated (for example, "Days' sales in inventory") or as expressing how often the "something" referred to in the previous paragraph happened. For example, if we think of TMA's receivables turnover as saying that the firm collected on its accounts receivable 2.8031 times during the year, then the corresponding Days' sales in inventory of $365/2.8031 = 130.2107$ is saying that TMA collected its accounts receivable about once every 130 days, on average.

Profitability Ratios

The profitability ratios shown here are trying to express how much money the firm made, either as a percentage of sales (i.e., *profit margin*) or as a percentage of capital invested in either all assets (i.e., *return on assets*) or just in the portion of the firm funded by equity (i.e., *return on equity*). All of these ratios rely on accounting statement items to measure both cash inflows and the amount of capital invested; as we discussed in the last chapter, accounting statements don't measure either of these very well, so the values produced for the formulas don't represent very good proxies for a true "rate of return."

Profitability Ratios

$$\text{Profit margin} = \frac{\text{net income}}{\text{sales}}$$

$$\text{Return on assets (ROA)} = \frac{\text{net income}}{\text{total assets}}$$

$$\text{Return on equity (ROE)} = \frac{\text{net income}}{\text{total equity}}$$

However, to the extent that the firms used for benchmarking a firm's profitability also suffer from the same problems, it may very well prove useful to compare these ratios. For example, if we know that TMA's ROE of $453/$1,602 = 0.2828 while the industry average ROE is 0.15, it really doesn't matter that neither of these numbers are really good measures of the rate of return to equity holders if the ordering of those unseen, "true" rates of return matches the ordering seen here.

QUIZ

Please use the income statement and balance sheets for AHS shown in Figures 4-7 and 4-8 to answer the next nine questions:

1. **Construct a common-size income statement for AHS. In this statement, what will be the value for taxable income?**
   A. 11.21%
   B. 17.25%
   C. 16.60%
   D. $1,660

2. **Construct common-size balance sheets for AHS for both 2010 and 2011. Percentage-wise, which of the following items has grown the most?**
   A. Accounts payable
   B. Accounts receivable
   C. Cash
   D. Notes payable

3. **Using 2010 as the base year, construct a common-base year balance sheet for 2011 for AHS. According to this statement, which of the following items has grown the most compared to its 2010 value?**
   A. Accounts payable
   B. Accounts receivable
   C. Cash
   D. Notes payable

AHS INC.			
2011 Income Statement			
($ in millions)			
Net sales		$	9625
Cost of goods sold			5225
Depreciation			1890
Earnings before interest and taxes		$	2510
Interest paid			850
Taxable income		$	1660
Taxes (35%)			581
Net income		$	1079
Dividends	$	679	
Addition to retained earnings		400	

FIGURE 4-7 · AHS income statement.

AHS INC.						
Balance Sheets as of December 31, 2010 and 2011						
($ in millions)						
	2010	2011			2010	2011
Assets				Liabilities and owners' equity		
Current assets				Current liabilities		
Cash	$ 1455	$ 260		Accounts payable	$ 1150	$ 2863
Accounts receivable	2460	3975		Notes payable	2600	1628
Inventory	1405	885		Total	$ 3750	$ 4491
Total	$ 5320	$ 5120				
Fixed assets				Long-term debt	7000	7600
Net fixed assets	$ 19,300	$ 21,720		Owners' equity		
				Common stock and paid-in surplus	5500	5700
				Retained earnings	8370	9049
				Total	$ 13,870	$ 14,749
Total assets	$ 24,620	$ 26,840		Total liabilities and owners' equity	$ 24,620	$ 26,840

FIGURE 4-8 · AHS balance sheets.

4. **Construct a combined common-size and common-base year balance sheet for 2011. What will be the common-base year value for the 2011 net fixed assets?**
   - A. 0.89
   - B. 0.92
   - C. 1.12
   - D. 1.32

5. **What will be the value of AHS's current ratio during 2011?**
   - A. 1.14
   - B. 1.42
   - C. 1.49
   - D. 1.53

6. **What will be the value of AHS's equity multiplier during 2011?**
   - A. 0.44
   - B. 0.56
   - C. 1.78
   - D. 1.82

7. **What will be the value of AHS's TIE during 2011?**
   - A. 2.75
   - B. 2.85
   - C. 2.95
   - D. 3.05

8. **What will be the appropriate value of AHS's inventory turnover ratio in 2011?**
   A. 4.56
   B. 4.78
   C. 5.32
   D. 5.90

9. **What will be the appropriate value of AHS's profit margin in 2011?**
   A. 9.34%
   B. 10.12%
   C. 11.21%
   D. 12.53%

10. **Suppose a firm had a *D/A* ratio of 0.4. Which of the following values would be equal to its *D/E* ratio?**
    A. 4/10
    B. 2/3
    C. 0.4/1.4
    D. 10/4

Part II

"I Will Gladly Pay You $2 Tomorrow for $1 Today": the Time Value of Money

chapter 5

Present and Future Value

CHAPTER OBJECTIVES

At the end of this chapter, the reader should be able to:

- Explain the advantages of using Excel or a financial calculator over calculating time value of money variables by hand

- Read and interpret cash flows depicted on a time line

- Calculate present value and future value for lump sums, annuities, and series of uneven cash flows

The *Time Value of Money* (TVM) is the central concept behind most of corporate finance, and we'll be using it later in this book to value shares of stock, bonds, and projects. In more advanced courses, it is even used to value entire companies.

In this chapter, we're going to focus on introducing the concepts behind TVM in a more general setting. In fact, most of the examples we'll use will come from *personal finance*, and you'll most likely find them very helpful in managing your own personal finances.

Many of you have already been introduced to TVM, perhaps in a basic accounting class, and are probably thinking, "I can skip this chapter." You might not want to do that because, as we go through the concepts of TVM, we're also going to do our best to simplify those concepts, put them into context, and tie them together into one cohesive "big picture."

Using a Financial Calculator or a Spreadsheet Program

If you're going to be tackling financial questions regularly, either as a career or for your own purposes, you should be using a spreadsheet program; their flexibility and built-in functions and tools make it easy to construct even the most complicated financial models.

Currently, the spreadsheet program of choice amongst business professionals is Microsoft Excel; the introduction of enhanced access to external data sources seen in the most recent versions, as well as the continued abundance of available third-party add-ons, make it likely that Excel will continue to be the financial tool of choice for quite some time to come.

Unfortunately, the academic world has lagged well behind the business world in adopting spreadsheets: if you're currently taking finance classes, it's a pretty good bet that your instructors are either using a financial calculator or doing the necessary math "by hand" when they work out examples in class. And they probably want you to do your homework the same way, right?

There are some very good reasons for doing the math by hand: looking at the formulas will help you understand the intuition behind what you're doing and why, and can help provide you guidance in answering those dreaded "What if…?" questions. However, the calculations necessary to solve most of the interesting financial problems can be quite tedious and repetitive; in some cases, it's actually *impossible* to solve directly for an answer, so you're reduced to using trial-and-error procedures that are definitely not fun.

So, we're going to use a hybrid approach to solving finance problems. When we initially encounter a particular type of problem, we will work it out by hand using the appropriate formulas; but, as we gain more familiarity with that type of problem, we'll use a shorthand notation based on calculator inputs. This same shorthand notation will also serve to indicate what the formula inputs for Excel would be, as well.

There are quite a few financial calculators on the market which could serve as the model for our shorthand notation, and they tend to fall into two general categories: general-purpose *programmable calculators*, such as the HP 49g+ or the TI-89, and dedicated "hard-wired" *financial calculators*, such as the HP 12c and the TI Business Analyst II Plus Professional. As a group, the programmable calculators tend to have a little more variation in their notational conventions due to the ability of end-users to create their own applications, so it's probably a good idea for us to use conventions based on the typical setup of one of the hard-wired calculators, instead, as they tend to be more consistent.

Of the hard-wired calculators, one of the best is the TI Business Analyst II Plus Professional. In addition to the features that most other calculators in this category share, it also has the ability to calculate *Net Future Value* (NFV), *Modified Internal Rate of Return* (MIRR), *modified duration, payback,* and *discounted payback,* all of which we'll cover in later chapters. Most hard-wired calculators *don't* calculate these values, but they are covered in almost all corporate finance textbooks, so modeling our notational conventions upon the assumption that our hypothetical calculator will be able to calculate these values would seem to be the best choice.

We will cover basic calculator setup and our notational conventions after we've discussed the TVM formulas.

Time Lines

When trying to make a financial decision, it is often helpful to have the relevant cash flows displayed graphically. The usual tool for doing this is called a *timeline*, and consists of a horizontal line with hash marks indicating the spacing of the time periods, period numbers along the top of the line, and cash flows occurring during a period indicated below the line, as shown below in Figure 5-1.

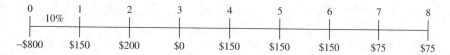

FIGURE 5-1 · Sample timeline.

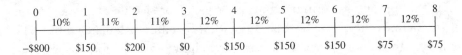

FIGURE 5-2 · Sample timeline with multiple interest rates.

The interest rate of 10 percent over the first line segment indicates the interest rate to be used when converting money between time 0 and time 1. While it is possible to use different interest rates for different time periods, listing only an interest rate for the first period like this indicates that we should use that same interest rate for all periods on a given problem (i.e., for all of the cash flows on a particular timeline). This assumption is the one that you'll use for virtually all of the problems you're likely to encounter, but, if you do happen upon the odd exception, the interest rates for each period will be listed separately as shown in the example in Figure 5-2.

Another feature that you'll sometimes see on a timeline is a wavy line segment such as that shown in Figure 5-3: this line segment is being used as a type of *spanning indicator*, and is a shorthand method of indicating that all the cash flows in the unlisted, intermediate periods are equal to those shown at the ends of the line segment. So, for example, the timeline in Figure 5-3 indicates that there are also cash flows of $200 at periods 3, 4, and 5.

You'll also see this spanning indicator being used to indicate an infinite set of cash flows at the end of a timeline, as shown in Figure 5-4.

Here, the wavy line segment, along with the infinity symbol over the last time period, indicates that the cash flow of $75 per period will last forever.

One final note about timelines: though textbooks try to be as precise as possible when referring to the timing of cash flows, they don't often explain that there are two different ways to refer to any particular time period. One method is to refer to a *point* in time, in which case you are being directed exactly to one of the vertical marks on a timeline; the other is to refer to a position in a relative manner, such as "the end of year 3" or "the beginning of year 4."

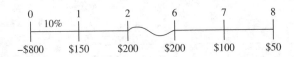

FIGURE 5-3 · Sample timeline with wavy line segment.

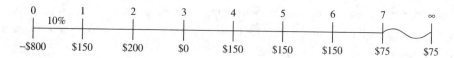

FIGURE 5-4 Sample timeline indicating perpetuity at the end.

What makes this particularly confusing sometimes is that multiple relative references will often refer to the same point in time. For example, look back at the relative references cited in the last paragraph and apply them to the timeline in Figure 5-4; you'll see that they both refer to the same point in time, the vertical hash mark with the "3" above it.

So, when you're reading a problem, be very careful to keep track of exactly when the cash flows occur, and to what time period you wish to move them.

The TVM Formulas

The most basic formula used in TVM is the one for computing the future value of a single sum of money (sometimes called a *lump sum*):

$$FV = PV \times (1+r)^T$$

where FV = future value
      PV = present value
       r = periodic interest rate
       T = number of periods

This formula is usually referred to simply as the *FV formula*. All other TVM formulas are simply reformulations or extensions to this one formula.

For example, dividing both sides of the FV formula by $(1 + r)^T$ yields the *PV formula*:

$$PV = \frac{FV}{(1+r)^T}$$

and summing this PV formula for an infinite number of constant-value cash flows, C, called a *perpetuity*, results in the following summation formula:

$$\text{Present value of a perpetuity} = \frac{C}{(1+r)^1} + \frac{C}{(1+r)^2} + \cdots + \frac{C}{(1+r)^\infty}$$

$$= \sum_{i=1}^{\infty} \frac{C}{(1+r)^i}$$

Since the terms inside the summation sign of this formula will converge toward 0 as i gets larger and larger, the entire summation will converge toward a finite amount, which we'll abbreviate as PVP:

$$PVP = \frac{C}{r}$$

One interesting feature of this formula that will pop up again and again is that *it will always give you a present value one length-of-time-between-payments in front of the first payment.* For example, if you have a perpetuity with payments that come once a quarter, the formula will gave you a present value one quarter in front of the first payment.

We can use the PVP formula, in turn, to derive the formula for the present value of an *annuity*, which is like a perpetuity except that it has a *finite* number, T, of constant-value cash flows, C. We do this by subtracting the present value of the perpetuity starting at time $T + 1$ from the present value of the perpetuity starting at time 1.

For example, suppose we had a 5-payment annuity; the present value at time 0 of its cash flows would be equal to those of a perpetuity starting at time 1 minus those of a perpetuity starting at time 6, shown graphically in Figure 5-5.

Mathematically, the present value of these cash flows will then be equal to

$$PVA = \frac{C}{r} - \left[\frac{C}{r} \times \frac{1}{(1+r)^T} \right]$$

$$= C \times \left[\frac{1 - \dfrac{1}{(1+r)^T}}{r} \right]$$

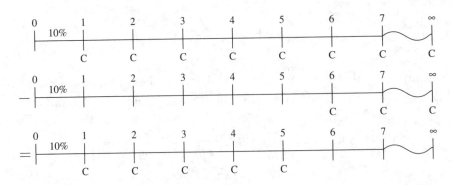

FIGURE 5-5 · Cash flows for a 5-payment annuity.

Why is there a "T" in this formula and not a "$T+1$"? Because, even though the perpetuity that we're subtracting starts at time $T+1$, when we use the perpetuity formula on it, we get a value one period before that first payment, at time T. Therefore, when we bring this value back to time 0, we're moving it T periods, not $T+1$.

Finally, we can take the value given by the PVA formula and then move it to any time period that we wish; specifically, we can use the FV formula to move it to the same point in time as the last payment of the annuity. This particular future value is what someone is usually referring to when they talk about the *Future Value of an Annuity (FVA)*.

$$FVA = PVA \times (1+r)^T$$

$$= C \times \left[\frac{1 - \frac{1}{(1+r)^T}}{r} \right] \times (1+r)^T$$

$$= C \times \left[\frac{(1+r)^T - 1}{r} \right]$$

So, to summarize, there are only five basic TVM formulas:

$$FV = PV \times (1+r)^T$$

$$PV = \frac{FV}{(1+r)^T}$$

$$PVP = \frac{C}{r}$$

$$PVA = C \times \left[\frac{1 - \frac{1}{(1+r)^T}}{r} \right]$$

$$FVA = C \times \left[\frac{(1+r)^T - 1}{r} \right]$$

Though most finance texts tend to make it look as if there are many more formulas than this by changing the variable names as they go from chapter to chapter, these five will handle most of the calculations you need to make. So don't be surprised when you find us repeatedly referring back to these five formulas throughout the rest of the book.

Calculator Setup and Notational Conventions

There are really only two things you need to do to set up a financial calculator to give you consistent answers: set the *payment per year* to "1," and set the number of decimal places displayed to "4." Both procedures should be explained in your calculator handbook.

Setting the *payment per year* to "1" will ensure that your calculator treats the interest rates you give it as the interest rate *per period*, and that it doesn't try to convert it to something you really don't want. We'll discuss this topic more, as well as how to do interest rate conversions yourself if you *do* need to do them, in the next chapter.

Setting the number of decimal places displayed to "4" actually doesn't change anything about how the calculator handles problems; instead, this setting is meant to ensure that you have enough precision in your numbers when you're doing a formula by hand or when you're taking an intermediate result and feeding it back into the calculator.

For our notational conventions, we are going to treat the calculator as if it were a "black box," a machine whose internal workings we know nothing about. Financial calculators encourage this approach by providing a set of dedicated keys for performing TVM functions, and taking this approach will allow us to describe our actions by listing which variables we input, and which we solve for.

If you'll glance back to the formula summary, you'll see that we used a total of five variables on the right-hand sides of our formulas: FV, PV, r, T, and C: these correspond to the keys you will usually see on your calculator's "TVM worksheet."

In addition to using FV and PV on the left-hand side of our TVM formulas, we also had three unique variables that weren't used on the right-hand side: PVP, PVA, and FVA. Most calculators (and most finance texts, for that matter) don't differentiate between different present values or different future values, using PV for PVP and PVA, and FV for FVA. We are going to differentiate between them so as to try and minimize any confusion concerning exactly which formula we're using; however, you will need to remember that there will only be two distinct buttons on your calculator for these five distinct present and future values.

Since most calculators have all the TVM keys act as their own "Enter" key, that's the approach we'll take, too. For example, if we need to enter a value of $300 as the future value, we'll indicate it by directing you to press "300 [FV]," which will correspond to typing in the number 300 and then pressing the FV key. To be consistent, we'll use those same square brackets to indicate all key presses.

The only other type of key entry that you would have to do, when using a calculator's TVM worksheet, would be to solve for the answer. While the TVM variables can act as their own "Enter" keys, they usually can't act as their own "Solve" or "Compute" key, so we'll explicitly indicate pressing such a key, which we'll call "[CPT]." For example, the direction "[CPT] [PV]" would indicate that you should press the CPT key, followed by the PV key.

After listing the keystrokes for computation in this manner, we'll also follow them with an "=" sign and the result: for example, "[CPT] [FVA] = $275" would tell you that computing the future value of a previously detailed annuity should give you an answer of $275.

Using the TVM Formulas

Of the five formulas we just derived, the PV and FV formulas are obviously much easier to use than the other three. Because of that, some students try to use them exclusively, converting every problem into multiple lump-sum problems. There are two reasons that this isn't a good idea:

First, there are several broad categories where doing this isn't possible: for example, solving for the interest rate on an annuity, or solving for the constant cash flow, C, in a perpetuity. If you come to depend on being able to do this for easier problems, it's going to hurt you when you come up against a problem where you can't use that approach.

Second, even on the problems that can be solved as a series of lump-sum problems, you're putting yourself at a serious disadvantage when you do so: solving 20 lump-sum problems isn't necessarily going to take you 20 times as long as solving for the present value of a 20-period annuity, but it will usually take you at least four to five times as long.

So, whenever possible, we do want to use the PVP, PVA, and FVA formulas; the key is going to lie in using them appropriately. For all three of these formulas, we need to make sure that we understand both *what* they're going to do to the cash flows we pass them, as well as *where* they're going to provide it.

The main value of all three of these formulas is that they will take a series of equal payments and convert them to a single lump sum for us: from our preceding discussion, remember that the PVP formula will give us a lump sum value one "length-of-time-between-periods" in front of the first payment of the perpetuity; the PVA formula, because of the way it's constructed from the PVP formula, *does exactly the same thing*, also giving us a value one length-of-time-between-periods in front of the first payment of the annuity; the FVA formula, on the other hand, will give us a value *at the same point in time as the last payment* (because that's the way we chose to construct it).

As we start to work with actual problems, we'll find that we often have "embedded annuities" (a series of constant, equal cash flows located in the middle of some nonconstant cash flows), or "trailing perpetuities" (a perpetuity that starts sometime after the first cash flow, but once it starts, continues on forever). Can we use the PVP, PVA, and FVA formulas on these? Yes! Will they give us a value where we want it? Probably not, but once they convert a series of cash flows to a single lump sum for us, it's pretty easy to move that lump sum to where we want it using the PV and FV formulas.

Example—Car Loan with Delayed First Payment

For our first example, suppose that we have just bought a new car, financing it for 60 months at 0.3 percent per month, but that our payments, shown in Figure 5-6, don't start for two months, and the last payment is, as shown, slightly different from all the others. If we wanted to value these payments at time 0, what would be the easiest way to go about this?

First, we would want to apply the PVA formula to the first 59 payments:

$$PVA = C \times \left[\frac{1 - \frac{1}{(1+r)^T}}{r} \right]$$

$$= -\$373 \times \left[\frac{1 - \frac{1}{(1+0.003)^{59}}}{0.003} \right]$$

$$= -\$373 \times \left[\frac{1 - \frac{1}{1.1933}}{0.003} \right]$$

$$= -\$373 \times \left[\frac{0.1620}{0.003} \right]$$

$$= -\$20,141.78$$

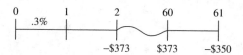

FIGURE 5-6 · Sample car loan.

Using our shorthand notation, this problem would be solved on a calculator by entering:

59	[T]
0.3%	[r]
-373	[C]
[CPT]	[PVA] = -20,141.78

This would convert our set of cash flows to those shown in Figure 5-7.
We can then convert the two remaining lump sums to time zero values using the PV formula, and then add them up:

$$PV = \frac{FV_1}{(1+r)^1} + \frac{FV_{61}}{(1+r)^{61}}$$

$$= \frac{-\$20,141.78}{(1.003)^1} + \frac{-\$350}{(1.003)^{61}}$$

$$= -\$20,081.53 + -\$291.55$$

$$= -\$20,373.08$$

On a calculator, these steps would be:

1	[T]
0.3%	[r]
-20,141.78	[FV]
[CPT]	[PV] = -20,373.08

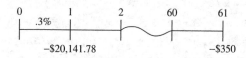

FIGURE 5-7 · Sample car loan with embedded annuity converted to lump sum.

and

61	[T]
0.3%	[r]
−350	[FV]
[CPT]	[PV] = −291.55

Summing these two intermediate values tells us that, given the interest rate of 0.3 percent per month, making the given stream of payments has a value equivalent to paying a single lump sum of $20,373.08 today.

Note that we were careful to keep all the cash flows negative in our calculations, indicating that we would be *paying* them. (If we had been doing this problem from the viewpoint of the lender, we would have kept them all positive to indicate that we would be *receiving* them.) For most of the problems dealing with personal finance, bonds, or stocks that you're likely to see, this isn't really necessary, as we're usually dealing with cash flows going in one direction only. The normal practice is to drop the negative signs on such problems, and that's what we'll usually do (though see the next example for a situation where we do need to keep track of the signs). We *will* have to consistently start keeping track of the signs again when we start talking about projects with both inflows and outflows, but that's still several chapters away.

Example—Retirement Calculation

As another example, suppose that you just turned 25 and are planning for your retirement. You hope to retire at the age of 60, and would like to be able to make end-of-month withdrawals from your retirement account of $2,500 per month for a 30-year period after that. If you plan on funding your retirement by making monthly deposits between now and when you retire, with the first monthly deposit occurring at the end of the coming month, how much must each deposit be if you can earn 1 percent per month in your retirement account? (And, yes: we're going to ignore taxes here.)

To set this up, you first need to make sure that you understand the timing of all the deposits and withdrawals, so set this up on a timeline and then compare it to the one shown in Figure 5-8.

Notice that all of the periods on the timeline are expressed in terms of months, even though the problem states them in terms of years. Whenever you use any

FIGURE 5-8 · Sample retirement problem.

of the TVM formulas, the inputs you enter must have what we'll refer to as *temporal congruence*: that is, any variables either measuring the number of time periods (i.e., *T*) or measuring units expressed in terms of per time period (i.e., *r* and C) must be converted to the same-length time period before you enter any of them into a TVM formula. In this problem, we have two annuities, one of deposits and one of withdrawals. Since both involve monthly payments, we will need to have *T* expressed in terms of months and *r* in terms of "per month." (Luckily, *r* is already given to us as a monthly rate: we'll discuss how to handle converting it if it's not, in the next chapter.)

The first step involves converting the annuity for the payments we *do* know, the withdrawals, into a lump sum. We have the choice of using either PVA or FVA formulas to do so; but, if we remember where those two formulas will place the lump sums, we can see that it will be better to use the PVA formula (because it will place the value at the same point in time as the last deposit, perfectly positioned for that value to be the FV of the deposit annuity). Solving for the PVA of the withdrawals yields:

$$PVA = C \times \left[\frac{1 - \frac{1}{(1+r)^T}}{r} \right]$$

$$= \$2{,}500 \times \left[\frac{1 - \frac{1}{(1+0.01)^{360}}}{0.01} \right]$$

$$= \$2{,}500 \times \left[\frac{1 - \frac{1}{35.9496}}{0.01} \right]$$

$$= \$2{,}500 \times \left[\frac{0.9722}{0.01} \right]$$

$$= \$243{,}045.83$$

On a calculator:

360	[T]
1%	[r]
2,500	[C]
[CPT]	[PVA] = 243,045.83

Applying the PVA formula in this manner converts our timeline to that shown in Figure 5-9.

Now, this is one of the few personal finance problems where the signs do matter, because it's one of a class of problems where we're both *paying* and *receiving* different cash flows. In this problem, we have to realize that the value of $243,045.83 at time 420 that we just calculated has to exactly offset the value of the deposits at the same point in time; that is, if the deposits are negative, then they have to have a future value of –$243,045.83. Knowing this lets us solve for the payment amount of the annuity of deposits:

$$FVA = C \times \left[\frac{(1+r)^T - 1}{r} \right]$$

$$-\$243,045.83 = C \times \left[\frac{(1+0.01)^{420} - 1}{0.01} \right]$$

$$= C \times 6,430.96$$

$$\frac{-\$243,045.83}{6,430.96} = C$$

$$-\$37.79 = C$$

On a calculator:

420	[T]
1%	[r]
–243,045.83	[FVA]
[CPT]	[C] = –37.79

So, you need to deposit $37.79 per month at the end of each of the next 420 months in order to fund your desired retirement.

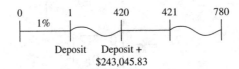

FIGURE 5-9 · Sample retirement problem with withdrawals converted to lump sum.

What About Annuities Due?

Annuities due, in case you've never heard of them, are simply annuities where the payments happen at the *beginning* of each period instead of the *end*, as they do with "ordinary" annuities.

There are adjusted versions of PVA and FVA for these types of annuities, as well as new rules concerning where those adjusted formulas will give you values on the timeline. However, they're probably not worth learning: you can usually handle almost all problems involving annuities due using the ordinary annuity formulas and a little creativity.

For example, consider the set of cash flows shown in Figure 5-10: is this an annuity?

Yes, and the question of whether it's an ordinary annuity or an annuity due only affects where we want to find the value of this annuity.

Suppose that, by default, we want to calculate the value at time 0. The easiest way to calculate this is to realize that the first payment of $150 is already where we want it: if we leave it alone for a moment, we can calculate the value of the other four payments as:

4   [T]
10%   [r]
150   [C]
[CPT]   [PVA] = 475.48

Notice where that $475.48 will be: one period in front of time 1, at time 0. Then all we have to do to find the total PV of all five payments is to add the first payment to this value: $475.48 + $150 = $625.48.

Or, consider another example: suppose we knew that the present value of this five-payment annuity due was $625.48 when the interest rate is 10 percent; how would we go about solving for the payment amount?

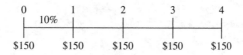

FIGURE 5-10 · Sample annuity due.

Well, once again we'd manipulate what we had to make it look like an ordinary annuity. If we move the $625.48 one period into the past using the PV formula, it becomes a value at time −1:

1	[T]
10%	[r]
625.48	[FV]
[CPT]	[PV] = 568.62

This allows us to rewrite our timeline as shown in Figure 5-11.

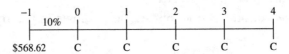

FIGURE 5-11 · Annuity due converted to ordinary annuity.

Notice that, even though the last payment occurs at time period 4, this is still a five-period annuity: *T* for an annuity is based upon how many payments there are, and not when they happen.

5	[T]
10%	[r]
568.62	[PV]
[CPT]	[C] = 150.00

QUIZ

1. The present value formula for an ordinary annuity gives you a value:
   A. One period before the first payment
   B. At the same point in time as the first payment
   C. One period after the last payment
   D. At the same point in time as the last payment

2. Suppose you finance $25,000 of the purchase price of a new car with a 48-month loan at 0.4 percent per month. What will your payments be?
   A. $373.24
   B. $416.67
   C. $469.49
   D. $573.47

3. Continuing the previous problem, suppose you also have the option of financing the car for 72 months at the same interest rate. If you chose this option, what would your payments be?
   A. $347.22
   B. $400.31
   C. $416.67
   D. $422.24

4. Suppose you are considering acquiring a house by assuming the remainder of the existing 30-year mortgage on the property. If there are 327 fixed monthly payments of $1,041.23 left to be paid, with the first payment being due exactly one month after you assume the loan, what price are you effectively paying for the house if your bank is quoting an interest rate of 0.5208 percent per month on similar loans?
   A. $16,659
   B. $163,354
   C. $169,108
   D. $340,482

5. What is the present value of a perpetuity of $100 per year if the first payment will be received one year from now and the appropriate interest rate is 8 percent per year?
   A. $0.80
   B. $12.50
   C. $125.00
   D. $1,250.00

6. Continuing the previous problem, what is the present value of this perpetuity if the first payment of $100 per year will not be received until five years from now, assuming that subsequent $100 payments will still occur once a year thereafter?

   A. $812.00
   B. $850.70
   C. $918.79
   D. $972.30

7. Suppose that you just turned 30 and are planning for your retirement. You hope to retire at age 67, and you would like to be able to make end-of-month withdrawals from your retirement account of $5,000 per month for a 20-year period after that. If you plan on funding your retirement by making monthly deposits between now and when you retire, with the first monthly deposit occurring at the end of the coming month, how much must each deposit be if you can earn 1 percent per month in your retirement account?

   A. $55.43
   B. $64.32
   C. $73.21
   D. $82.10

8. Continuing the previous problem, how much must each deposit be if you can earn only 0.5 percent per month in your retirement account?

   A. $134.82
   B. $227.82
   C. $343.82
   D. $427.82

9. What would be the present value of a yearly annuity of $105 per year for 10 years if the appropriate rate of interest is 4.5 percent per year and the first payment starts one year from today?

   A. $720.73
   B. $830.84
   C. $840.85
   D. $950.96

10. What would be the present value of a yearly annuity of $105 per year for 10 years if the appropriate rate of interest is 4.5 percent per year and the first payment arrives today?

    A. $636.83
    B. $705.05
    C. $774.79
    D. $868.22

Compounding and Interest Rate Conversion: When What You've Got Isn't What You Need

At the end of this chapter, the reader should be able to:

- Explain the difference between effective and nominal interest rates
- Explain how APRs are constructed
- Convert between nominal and effective interest rates

As we discussed in the last chapter, using any *Time Value of Money* (TVM) formula requires that *temporal congruence*, the agreement on a time period amongst all the variables dealing with time, holds. In this chapter, we'll discuss what our choices are when we don't have temporal congruence, and how to convert interest rates if necessary.

Interest Rate Flavors

All interest rates can be described using the two-dimensional grid shown in Figure 6-1.

In this grid, the vertical dimension consists of two absolute categories: *effective* interest rates are true interest rates, ones that can be used in TVM formulas; *nominal* interest rates are rates "in name only" because they cannot be used as such in TVM formulas. Nominal rates are usually somehow constructed from effective rates, but the mathematical procedures used to produce them are not sufficiently rigorous to ensure that the results are also effective rates.

The horizontal dimension of this grid measures a continuum of relative periods of time associated with multiple rates. Since this continuum is relative, a particular rate's placement depends upon what it's being compared to; for example, a monthly rate would lie to the right of a weekly rate, but to the left of a quarterly rate, and so forth.

Whenever we are given a rate in a problem, we should determine (a) where that rate is on this grid; (b) whether it's the rate that we need, and, if necessary, how to get from (a) to (b).

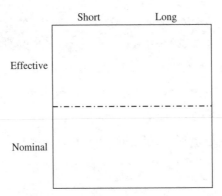

FIGURE 6-1 • The universe of interest rates.

APRs Explained

Benjamin Disraeli, the prime minister of the British Empire from 1874–1880, uttered the famous quote that, "There are three types of lies—lies, damn lies, and statistics." To this list, we need to add a fourth: the *Annual Percentage Rate* (APR).

The use of the APR in the United States arose from the "Truth in Lending" provisions of the Consumer Credit Protection Act, which was passed by the U.S. Congress in 1968. This act was intended to protect consumers by requiring lenders to provide information about credit terms and to express the cost of credit in a consistent manner; that is, as an APR.

APRs are comparable across lenders, in that an APR of 21 percent on one credit card does indicate that the borrower will pay more on this credit card than on one that quotes, say, an APR of 18 percent. But neither of these quoted rates can be used as is by the borrower to calculate how much interest he or she will pay, except under a very special set of circumstances, which we'll cover below.

As with other nominal rates, the reason that an APR is not a real rate is due to how it's constructed: the lender takes the effective rate per payment period and multiplies it by the number of payment periods in a year. Since most consumer loans require monthly payments, this means that most quoted APRs are constructed by taking the monthly effective rate and multiplying it by 12.

What's wrong with this? Well, it does capture the amount of interest you would pay on the amount of borrowed principal, normally referred to as the *simple interest*, but it fails to account for any "interest on interest" that accrues and is added to the principal. This process is referred to as *compound interest*, and underlies all of the TVM formulas, including the annuity formulas used by the lenders to calculate your loan payments.

Not surprisingly, this implicit use of compound interest in the TVM formulas implies that the formula for calculating the amount of compound interest accruing to a loan during a year, for example, can be calculated using the FV formula. If we substitute PV $\times (1 + r_{annual})$ into the formula for FV, set T equal to 12 (because there's 12 months in a year), and use the monthly rate, $r_{monthly}$, as the interest rate on the right-hand side of the equation, r_{annual} will represent the annual rate of growth in money, which is really just what an interest rate is:

$$FV = PV \times (1+r)^T$$
$$PV \times (1+r_{annual}) = PV \times (1+r_{monthly})^{12}$$
$$1+r_{annual} = (1+r_{monthly})^{12}$$
$$r_{annual} = (1+r_{monthly})^{12} - 1$$

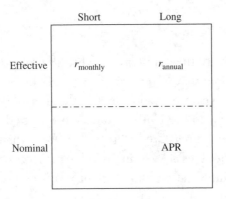

FIGURE 6-2 · Positioning of $r_{monthly}$, r_{annual}, and APR.

So, while the APR would state the quoted annual interest rate on a credit card which charges 1.5 percent interest per month as $12 \times 1.5\% = 18\%$, the calculations above would tell us that the actual annual effective rate would be equal to $(1.015)^{12} - 1 = 0.1956$, or 19.56%.

Referring once again to our two-dimensional grid, the relationships between the effective monthly rate, the effective annual rate, and the APR are shown in Figure 6-2. So, how do you know that you're being quoted an APR or some other nominal rate instead of an effective rate? Well, there are two common conventions for quoting a nominal rate:

1. Explicitly state that the rate is an APR or some other nominal rate.

2. Quote the rate, but follow it up with a phrase indicating that this rate is constructed from smaller effective rates, such as, "compounded weekly"; for example, "10%, compounded monthly" implies that the 10 percent rate is a nominal rate and that it was constructed from effective monthly rates, so you can "deconstruct" it by dividing back by 12 to get the effective monthly rate.

If neither of these caveats applies to a rate that you're given, then you should assume that it's an effective rate, and that it's for the length of time period that you need.

Just Because You Have a New Toy Doesn't Mean You *Have* To Use It!

To summarize the discussion on APRs above, the methods for converting back and forth between various rates that we're likely to see are shown in Figure 6-3.

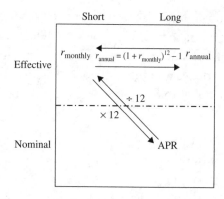

FIGURE 6-3 · Conversion techniques for APR and monthly interest rates.

Notice that, if you're given an APR and you need an effective monthly rate, all you have to do is divide the APR by 12 to get what you need. And, most of the time when you're dealing with a consumer finance problem involving a car loan, or a house mortgage, or credit card payments, or something similar, the monthly rate *is* the rate you want.

Even if you are being given an effective rate *other* than what you need, either explicitly or implicitly via a nominal rate constructed from a different effective rate, you still might not have to use the interest rate conversion formula. Specifically, if you're dealing with a lump-sum problem, there's an easier way to handle temporal incongruence.

Even though all five TVM equations have T in them, it means a *different* thing for the lump-sum equations (i.e., PV and FV) than it does for the equations that deal with series of payments (i.e., PVP, PVA, and FVA). In the lump-sum equations, T is measuring *how far you need to move the lump sum*; in the other equations, it's measuring *how many payments there are*.

For the equations involving payments, this means that we are *not* free to change T; its value is locked in to be the number of payments involved in the problem (and, no, getting 30 yearly payments on a mortgage is not the same as getting 360 monthly payments; think of the effect on interest accrual due to the difference in timing).

However, for the lump-sum equations, we are free to change the units of measurement we're using to describe T because, since we're using T to measure distance, doing so has no detrimental effect on the problem (for example, "12 months" means the same thing as "1 year," doesn't it?). So, if we get a problem where the effective rate is given to us in a different time denomination than T is, it's going to be much simpler for us to convert T than to use the interest conversion formula.

For example, suppose we're asked to find the present value of $1,000 to be received in five years if the APR is 6 percent. The 6 percent APR is easily converted to a monthly effective rate of 6%/12 = 0.5% per month. We could then turn around and convert this monthly rate to an *Effective Annual Rate* (EAR) so that we could keep T equal to five years, but it would be easier just to do the problem like this:

60 (months)	[T]
0.5% (per month)	[r]
1000	[FV]
[CPT]	[PV] = 741.37

Dealing with Other Nominal Rates

More generally, the interest rate conversion formula for going back and forth between effective interest rates for different lengths of time can be written as:

$$r_{long} = (1 + r_{short})^m - 1$$

where r_{long} = the effective interest rate for the *longer* period of time
r_{short} = the effective interest rate for the *shorter* period of time
m = the number of short periods in a long period

So, for example, if you knew that the one-year effective rate (commonly referred to as the EAR) was 13 percent, but wanted to find the three-year effective rate, you would calculate it as $(1.13)^3 - 1 = .4429$, or 44.29 percent, because there are three single years in a three-year period.

This formula could also be easily rewritten to allow for the situation where you know r_{long} and need to solve for r_{short}:

$$r_{long} = (1 + r_{short})^m - 1$$
$$1 + r_{long} = (1 + r_{short})^m$$
$$\sqrt[m]{1 + r_{long}} = 1 + r_{short}$$
$$\sqrt[m]{1 + r_{long}} - 1 = r_{short}$$

For example, if you knew that the EAR was 12 percent, but wanted to find the quarterly effective rate, you could calculate it as $(1.12)^{1/4} - 1 = 0.0287$, or 2.87 percent per quarter. (Remember that the "mth" root of something is the same as the "$1/m$th" power, which is the fact that we're using here.)

If we were going to be doing only personal finance problems throughout the rest of this text, we'd probably have just kept our interest conversion equation in the form specific to converting back and forth between r_{annual} and $r_{monthly}$; however, as we'll see again and again in later chapters, corporate finance involves many interest rate conversions between other pairs of effective rates, too, so the more general form that we've developed here is much better suited for our purposes.

For example, bond rates (usually called *yields*, because they represent the rate to be *earned*, from the viewpoint of the bond purchaser) are quoted in terms of a nominal annual interest rate based on two payments (and, therefore, two interest compounding periods) a year. If someone quotes a nominal annual yield of 8 percent on a bond with semiannual payments, you need to first divide the nominal 8 percent annual yield by 2 (the number of six-month periods in a year) to get the effective six-month rate of 4 percent, then use the interest rate conversion formula to determine that they are really telling you that the *Effective Annual Yield* (EAY) is $(1.04)^2 - 1 = .0816$, or 8.16 percent.

A Caution on Using Calculators or Textbook Formulas to Convert Rates

If you'll closely examine the conversion techniques shown in Figure 6-4, you'll notice that both the conversion from nominal long to effective short and the conversion from effective short to effective long use m.

However, these two instances of m don't have to have the same value: for example, we could be given a nominal annual rate based on monthly compounding, but need an effective five-year rate. By converting the nominal annual rate to

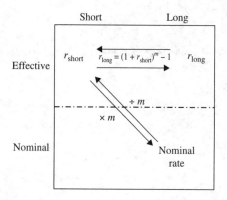

FIGURE 6-4 · Conversion techniques for interest rates in general.

the effective monthly rate separately from the conversion of the effective monthly rate to an effective five-year rate, we are able to accommodate differences in the value of m between the two parts of problems such as this one.

One of the pitfalls of using either a calculator's built-in interest conversion worksheet or the interest conversion formula given in a textbook is that both of these sources try to do everything for you. Normally, that's a good thing, but in trying to do everything for you they also make the assumption that m is going to be the same in both parts of every problem, which allows them to perform the conversion from nominal long rate to effective long rate in one step as shown in Figure 6-5.

If the two values of m are *not* the same, then doing everything in one step like this will probably cause problems: most calculators only have one place to enter m, and the formulas in most textbooks don't give you any easy way to tell which instance of m is which.

Will you always get into trouble if you use a calculator or your textbook's formula to do this conversion in one step like this? No; in fact, you'll usually be OK, because the m's of the two parts usually are the same, but you will have to be on the lookout for the odd exception.

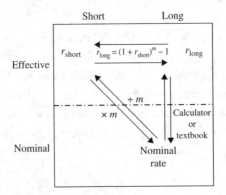

FIGURE 6-5 · The conversion technique used by calculators and textbooks.

QUIZ

1. Which of the following pairs of interest rate quotations represents a pair of different quotes that we could switch back and forth between using only division and multiplication (i.e., without using a formula involving powers or roots)?

   A. The effective monthly rate and the EAR
   B. The APR and the EAR
   C. The nominal quarterly rate and the effective quarterly rate
   D. The effective monthly rate and the APR

2. Everything else held constant, decreasing the number of compounding periods during a year for a given nominal rate will cause:

   A. The effective rate per compounding period to increase and the EAR to decrease
   B. The effective rate per compounding period to decrease and the EAR to increase
   C. The effective rate per compounding period and the EAR to increase
   D. The effective rate per compounding period and the EAR to decrease

3. Suppose you are considering an investment that has an APR, based on monthly compounding, of 6.5 percent. What would be the effective two-year rate of return on this security?

   A. 13.84%
   B. 14.37%
   C. 88.36%
   D. 95.66%

4. If you want your money to triple (i.e., increase by 200 percent) in four years, what APR (based on monthly compounding) would you need to earn?

   A. 22.07%
   B. 27.78%
   C. 31.95%
   D. 60.00%

5. A three-year annuity of twelve $5,000 quarterly payments will begin 2.75 years from now (i.e., the first payment will be 2.75 years from now). If the discount rate is 8 percent compounded monthly, what is the current value of this annuity?

   A. $43,285
   B. $52,833
   C. $55,017
   D. $60,000

6. If a bank wanted to quote an APR of 6.25 percent based on monthly compounding for its savings accounts, what EAR would it have to pay?

   A. 6.00%

   B. 6.25%

   C. 6.43%

   D. 6.56%

7. What quoted interest rate, if compounded daily, would be equal to an EAR of 7.50 percent?

   A. 6.50%

   B. 6.75%

   C. 7.00%

   D. 7.23%

8. Bonds usually pay interest twice a year (i.e., every six months), so their interest rates are usually quoted as a nominal annual rate compounded biannually. If a bond is quoted as paying an interest rate of 8 percent, what would the EAR be?

   A. 7.50%

   B. 8.16%

   C. 8.71%

   D. 11.30%

9. Stocks usually pay dividends quarterly, so their *dividend yields* (i.e., dividends expressed as interest rates based on the stock price) are usually quoted as a nominal annual rate compounded quarterly. If a stock is quoted as yielding 12 percent per year, what would the EAR be?

   A. 10.52%

   B. 11.37%

   C. 12.56%

   D. 13.03%

10. An elderly woman is considering a "reverse mortgage," in which her bank will pay her $1,500 per month for the rest of her life. In exchange for this, the bank gets ownership of her home on her death, but nothing else, no matter how long she lives. Her home is currently worth $150,000 and, due to an extremely stable real estate market in her town, is expected to retain (but not increase) that value in the future. If the appropriate APR for this reverse mortgage is 10 percent, and if the first $1,500 payment will be received exactly one month after she signs the paperwork, the bank will make money on this deal only if it gains ownership of the home in less than (round your answer down to the closest month):

    A. 2 years, 9 months

    B. 6 years, 1 month

    C. 8 years, 4 months

    D. 12 years, 6 months

chapter 7

Payment Composition and Amortization Schedules

CHAPTER OBJECTIVES

At the end of this chapter, the reader should be able to:

- Compare and contrast pure discount loans, interest-only loans, and amortized loans
- Calculate payment components for pure discount loans
- Calculate payment components for interest-only loans
- Calculate payment components for constant-payment loans
- Calculate payment components for constant-principal loans

As loans are repaid over time, the composition of the payments, in terms of how much of each goes toward principal repayment and how much goes toward interest, may change. Keeping track of these changing amounts is important for several reasons:

1. From the viewpoint of the corporate borrower, interest will be tax-deductible, but principal won't be.

2. From the viewpoint of the lender or investor, interest will be taxable, but principal won't be.

3. If a loan is repaid early, the repayment amount will be equal to the principal that has not been repaid, plus any accrued but unpaid interest.

4. The amount of outstanding principal may have regulatory implications, particularly for financial institutions such as banks or thrifts.

For these and other reasons, being able to model the amount if principal and interest contained in each payment on a loan is important. How we undertake that modeling will differ based on the type of loan:

1. In a *pure discount loan*, all interest and principal is repaid at the maturity date.

2. In an *interest-only loan*, all intermediate payments consist of only interest and all principal is repaid at the end.

3. With an *amortized loan*, each payment contains some principal and interest, with the interest being calculated based on how much principal is still outstanding at the time of each payment. Theoretically, the amount of principal repaid in each payment can be set according to any scheme that the lender and borrower agree to; pragmatically, most loans of this type are set up to be *constant-payment loans* or *constant-principal loans*, both types of which we'll explain later.

Calculating Payment Components for Pure Discount Loans

Pure discount loans are essentially lump-sum *Time Value of Money* (TVM) problems, with the amount to be repaid set equal to the future value of the loan amount. To calculate how much of the repaid amount is interest, we simply take the difference between *Future Value* (FV)—the amount repaid, and *Present Value* (PV)—the amount borrowed.

For example, suppose you had borrowed $1,000 via a pure discount loan at 8 percent interest per year and were going to pay it back in three years. At the end of the three years, you would repay:

$$FV = PV(1+r)^T$$
$$= \$1000(1.08)^3$$
$$= \$1,259.72$$

Of this, $1,259.72 − $1,000 = $259.72 would be interest and $1,000 would be principal.

Notice that this approach works whether the loan is repaid on time or early. With these loans, the interest accrues fairly smoothly through time, so the amount to be repaid at any point in time is going to be the FV at that time.

This discussion, of course, assumes that the loan doesn't call for any penalties for early repayment. Since the Predatory Lending Consumer Protection Act of 2002 put a pretty severe cap on lenders' use of prepayment penalties, these are becoming increasingly rare, so it's not something we need to worry about.

Calculating Payment Components for Interest-Only Loans

This type of loan calls for the borrower to make a certain number of interest-only payments at specified intervals throughout the life of the loan and then to repay all principal, as well as the last interest payment, at maturity.

Effectively, the payments on this type of loan consist of an annuity, plus an extra lump sum at the same time as the last annuity payments, as shown in Figure 7-1. The annuity payments are calculated by multiplying the principal by the effective periodic rate for the length of time between payments:

$$C = r \times \text{principal}$$

With this type of loan, calculating the remaining principal and accrued unpaid interest is trivial; none of the principal is paid until the end, and the most accrued interest that can be owed at any given time is equal to C.

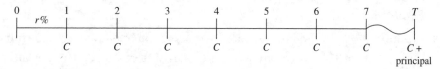

FIGURE 7-1 · Cash flows of an interest-only loan.

Amortized Loans: Constant-Payment Loans

Constant-payment loans, those which involve repayment through a stream of fixed, constant payments throughout the life of the loan, are by far the most common types of amortized loans, particularly for consumers. If you're making a mortgage payment on a fixed-rate loan, or if you have a car loan, then you're making payments on a constant-payment loan.

With amortized loans, the amount of interest paid is neither a single amount, like it is with pure discount loans, nor a constant amount, as it is with interest-only loans. As a result, we need to have a more systematic approach for keeping track of exactly how much interest and principal is repaid in each payment than the rather *ad hoc* approaches that we've used so far in this chapter. We achieve this through the use of what's called an amortization table, an example of which is shown in Figure 7-2. This amortization table was constructed for the following problem:

Assume that you have borrowed $25,000 at 10 percent interest per year, and that it will be repaid in 10 equal payments at the end of each of the next 10 years.

Each row of this table was constructed using the following six steps:

1. Calculate the payment amount by treating the amount borrowed as the present value of an annuity. For this problem, the payment amount would be solved for by:

10	[T]
10%	[r]
$25,000	[PVA]
[CPT]	[C] = $4,068.63

2. For each payment in turn, determine the amount of principal outstanding (the *Beginning Balance*) during the period for which the payment comes at the end. Note that, for the first payment, the entire amount borrowed would have been outstanding during the first period, $25,000; for all later payments, this amount will be equal to the remaining principal after the previous payment has been made (the previous period's *Ending Balance*).

3. Multiply the periodic interest rate by this *Beginning Balance* to determine how much of this payment will go toward interest (i.e., the *portion of payment toward interest*). For the first row, $25,000 × 10% = $2,500.

Payment number	Beginning balance	Payment	Portion of payment toward		Ending balance
			Principal	Interest	
1	$25,000.00	$4,068.63	$1,568.63	$2,500.00	$23,431.37
2	$23,431.37	$4,068.63	$1,725.50	$2,343.14	$21,705.87
3	$21,705.87	$4,068.63	$1,898.05	$2,170.59	$19,807.82
4	$19,807.82	$4,068.63	$2,087.85	$1,980.78	$17,719.97
5	$17,719.97	$4,068.63	$2,296.64	$1,772.00	$15,423.33
6	$15,423.33	$4,068.63	$2,526.30	$1,542.33	$12,897.03
7	$12,897.03	$4,068.63	$2,778.93	$1,289.70	$10,118.09
8	$10,118.09	$4,068.63	$3,056.83	$1,011.81	$7,061.27
9	$7,061.27	$4,068.63	$3,362.51	$706.13	$3,698.76
10	$3,698.76	$4,068.63	$3,698.76	$369.88	$0.00

FIGURE 7-2 · Sample amortization table for fixed-payment loan.

4. Deduct this amount from the constant payment amount to determine how much of this payment will go toward principal (i.e., the *portion of payment toward principal*). For the first row, this is equal to $4,068.63 − $2,500 = $1,568.63.

5. Deduct the amount in step 3 from the *Beginning Balance* to get the *Ending Balance*. After the first payment, we are left with $25,000 − $1,568.63 = $23,431.37.

6. Go to the next row, copy the *Ending Balance* you just computed to the next period's *Beginning Balance*, and repeat steps 2 through 6.

Amortized Loans: Constant-Principal Loans

Constant-payment loans require that the amount repaid toward the principal each time is equal to $1/T$ times the original balance of the loan, so that the principal is repaid smoothly in equal amounts throughout the life of the loan.

Constructing the amortization for this type of loan is very similar to the process we followed above for fixed-payment loans, with one large difference: instead of knowing the payment amount and then "backing out" the principal and interest portions as we did above, for constant-principal loans we *start* with the principal repaid in each payment and then add the interest to determine the payment amount. As payments are made, the outstanding principal goes down, causing both the interest portion and the total payment to decline over time.

| Payment number | Beginning balance | Payment | Portion of payment toward | | Ending balance |
			Principal	Interest	
1	$25,000.00	$5,000.00	$2,500.00	$2,500.00	$22,500.00
2	$22,500.00	$4,750.00	$2,500.00	$2,250.00	$20,000.00
3	$20,000.00	$4,500.00	$2,500.00	$2,000.00	$17,500.00
4	$17,500.00	$4,250.00	$2,500.00	$1,750.00	$15,000.00
5	$15,000.00	$4,000.00	$2,500.00	$1,500.00	$12,500.00
6	$12,500.00	$3,750.00	$2,500.00	$1,250.00	$10,000.00
7	$10,000.00	$3,500.00	$2,500.00	$1,000.00	$7,500.00
8	$7,500.00	$3,250.00	$2,500.00	$750.00	$5,000.00
9	$5,000.00	$3,000.00	$2,500.00	$500.00	$2,500.00
10	$2,500.00	$2,750.00	$2,500.00	$250.00	$0.00

FIGURE 7-3 · Sample amortization table for fixed-principal loan.

For example, let's consider the same loan we used in the previous example ($25,000 at 10 percent repaid in 10 annual payments), but let's now assume that it is a fixed-principal loan. Constructing the amortization table for this loan will now have a very different set of figures, shown in Figure 7-3.

This table was constructed using the following five steps:

1. Determine the amount or principal repaid each period by dividing the principal by the number of payments. For this example, this would be equal to $25,000/10 = $2,500.

2. For each payment, first determine the amount of principal outstanding (the *Beginning Balance*) during the period for which the payment comes at the end. *Note that this step will yield the same number, $25,000, for the first row that we saw in the previous example, but that all subsequent Beginning Balance amounts will be different.* As before, this amount will still be equal to the remaining principal after the previous payment has been made (the previous period's *Ending Balance*), but we don't have to wait to fill in this column until after we calculate each payment. We know that principal is going to start at $25,000 and decline by $2,500 each year, so we can go ahead and fill in all these values as $22,500 for the second payment, $20,000 for the third payment, and so forth.

3. Multiply the periodic interest rate by this *Beginning Balance* to determine how much of this payment will go toward interest (i.e., the *portion of payment toward interest*). For the first row, $25,000 × 10% = $2,500.

4. Add the principal portion from step 2 to the interest portion from step 3 to determine the total payment for this period. For the first row, this is equal to $2,500 + $2,500 = $5,000.

5. Go to the next row and repeat only steps 3 through 5.

A Final Note on Amortized Loans

Constructing an amortization table can be a lot of work if all you're really interested in is just a small part of that table, such as the balance remaining on a loan after a certain number of payments are made. If you're dealing with a fixed-principal loan, or just about any other less-common type of amortized loan, you're out of luck; you basically have to build the whole table (or, at least, get Excel to do it for you).

However, if you're working with a fixed-payment loan, there are shortcuts available to you. These shortcuts exist because a fixed-payment loan is, at heart, just an annuity. Because of that, you can always:

- Calculate the remaining principal after any payment by calculating the present value of the remaining payments.

- Calculate how much interest will be paid over the remaining payments by summing up the remaining payments and subtracting the remaining principal that you just calculated.

For example, returning to our previous example of a $25,000 fixed-payment loan at 10 percent per year to be repaid through 10 annual payments, suppose that we hadn't yet prepared the amortization table, but we wanted to know what the remaining balance of the loan was after we'd made seven payments. We would just have to solve the following problem:

3   [T]
10%   [r]
$4,068.63   [C]
[CPT]   [PVA] = $10,118.09

Note that this is the same value as calculated for the *Ending Balance* after the seventh payment in Figure 7-2.

If we also wanted to calculate the sum of the interest payments yet to be made at that same time (i.e., after payment 7), we could do so by taking ($4,068.63 × 3) − $10,118.09 = $2,087.81. This value is equal, except for a rounding error, to what we would obtain by adding the interest portions of payments 8, 9, and 10 from Figure 7-2:

$$\$1,011.81 + \$706.13 + \$369.88 = \$2,087.82$$

Finally, please note that this example assumes that the loan is being repaid early on exactly the date that a payment is due (which happens fairly frequently, by the way). If this is the case, then you simply have to find the present value of the annuity of remaining payments as shown above. However, if the loan is being repaid on other than a normal payment date, then you will still use the present value of an annuity formula but will also need to use the lump-sum formula to move the resulting value to the right point in time.

QUIZ

1. Everything else held constant, which of the following types of loans will require you to pay the least total interest throughout the life of a loan?

   A. Pure discount loan
   B. Interest-only loan
   C. Constant-payment loan
   D. Constant-principal loan

2. Suppose you borrowed $5,000 via a pure discount loan at 4.25 percent interest per year and were going to pay back both principal and interest in three years. How much interest would you pay?

   A. $664.98
   B. $1,540.81
   C. $6,540.81
   D. $5,664.98

3. Returning to the loan described in problem 2, suppose that, instead of a pure discount loan, you had borrowed the money through an interest-only loan with a nominal interest rate of 5.50 percent, compounded semiannually, and that the loan required payments every six months. What would the amount of your periodic interest payment be?

   A. $27.50
   B. $55.00
   C. $137.50
   D. $275.00

4. Suppose that you finance $30,000 of the purchase price of a new car for 60 months at an APR of 4.9 percent. If you repay the loan in 60 monthly payments, how much total interest will you have paid at the end of the 60 payments?

   A. $3,885.82
   B. $7,350.00
   C. $63,500.09
   D. $88,200.00

5. Suppose that you buy a new house, financing $110,000 of the purchase price with a 30-year mortgage at an APR of 7.5 percent, which is to be repaid in 360 equal monthly payments. If you buy the house in July, but make your first payment in August, you will make your first five payments during the first "calendar year" that you own the house. How much total interest for this loan will you be able to claim on your taxes for the *second* calendar year that you own the house?

   A. $6,540.14
   B. $7,080.14
   C. $8,183.53
   D. $9,104.30

6. Suppose that you borrow $100,000 in the form of a constant-principal loan that calls for repayment of the loan via 20 annual payments, with the first payment occurring one year from today. If this loan carries an interest rate of 6 percent, what will be the amount of principal repaid each year?

A. $5,000

B. $6,000

C. $8,000

D. $10,000

7. Continuing the previous problem, how much interest will be in the third payment?

A. $600

B. $1,200

C. $1,800

D. $5,400

8. Suppose you have taken out $65,000 in student loans to get through college. You are now faced with repayment of those loans, and that repayment will take the form of equal monthly payments for the next 10 years. If the APR on student loans is 6.25 percent, what will be your monthly payment?

A. $280.70

B. $487.23

C. $729.82

D. $1,563.58

9. Continuing the previous problem, how much of your first payment will be interest?

A. $105.44

B. $338.54

C. $428.90

D. $730.21

10. Continuing the previous two problems, how much total interest will you pay throughout the life of this loan?

A. $4,565.98

B. $6,886.73

C. $8,684.03

D. $22,578.48

Part III

Valuation

chapter 8

Valuing Bonds

CHAPTER OBJECTIVES

At the end of this chapter, the reader should be able to:

- Explain the conventions of bond quotations
- Price a bond
- Explain the difference between coupon rate and yield to maturity and solve for each
- Calculate a bond's current yield and capital gains yield

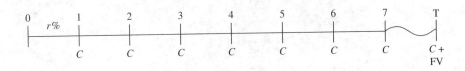

FIGURE 8-1 · Sample bond cash flows.

A *bond* is tangible evidence of debt issued by a corporation or a governmental body, and represents a loan made by investors to the issuer. In fact, bonds are the most prevalent example of the interest-only type of loan discussed in the previous chapters, with investors receiving exactly the same two sets of cash flows that we discussed previously, albeit cloaked in a new lingo: the periodic interest payments are referred to as the *coupon* payments, and the principal returned at maturity is usually referred to as the *par value* or *face value*. (Sort of makes you understand why we've been using "C" to stand for annuity payments and "FV" for future value, doesn't it?) These cash flows are shown in Figure 8-1.

The Conventions of Bond Quotations

Bonds have been around a long time; long enough, in fact, for there to be a rather elaborate set of customary rules concerning how they're quoted, much of which was set down well before most of us were born. As a result of their age, some of these quotation conventions seem a bit nonsensical in an era of high-speed computers and pervasive broadband communication, but we need to understand them in order to interact with the bond markets.

For example, bond prices for corporate and government bonds are typically quoted as a percentage of the bond's face value, with the added complication that fractional portions of prices are quoted as actual fractions: corporate bonds are quoted in 1/8 increments, while U.S. government bonds are usually quoted in 1/32 increments. So, if you receive a quote of 101 1/8 on a corporate bond, you need to convert that by taking 101.125 percent of par ($1,000), or $1,011.25, before you can start analyzing it.

Another convention is based on the fact that most bonds carry a face value of $1,000. This value is typical enough that most finance texts expect you to assume that it will be $1,000 unless specifically told otherwise. For conformity's sake, we'll do the same, too.

Another confusing aspect of how people refer to bonds deals with a bond's maturity, which is always quoted in terms of how many periods are left when you're pricing it. For example, suppose that it's now 2007 and you're talking about an annual-coupon bond that was issued in 1997 with an original 30-year maturity; since this bond has 20 years left until maturity, it would be referred to as a 20-year bond, not as a 30-year bond. The rationale here is that those first 10 payments are gone; they're not going to go to whoever buys the bond today, so that person should use $T = 20$ (see later) when pricing the bond.

Finally, we need to understand how bond rates are quoted; as we'll discuss later, there are actually several different types of rates quoted concerning bonds. Without exception, all of these are quoted on a nominal annual basis, even though the majority of bonds pay interest semiannually. As per our previous discussion concerning APRs and other nominal rates, we *cannot* use any of these nominal rates in calculations and should, instead, divide any such rates by two to get the effective six-month rate before using these rates in any type of bond calculation.

The Mathematics of a Bond

If bonds consisted of any arbitrary combination of an annuity of coupon payments and a lump-sum face value, we would have a great deal of difficulty in analyzing them. But we're in luck, because the combination of these two parts *isn't* arbitrary: in every bond, T for the annuity part of the cash flows will be numerically equal to T for the lump-sum part.

This allows us to write the sum of the present values of these two parts as one large equation, where T has a common value throughout:

$$PV_{bond} = C \times \left[\frac{1 - \frac{1}{(1+r)^T}}{r}\right] + \frac{FV}{(1+r)^T}$$

To make this equation a little more readable, as well as making the intuition that we're going to go over in a moment easier to obtain, the ultimate divisor r in the annuity portion of the formula above is usually distributed out to produce this version:

$$PV_{bond} = C \times \left(\frac{1}{r} - \frac{1}{r(1+r)^T}\right) + \frac{FV}{(1+r)^T}$$

This is the bond pricing formula that we'll be using throughout the rest of the book. Notice that it is the first *Time Value of Money* (TVM) equation that actually uses all five of the variables found in the other TVM formulas.

However, before we start using it, we need to talk about another convention concerning bonds: Which rates are quoted?

There are Rates, and then there are Rates that aren't Really Rates...

If you'll refer back to the last chapter, you'll remember that we said that the annuity payments on an interest-only loan (a category which bonds fall into) can be calculated by multiplying the effective periodic rate for the length of time between payments by the principal. In the case of bonds, that would be:

$$C = r \times FV$$

However, we need to be a little more specific here. The r inside the coupon payment, C, is different than all the other r that's everywhere else in the bond pricing equation that we just developed; to keep the two clear, let's call the r inside the coupon payment r_{coupon} and the other r the "going rate of interest." (You also sometimes hear that other r referred to as the *Yield to Maturity* (YTM), particularly when it's being solved for; but we'll talk more about that later.) The going rate of interest will change throughout the life of the bond in response to changes in either the macroeconomic environment or in the issuing entity's fortunes. As we'll discuss later in this book, the going rate of interest acts as compensation for the issuing entity's risk: if the chance of default goes up, making the bond more risky, then the going rate of interest will go up, too, to compensate.

The r_{coupon}, on the other hand, will *not* change once the bond is issued. After issuance, the dollar coupon, C, is a contracted obligation to the issuing firm or organization, and it cannot be changed (with the exception of variable-rate bonds, which we'll discuss later).

"Whew!," you say, "Wait a minute! If r_{coupon} isn't going to change, if all we really care about is the dollar coupon C, and if the bond pricing formula didn't have r_{coupon} in it to start with, why in the world are we even talking about it in the first place? Isn't it just going to confuse us?"

You're right, but bond markets don't quote C, they quote a nominal r_{coupon}. They're the ones who are going to be confusing us, so it's a good idea to make sure that we know what to do with what we're going to receive.

When we receive an r_{coupon}, we will first need to convert it to an effective six-month rate if it's being quoted on a semiannual bond; then, we'll need to multiply it by the face value to get the dollar coupon per period.

For example, if we're analyzing a bond that we're told is "paying a semiannual coupon of 9%," our first step will be to divide that quoted 9 percent by 2 to get the effective six-month rate: 9%/2 = 4.5%. We'll then turn around and multiply that percentage by $1,000 (since face value is not otherwise quoted) to get the semiannual dollar coupon, C: 4.5% × $1,000 = $45 per six-month period.

On the other hand, if we had been told that the bond was paying an *annual* coupon of 9 percent, then we would have skipped the step of dividing by 2 and would have immediately calculated C: 9% × $1,000 = $90 per year.

In either case, we can just throw r_{coupon} away once we've calculated C, right? Well, we don't need it (or ever want to use it) as a mathematical variable in a TVM formula anymore, but there *is* still some valuable intuition to be gained from it.

It turns out that, even though r_{coupon} is fixed now, it wasn't always fixed. Earlier, before the company or organization sold the bonds for the first time, they chose r_{coupon} very carefully. To see what value they would have wanted to choose, let's substitute r_{coupon} × FV for C into our bond pricing formula:

$$PV_{bond} = (r_{coupon} \times FV) \times \left(\frac{1}{r} - \frac{1}{r(1+r)^T} \right) + \frac{FV}{(1+r)^T}$$

If we set r_{coupon} equal to the current value of r at that time, this formula simplifies a lot:

$$PV_{bond} = (r \times FV) \times \left(\frac{1}{r} - \frac{1}{r(1+r)^T} \right) + \frac{FV}{(1+r)^T}$$

$$= FV \times \left(\frac{1}{1} - \frac{1}{1(1+r)^T} \right) + \frac{FV}{(1+r)^T}$$

$$= FV - \frac{FV}{(1+r)^T} + \frac{FV}{(1+r)^T}$$

$$= FV$$

That is, if the coupon rate is set equal to the going rate of interest at the time of issuance, the bond will sell for the same amount as the face value. Since this will make the bond's cash flows *exactly* equal to those of an interest-only loan from the viewpoint of the issuer, and will thereby greatly simplify the necessary bookkeeping, issuers want to set the coupon rate equal to the going rate of interest.

So, where does all this leave us, and how does it affect any intuition we might get from keeping r_{coupon} in mind after the bond has been issued? Let's take a look back at the bond pricing formula again, without the substitution that we just performed:

$$PV_{bond} = C \times \left(\frac{1}{r} - \frac{1}{r(1+r)^T} \right) + \frac{FV}{(1+r)^T}$$

In terms of being on the top or bottom of fractions, where are all the r's that can change after issuance? On the bottom. So, after a bond has been issued, what is going to happen to the price of the bond price if r goes up? It's going to go down, and vice-versa. Therefore, knowing what r was equal to when the bond was issued (i.e., the coupon rate) will give us a rough idea of the range that the price should be in.

For example, if we are asked to price a bond with an annual 8 percent coupon when the going rate of interest on such bonds is 9 percent, we would know that the price we get should be *less* than par before we do any calculations. Because rates have gone *up* from 8 percent to 9 percent since the bond was issued, the price must have gone *down*.

Likewise, if we are asked to price a bond with a coupon of 9.5 percent when the going rate of interest on such bonds is 8.3 percent, we would know that the price we get should be *greater* than par before we do any calculations. Because rates have gone *down* from 8 percent to 9 percent since the bond was issued, the price must have gone *up*.

Furthermore, this causation works the other way, too: if a problem tells you that a bond is selling at a *discount* (i.e., for less than face value), it is also telling you that rates must have gone up since the bond was issued; in other words, that the going rate of interest on this bond must be greater than the coupon rate. (The equivalent terminology for a bond selling for *more* than face value is *selling at a premium*.)

Solving for Bond Price

Now that we've covered the environment and conventions of bond quotations, we're ready to put it all together and actually start using the bond pricing formula.

Suppose that someone is selling a 10-year bond with a semiannual coupon of 9 percent, when the going rate on such bonds is 7 percent. How much would you be willing to pay for this bond?

Before we can use the bond pricing equation, we need to once again make sure that we've got temporal congruence: for bonds, r, T, and C all need to agree in terms of the time period involved.

Both r and the coupon rate are quoted on an annual basis, but we're also told that the bond makes semiannual coupon payments, implying that a *nominal* annual basis, derived using six-month rates, is being used for quoting both rates.

This means that we're actually being told that $r = 7\%/2 = 3.5\%$ per six-month period, and that the coupon dollar amount, C, is equal to $(9\%/2 \times \$1,000) = \$45$ per six-month period. Similarly, we'll calculate T as (10 years × 2 six-month periods per year) = 20 six-month periods.

Since all three are being implicitly stated in terms of a six-month period, temporal congruence holds and we can proceed with using the bond pricing equation:

$$PV_{bond} = C \times \left(\frac{1}{r} - \frac{1}{r(1+r)^T} \right) + \frac{FV}{(1+r)^T}$$

$$= \$45 \times \left(\frac{1}{0.035} - \frac{1}{0.035(1.035)^{20}} \right) + \frac{\$1,000}{(1.035)^{20}}$$

$$= \$45 \times (28.5714 - 14.3590) + \$502.5659$$

$$= \$1,142.12$$

Or, using our calculator-based notation conventions:

20	[T]
3.50%	[r]
$45	[C]
$1,000	[FV]
[CPT]	[PV] = $1,142.12

With either method, note that the price we calculated is greater than the assumed face value, $1,000, which we should expect, given that the going rate of interest on this bond has gone down from 4.5 percent to 3.5 percent since issuance.

Solving for Anything But Bond Price

If you want to solve for any of the right-hand side variables in the bond pricing equation, you're probably going to be better off using a calculator, or Excel, than trying to do it by hand. While you can solve directly for C, solving for either r or T is going to involve a lot of trial-and-error.

For example, suppose you are analyzing an eight-year, annual coupon bond carrying a 12 percent coupon rate that is selling for $1,240; what would be the YTM (i.e., the r that would make the problem work out right)?

If you try to set this up as an equation, you're going to get to the following step and be stumped:

$$PV_{bond} = C \times \left(\frac{1}{r} - \frac{1}{r(1+r)^T} \right) + \frac{FV}{(1+r)^T}$$

$$\$1,240 = \$120 \times \left(\frac{1}{r} - \frac{1}{r(1+r)^8} \right) + \frac{\$1,000}{(1+r)^8}$$

On the other hand, doing this on a calculator is a breeze:

8	[T]
$1,240	[PV]
$120	[C]
$1,000	[FV]
[CPT]	[r] = 7.8477%

The Parts of YTM

Let's go back to the first bond that we priced earlier, a 10-year bond with a semiannual coupon of 9 percent when the going rate on such bonds is 7 percent. As you remember, we calculated the price of this bond as $1,142.12.

Intuitively, the reason that this bond is selling at a premium is because it's paying coupon payments of $45 per six-month period when brand-new, otherwise equivalent bonds are only paying $35 per six-month period. That is, it's the abnormally high coupon rate that makes this bond's price "abnormal" (i.e., greater than face value).

But, if you buy this bond, you're getting a deal then, right? No, because it's priced higher than those other new bonds; they're going to be selling for exactly $1,000 (because their coupon rates are exactly equal to the current going rate), while this one sells for a good deal more.

How much more? Well, enough so that if you buy and hold this bond until maturity, you will earn exactly the same 3.5 percent per six-month period rate of return that the owners of the other bonds will. However, you won't earn it in exactly the same way that they will.

You see, the YTM on a bond actually has two components: one part is composed of the rate of return you expect to earn in the form of interest, while the other part consists of the expected percentage change in price between the time you buy the bond and when you expect to sell it. These two parts are referred to as the *current yield* and the *expected capital gains yield*, respectively:

$$YTM = \text{current yield} + \text{expected capital gains yield}$$

The current yield is calculated by dividing the dollar coupon, C, by the current price:

$$\text{Current yield} = \frac{C}{PV_{bond}}$$

For the bond in our example, this will be equal to $45/$1,142.12 = 0.0394, or 3.94 percent per six-month period. For one of those otherwise equivalent, just-issued bonds that we were talking about, the current yield will be equal to $35/$1,000 = 0.035, or 3.50%.

To calculate the capital gains yield, we estimate what the price of a bond would be one period from now *if the current going rate of interest remained unchanged*, and then we compute the capital gains yield as the expected percentage change in price.

For our sample bond, one period from now it will only have 19 coupon payments left, so we will have to price it as a "9.5 year" semiannual bond:

19	[T]
3.50%	[r]
$45	[C]
$1,000	[FV]
[CPT]	[PV] = $1,137.10

Notice that the price is expected to go down; or, more precisely, *notice that the price is expected to get closer to face value*. This is happening because a 19-period bond paying $45 per period is a little more like all the otherwise equivalent bonds than a 20-period bond is; as time passes, this bond's "abnormality" (in the form of different-than-everyone-else coupon payments) will "bleed off" until, at maturity, right after the last coupon payment has been made but before the $1,000 face value is repaid, this bond will look just like all the other bonds, and sell for the same $1,000 face value that they're selling for.

This expected decline in the price of the bond translates into an expected capital gains yield of ($1,137.10 – $1,142.12)/$1,142.12 = –0.0044, or –0.44%, using the general formula for the expected change in price as a percentage of starting value:

$$\text{Expected capital gains yield} = \frac{\text{price}_{\text{tomorrow}} - \text{price}_{\text{today}}}{\text{price}_{\text{today}}}$$

If we add this expected capital gains yield to the current yield that we previously calculated, we get 3.94% + (–0.44%) = 3.50%.

So, if we invest in this bond, we expect to get the same 3.50 percent rate of return per six-month period that we would earn from buying the other bonds, the ones paying only $35 a period.

How do we know that the total return to those other bonds will only be 3.50 percent? We only calculated their current yields, not their expected capital gains yields, right?

Well, a little thought shows why we don't need to, if they're selling at par right now, and if rates don't change for the next period, what are they going to sell at then? Still par. So the expected change in price will be zero.

In general, bonds selling at a premium can be expected to decline in price as they approach maturity; bonds selling at par can be expected to remain at par; and bonds selling at a discount can be expected to *increase* in price as they near maturity. An example of the exact paths followed by two specific bonds when the YTM is 8.25 percent is shown in Figure 8-2.

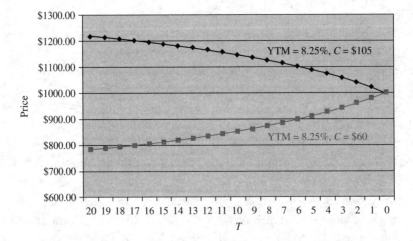

FIGURE 8-2 · Sample bond price curves as maturity approaches.

QUIZ

1. Investors would be thinking correctly if they decided to sell a particular type of bond because they thought that:

   A. Bond prices were about to *fall* due to a coming *decrease* in rates.
   B. Bond prices were about to *rise* due to a coming *decrease* in rates.
   C. Bond prices were about to *fall* due to a coming *increase* in rates.
   D. Bond prices were about to *rise* due to a coming *increase* in rates.

2. A bond selling at a discount should have:

   A. A coupon rate higher than the YTM
   B. A coupon rate lower than the YTM
   C. A coupon rate equal to the YTM
   D. A current yield equal to the YTM

3. You are considering buying a 17-year, annual-coupon bond that has a coupon rate of 7 percent and a YTM of 6 percent. What should be the price of this bond?

   A. $838.79
   B. $1,000.00
   C. $1,057.17
   D. $1,104.77

4. You are considering buying a 15-year, semiannual-coupon bond that has a coupon rate of 8.25 percent and a YTM of 9.25 percent. What should be the price of this bond?

   A. $919.74
   B. $1,106.08
   C. $1,128.46
   D. $1,997.19

5. You are considering buying a 14-year, semiannual-coupon bond that has a coupon rate of 8.25 percent and a YTM of 8.25 percent. What should be the price of this bond?

   A. $1,000.00
   B. $1,106.08
   C. $1,128.46
   D. $1,997.19

6. You are considering buying a 23-year, annual-coupon bond that has a coupon rate of 6.20 percent and a YTM of 8.25 percent. What should be the current yield of this bond?

   A. 6.20%
   B. 7.25%
   C. 7.75%
   D. 7.83%

7. You are considering buying an 8-year, semiannual-coupon bond that has a coupon rate of 10.25 percent and a YTM of 9.00 percent. What should be the current yield of this bond?

   A. 8.23%
   B. 8.88%
   C. 9.58%
   D. 9.90%

8. You are considering buying a 20-year, annual-coupon bond that has a coupon rate of 9 percent and is currently selling for $1,134.89. What is the YTM on this bond?

   A. 7.07%
   B. 7.66%
   C. 7.88%
   D. 9.00%

9. You are considering buying an 8-year, semiannual-coupon bond that has a coupon rate of 8 percent and is currently selling for $834.89. What is the YTM on this bond?

   A. 4.00%
   B. 5.59%
   C. 8.22%
   D. 10.45%

10. Twelve years ago, XYZ Corp. sold a 20-year, annual-coupon bond with a coupon rate of 7.25 percent. What should be the price of this bond today if the current YTM is 6.50 percent?

   A. $1,020.91
   B. $1,045.67
   C. $1,061.19
   D. $1,082.64

chapter **9**

Valuing Stocks

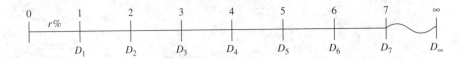

FIGURE 9-1 • Sample stock cash flows.

As with bonds, stocks represent a claim against the assets of the company. However, stocks differ from bonds in two important ways:

1. As long as the firm doesn't go bankrupt, bond cash flows are guaranteed and constant; stockholders' cash flows are neither.

2. Bondholders' cash flows last for a finite time; as long as the firm doesn't go bankrupt, stockholders' cash flows can potentially last forever.

Because of these two factors, pricing a stock involves pricing a potentially infinite stream of uneven cash flows, called *dividends*, and designated in Figure 9-1 by the variables D_1, D_2, and so forth.

Unfortunately, pricing such a stream of dividends with a closed-end formula is impossible unless there's some type of smoothness or pattern to them. Accordingly, much of this chapter will be devoted to justifying and explaining a reasonable set of assumptions that will allow us to get an acceptably close-enough approximation to the value of a stock.

The Conventions of Stock Quotations

Fortunately, the infrastructures of the global stock markets have been subjected to a spate of recent modernization efforts, which have left these markets with far fewer "legacy" conventions than the bond markets have. For example, stock prices are now quoted on a decimal basis, rather than through a fractional quotation system similar to the ones used in the bond markets.

However, stock return quotations (and statistics such as *dividend yield*, which is in the format of a return, and which we'll discuss later) are often still quoted in nominal annual terms. Given that most stocks pay dividends quarterly, you will have to remember to divide these quoted rates by four before using them in an equation.

The only other thing that students find confusing about stock market quotes is that they often provide two prices: a *bid price* and an *ask price*. The bid price is the price that a market maker or a dealer will pay for the stock, so it's the price you, the investor, could *sell* for; the ask price is the price that the market maker or dealer will sell for, so it's the price you would pay to *buy*.

Which price should you use in your calculations? Well, to the extent that you'll usually be considering buying a stock, using the ask price would be best.

The Mathematics of a Stock: Constant Dividends

To start working toward a good stock pricing equation, let's assume for a moment that all of the dividends in Figure 9-1 are constant and equal to D (with no subscript, because all the dividends are the same). If that were the case, then we'd be able to solve for the stock price using the equation for the present value of perpetuity:

$$PV_{stock} = \frac{D}{r}$$

As with the previous times we've made use of the perpetuity formula, we have to remember that this will always give us a value one length-of-time-between-dividends in front of the first dividend. We also have to ensure that temporal congruence holds.

For example, suppose you're considering buying a share of stock that is expected to pay a dividend of $1 per share, per quarter forever. If the appropriate effective *annual* rate of return on such stocks is 12 percent, then in order to price this stock we would first have to compute the effective *quarterly* rate to satisfy temporal congruence: $r = (1.12)^{¼} - 1 = 0.0287$, or 2.87 percent per quarter.

With this, we could then solve for the value of the stock:

$$PV_{stock} = \frac{D}{r}$$
$$= \frac{\$1}{0.0287}$$
$$= \$34.80$$

This value of $34.80 would be valid at the point in time exactly one quarter before the first dividend of $1 was to be received. So, if the first dividend was simply identified as D_1, and we were being asked to find the price at time "0," this would be the answer, because the operating assumption in such situations is always that the person selling the stock at time 0 will keep the last dividend.

But, what if you were buying a stock on, say, any day other than exactly one quarter before the next dividend? (Even though many textbook problems assume you're exactly one period before the next dividend, you'd be surprised how many times it doesn't work out that way in the real world.) What if, for example, you were still dealing with the stock discussed in the previous example, but you were considering buying it two months before the next dividend? Would that change the calculations?

Well, it wouldn't *change* them, but it would *add* to them; you would still want to use the perpetuity formula to convert the infinite stream of $1 dividends into a single lump sum, but now that lump sum wouldn't be positioned exactly where you wanted it. The stream of cash flows facing you would be those shown in Figure 9-2, where the time periods are numbered in months relative to your current position.

When you do apply the perpetuity formula to these dividends, it will give you the value of $34.80, but that value will be at time "−1 month" relative to the present, as shown in Figure 9-3.

Moving that $34.80 to the present time will only require a straightforward application of the *Future Value* (FV) formula for a lump sum, but before you can use that formula with $T = 1$ month you will need to compute the monthly rate: $r = (1.0287) - 1 = 0.0095$, or 0.95 percent per month.

After that, finding the value at time 0 is trivial:

1	[T]
0.95%	[r]
$34.80	[PV]
[CPT]	[FV] = $35.13

Using a perpetuity formula to value stocks like this is fairly simple, but it's not too realistic. In the real world, dividends do not remain constant forever, nor does anyone expect them to. In order to move closer to a method for valuing stocks that is more plausible, we need to allow for the possibility of dividends changing over time. As a first stab, let's assume that dividends grow at a constant growth rate, g, from period to period.

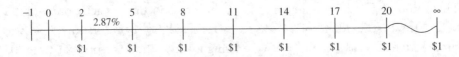

FIGURE 9-2 · Stock with quarterly $1 dividends when the next dividend is two months away.

FIGURE 9-3 · Stock after application of perpetuity formula.

The Mathematics of a Stock: Constantly Growing Dividends

A more general form of the perpetuity formula is available that handles situations where the dividends do not stay constant, but instead grow at a constant growth rate, g, so that:

$$D_1 = D_0 \times (1+g)$$
$$D_2 = D_1 \times (1+g) = D_0 \times (1+g)^2$$
$$D_3 = D_2 \times (1+g) = D_0 \times (1+g)^3$$

and so on. Notice two things about this stream of dividends: first, even though D_0 is *still* going to remain with the seller, we may need to use it to determine D_1.

Second, note that there are two alternative ways of calculating each dividend: one based on the immediately preceding dividend and one based on D_0. Both ways will come in handy in different situations, as we'll see below.

If the dividends reflect this property of growing at a constant rate, then the sum of their present values, the price of the stock, is said to be the present value of a *constantly growing perpetuity*. In general, the present value of any such constantly growing perpetuity can be simplified as:

$$
\begin{aligned}
\text{Present value of a} \\
\text{constantly growing perpetuity}
\end{aligned}
= \frac{C_1}{(1+r)^1} + \frac{C_2}{(1+r)^2} + \cdots + \frac{C_\infty}{(1+r)^\infty}
$$

$$
= \frac{C_0(1+g)^1}{(1+r)^1} + \frac{C_0(1+g)^2}{(1+r)^2} + \cdots + \frac{C_0(1+g)^\infty}{(1+r)^\infty}
$$

$$
= \sum_{i=1}^{\infty} \frac{C_0(1+g)^i}{(1+r)^i}
$$

$$
\text{PVCGP} = \frac{C_1}{r-g}
$$

So as to conform to the notation that you're going to see in other textbooks, we'll write this as the same *constant-growth stock pricing formula* that they use:

$$P_0 = \frac{D_1}{r-g}$$

As before, note that this formula will also always give you a value one period before the first dividend. In fact, this is true in an even more general way:

$$P_i = \frac{D_{i+1}}{r-g}$$

The price at any time i will be equal to the *next* dividend divided by $(r-g)$.

The only really tricky part of using this formula is making sure that you've got the right dividend. To do so, you need to learn to differentiate between the ways that problems will refer to both D_0 and D_1.

If the dividend is referred to in the past tense, as in, "The dividend just paid *was*...," or, "The last dividend *was*...," you're being given D_0, and will need to multiply it by $(1+g)$ before using this formula. On the other hand, if the dividend is referred to in the future tense, as in, "You expect the next dividend *to be*...," or "Future dividends *will start* at...," then you're being explicitly given D_1, and should not multiply it by $(1+g)$ before using it in the equation.

For example, suppose you're evaluating a stock that just paid a quarterly dividend of $0.57, you expect future dividends to increase at a rate of 5 percent per quarter, and you think that the appropriate quarterly rate of return on this stock is 8 percent. How much would it be worth?

Since you're being given D_0, you must first use it to find $D_1 = \$0.57 \times (1.05) = \$0.5985$. Then you can put it into the constant-growth stock pricing formula:

$$P_0 = \frac{D_1}{r-g}$$
$$= \frac{\$0.5985}{0.08-0.05}$$
$$= \frac{\$0.5985}{0.03}$$
$$= \$19.95$$

Please notice that we were very careful to use all four decimal places of D_1 in the constant-growth pricing formula; until now, we've been pretty lax about how much precision we use when carrying intermediate answers forward, but this is the one place where you don't want to do that.

In a very real way here, D_1 is acting as "representative of its class"; that is, when we put it in the numerator of the pricing formula, it's not just there on its own account, it's there representing itself *and* the rest of the infinite stream of dividends for which it is serving as a proxy. If you round this dividend to the closest penny, you're going to put an unacceptable amount of error in the computed price.

For instance, suppose that we had rounded D_1 to $0.60 after we computed it. This would have given us a price of:

$$P_0 = \frac{D_1}{r-g}$$

$$= \frac{\$0.60}{0.08 - 0.05}$$

$$= \frac{\$0.60}{0.03}$$

$$= \$20$$

Yes, it's only off by $0.05, but when you consider that stocks normally trade in lots of 100 shares, and that many people buy multiple lots at a time, such small rounding errors can have a fairly significant impact. Plus, think about how big the error would have been if we'd rounded D_1 down to $0.59 instead of to the nearest penny.

The Mathematics of a Stock: Constantly Shrinking Dividends

The constant-growth stock formula that we just developed is perfectly valid for instances of *negative* dividend growth, too.

For example, suppose you are considering buying shares in KAD, Inc. KAD's next yearly dividend is expected to be $2.50 per share, and all subsequent dividends are expected to shrink by 7 percent per year for the foreseeable future. If the appropriate rate of return on this stock is 12 percent, what should it be selling for?

Here, we've been explicitly told D_1, so we don't need to solve for it. Instead, we can just use the constant-growth stock formula, taking great care to treat the negative growth rate correctly:

$$P_0 = \frac{\$2.50}{0.12 - (-0.07)}$$

$$= \frac{\$2.50}{0.12 + 0.07}$$

$$= \frac{\$2.50}{0.19}$$

$$= \$13.16$$

What $g > r$ Really Means

As we've just seen, there's no problem with g being negative; but, can it be too large? Yes; if $g > r$, the formula will "blow up" by giving you a negative answer.

For instance, suppose you've been asked to analyze a stock with a required rate of return of 8 percent that just paid an annual dividend of $2.00 per share. If the anticipated growth rate in dividends is 10 percent per year, what value will the constant-growth stock formula give us?

Well, first we need to calculate $D_1 = \$2.00 \times (1.10) = \$2.20$. Then, inserting this into the constant-growth stock valuation formula will give us:

$$P_0 = \frac{\$2.20}{0.08 - 0.10}$$
$$= \frac{\$2.50}{-0.02}$$
$$= -\$125$$

So, what exactly does this mean? Does a negative price mean that someone would have to be *paid* to get them to take this stock?

No. What it really means is that the formula is not valid if $g > r$. A negative number such as this is actually indicating that the stock has an infinitely *positive* value.

To see why, look back at our original formulation of a general constant-growth perpetuity formula. One of the intermediate steps was:

$$\text{Present value of a constantly growing perpetuity} = \sum_{i=1}^{\infty} \frac{C_0(1+g)^i}{(1+r)^i}$$

In this version of the formula, it's easy to see that g and r are going to have opposing impacts on the present value of any perpetuity, including the stock that we're talking about. As long as $r > g$, then the numerator of these fractions is going to grow slower than the denominator; mathematically, this means that, as the dividends get farther and farther out in time, their dollar value is growing, but the interest rate is growing at a quicker rate, which makes each dividend's present value get smaller and smaller. Any *infinite* series like this, where the individual parts are getting smaller and smaller, will have a finite sum.

However, if $g > r$, then the dividends are growing so fast that even their present values are growing, too. Taking the sum of an infinite series where the parts are getting bigger and bigger like that will yield $+\infty$.

The Mathematics of a Stock: Nonconstant Dividends

In reality, we do think that, on average, dividends will tend to go up more often than they will go down (due to the effects of inflation, if nothing else), so using the assumption of a constant growth rate as we just did will give us a good first approximation to stock price. However, if we want to get as precise an estimate of stock price as possible, we have to admit that, while stock dividends do *tend* to follow a consistent pattern of growth, it's only in a very loose way. If you plotted a trend line for dividends across time, the actual dividends would show a *lot* of variation around that trend. So, assuming constant growth when we know it isn't so is going to impose error on our estimated stock price.

However, we face a dilemma: if we *don't* assume that dividends are growing at a constant rate, there's not enough consistency in the dividend stream to be able to find a closed-form equation for the present value of the infinite dividend stream.

So, what do we do? We try to estimate the first few dividends as precisely as possible, and then, wrongly (but knowing full well what we're doing), we assume a constant growth rate for the rest of the dividends even though we know that there isn't going to be one. By doing this, we "push" the error associated with the wrongful assumption of constant growth far enough into the future so that its impact on our price estimate is reduced.

Could we reduce that error further by estimating the first 10 or even the first 100 dividends as precisely as possible? Yes, but it probably wouldn't be worth it, because, as we try to estimate exact dividends that are further and further into the future, there's going to be more and more error in each one, anyway. (Think about whether you're likely to be a better guesser about what's going to happen next year or about what's going to happen 10 years from now, and you'll realize why.)

So, as far as estimating the price of a stock is concerned, there *isn't* any such thing as a nonconstant-growth stock; there's just stocks that have constant growth from the beginning, which we covered in the last section, and stocks that *start out* with nonconstant-growth dividends, but even they will be assumed to have constant-growth dividends past a certain point in the future.

Our methodology for pricing such stocks will go as follows:

1. Estimate all the nonconstant dividends as precisely as possible.
2. Estimate the first constant-growth dividend.

3. Use that first constant-growth dividend in the constant-growth pricing equation to find the value of the infinite "tail" of constant-growth dividends.

4. That value will (usually) be at the same point in time as the *last* nonconstant-growth dividend. Add those two values together.

5. Sum the present values of the finite set of lump sums represented by the number calculated in step 4 and any other, earlier nonconstant-growth dividends.

For example, suppose you estimate that the next three quarterly dividends paid to XYZ Corp. will be $1.00, $1.25, and $1.75, respectively, and you decide to assume that all subsequent dividends will grow at a constant rate of 5 percent per quarter, indefinitely. If the required rate of return on the shares of XYZ stock is 14 percent, what should be its price?

Going through the five steps listed earlier:

1. We don't need to estimate the nonconstant-growth dividends, because we're given them: $D_1 = \$1.00$, $D_2 = \$1.25$, $D_3 = \$1.75$.

2. The first constant-growth dividend, D_4, should be equal to $\$1.75 \times 1.05 = \$1.8375$.

3. We can use the constant-growth pricing equation to get P_3:

$$P_3 = \frac{D_4}{r-g}$$
$$= \frac{\$1.8375}{0.14-0.05}$$
$$= \frac{\$1.8375}{0.09}$$
$$= \$20.4167$$

(Notice that we're not getting P_3 because we want a price at time 3, but because it's all we can get with D_4.)

4. Add the two values at time 3, D_3 and P_3: $\$1.75 + \$20.4167 = \$22.1667$

5. Find the present values of the three cash flows we have left, then add them up:

1	[T]
14%	[r]
$1.00	[FV]
[CPT]	[PV] = $.8772

2	[T]
14%	[r]
$1.25	[FV]
[CPT]	[PV] = $.9618

3	[T]
14%	[r]
$22.1667	[FV]
[CPT]	[PV] = $14.9619

$$.8772 + \$.9618 + \$14.9619 = \$16.80$$

Dividend Yield and Expected Capital Gains Yields on Stocks

As we saw with bond *Yield to Maturity* (YTMs) in the last chapter, stocks' required rates of return have two parts:

$$r = dividend\ yield + expected\ capital\ gains\ yield$$

The dividend yield is directly analogous to the bonds' current yield:

$$\text{Dividend yield} = \frac{D_1}{P_0}$$

and the expected capital gains yield is also computed the same way:

$$\text{Expected capital gains yield} = \frac{P_1 - P_0}{P_0}$$

Now, we *can* use this formula to directly estimate the expected capital gains yield, but it's usually easier to calculate the dividend yield and then "back out" the expected capital gains yield by subtracting dividend yield from r.

For example, if we continue the problem from the previous section, we already have $P_0 = \$16.80$. We could value the stock at time 1 by dropping D_1 (because in pricing the stock at time 1, we assume that D_1 will stay with the seller) and move all the remaining cash flows one period closer to us before finding their present value:

1   [T]
14%   [r]
$1.25   [FV]
[CPT]   [PV] = $1.0965

2   [T]
14%   [r]
$22.1667   [FV]
[CPT]   [PV] = $17.0566
$1.0965 + $17.0566 = $18.15

With this, we can calculate the expected capital gains yield as:

$$\text{Expected capital gains yield} = \frac{P_1 - P_0}{P_0}$$

$$= \frac{\$18.15 - \$16.80}{\$16.80}$$

$$= 0.0805, \text{ or } 8.05\%$$

However, since we already had P_0, it would have been easier to first calculate dividend yield:

$$\text{Dividend yield} = \frac{D_1}{P_0}$$

$$= \frac{\$1.00}{\$16.80}$$

$$= 0.0595, \text{ or } 5.95\%$$

and then calculate the expected capital gains yield as:

$$\text{Expected capital gains yield} = r - \text{dividend yield}$$

$$= 14\% - 5.95\%$$

$$8.05\%$$

QUIZ

1. Suppose that you were calculating the dividend yield on a stock you were considering buying, and you intended to "back out" the expected capital gains yield as described in the previous section. Using the bid price instead of the ask price (or instead of calculating P_0 yourself) as P_0 in your calculation would cause:

    A. Both the dividend yield and the expected capital gains yield to be too high
    B. Both the dividend yield and the expected capital gains yield to be too low
    C. The dividend yield to be too high and the expected capital gains yield to be too low
    D. The dividend yield to be too low and the expected capital gains yield to be too high

2. In order for the constant-growth stock pricing formula to work correctly, you need to have:

    A. $g > r$
    B. $g < r$
    C. $r - g < 0$
    D. $g - r > 0$

3. Suppose you're considering buying a stock that is expected to pay a dividend of $1.25 per share, per year. If the appropriate rate of return on this stock is 15 percent, what should it sell for?

    A. $0.10
    B. $8.33
    C. $10.42
    D. $12.88

4. Suppose you're considering buying a stock that is expected to pay a dividend of $0.80 per share, per year. If the stock is selling for $8.68, what is the appropriate rate of return on this stock?

    A. 9.22%
    B. 13.67%
    C. 14.40%
    D. 15.70%

5. Suppose you're evaluating a stock that just paid a quarterly dividend of $1.25. You expect future dividends on this stock to increase at a rate of 4 percent per quarter, and you think the appropriate rate of return on this stock is 12 percent per quarter. How much would it be worth?

    A. $15.63
    B. $16.25
    C. $41.67
    D. $43.33

6. Suppose you're evaluating a stock, and you expect the next dividend to be $0.57. You expect future dividends on this stock to increase at a rate of 2 percent per quarter, and you think the appropriate rate of return on this stock is 4 percent per quarter. How much would it be worth?

    A. $11.40
    B. $11.84
    C. $19.00
    D. $28.50

7. Suppose you are considering buying shares in IMT, Inc. IMT's next yearly dividend is expected to be $1.50 per share, and all subsequent dividends are expected to shrink by 10 percent per year for the foreseeable future. If the appropriate rate of return on this stock is 8 percent, what should it be selling for?

    A. $8.33
    B. $11.56
    C. $28.45
    D. $75.00

8. Suppose you estimate that the next three quarterly dividends paid to ILHS Corp. will be $2.00, $2.25, and $2.50, respectively, and you decide to assume that all subsequent dividends will grow at a constant rate of 2 percent per quarter indefinitely. If the required rate of return on the shares of ILHS stock is 8 percent per quarter, what should be its price?

    A. $39.50
    B. $46.65
    C. $53.75
    D. $56.95

9. Suppose that you estimate that LOHI Corp. will skip its next three annual dividends, but then resume paying a dividend, with the first dividend paid being equal to $1.00. If all subsequent dividends will grow at a constant rate of 6 percent per year and the required rate of return on LOHI is 14 percent per year, what should be its price?

    A. $6.35
    B. $8.44
    C. $10.37
    D. $12.50

10. Continuing the previous problem, what is LOHI's expected capital gains yield over the next year?

    A. 10.34%
    B. 11.85%
    C. 12.08%
    D. 14.00%

chapter 10

Valuing Projects: The Capital-Budgeting Decision Rules

CHAPTER OBJECTIVES

At the end of this chapter, the reader should be able to:

- Calculate and use the net present value decision rule
- Calculate and use the payback decision rule
- Calculate and use the discounted payback decision rule
- Calculate and use the average accounting return decision rule
- Calculate and use the internal rate of return decision rule
- Calculate and use the modified internal rate of return decision rule
- Calculate and use the profitability index decision rule

So far, all the applications of *Time Value of Money* (TVM) that we've been discussing have been equally applicable to multiple areas of finance. In this chapter, we are going to start focusing more precisely on using TVM to make corporate finance decisions; more specifically, we will be focusing on decision rules for making *capital budgeting* decisions, the choices involving which projects a firm should invest in.

We will discuss several decision rules, but one, the *Net Present Value* (NPV) rule, will stand out for both its simplicity of computations and its intuitive appeal. However, though NPV is arguably the *best* decision rule, there are plenty of reasons why it shouldn't necessarily be the *only* decision rule that a firm uses. So, as we discuss the other decision rules, realize that they're not necessarily *alternatives* to NPV; they're more like *complements*. We will discuss how they can be used in conjunction with one another after we've discussed each rule individually.

As we discuss each rule, we will take a uniform approach of clearly identifying:

1. How to calculate the statistic.
2. An appropriate benchmark value to be used in the decision rule.
3. The valid ranges for acceptance and rejection of a project by this rule. (As we'll see, bigger isn't always better with some of these decision rules.)

However, before we can actually start discussing all the decision rules, we need to talk about moderating our practice to this point of ignoring the signs of the cash flows, and we need to add a little more functionality to the shorthand notation that we've been using.

Why Cash Flow Signs Matter Now

Since Chapter 5, we've been using the TVM formulas a lot, and in most of those cases, we've more or less ignored the direction of the cash flows. There were several valid reasons for doing this. First, many of the problems only involved cash flows in one direction; for instance, when we price a bond, the same person who will receive the coupon payments is also the person who has the right to receive the face value. Second, the sign of those cash flows was often implicit in the action we were talking about; if you *buy* a stock, it's understood that you will be the one *receiving* its dividends, and so forth. As long as it was safe to assume that these circumstances held, dropping the negative signs from our calculations just made sense, because it saved us time and reduced the complexity of our calculations.

Now that we're going to be considering potential projects to invest in, this assumption is no longer valid. Projects will always have two sets of cash flows, one positive and one negative, and the role of the decision rules that we're going to be discussing in this chapter will be to determine if the positive outweighs the negative. So, in order for these rules to work right we have *got* to start keeping consistent track of which type of cash flow is which; we'll do so by assigning all cash *inflows* (money that the firm receives) a *positive* sign, and all cash *outflows* (money paid by the company) a *negative* sign.

Notational Conventions, Part 2

The TVM worksheet present in most financial calculators has been fine, so far, for the types of TVM problems we've been dealing with. Sometimes we had to use the worksheet two or three times in a single problem, but that was usually because we needed an intermediate calculation as an input to another TVM equation.

In this chapter, we will generally be using the more simplistic TVM equations (i.e., PV and FV), but we'll find ourselves having to use them repeatedly, with only small variations in inputs, within the same problem.

We're also going to run up against a problem concerning the consistency (or, rather, the inconsistency) of the cash flows in most projects. If you thought the cash flows of stocks jumped around a lot, wait until you see what *project* cash flows do. If we stick with the TVM worksheet, these inconsistent cash flows will be a problem for us if we want to solve for a "common" r or T value, because the TVM worksheet won't let us enter multiple cash flows unless they're in the form of an annuity. (The one notable exception to this has been when we used the TVM worksheet to simultaneously solve the annuity/lump-sum problems inherent in a bond, but that required a degree of agreement between the inputs to the annuity and the lump-sum problems which is *highly* unlikely to occur in other circumstances.)

Luckily, most financial calculators also have built-in worksheets specifically designed for computing NPV in problems with multiple nonconstant cash flows; in many cases, they will also calculate most of the other decision rule statistics that we're going to be discussing, too.

To make these worksheets as flexible as possible, they are usually divided into two parts: one for input, which we'll refer to as the *Cash Flow* (CF) worksheet;

and one or more for calculating decision statistics. We'll go over the conventions concerning the CF worksheet here, but we'll wait to cover the conventions on the various decision rules until we discuss them.

The CF work sheet is usually designed to handle inputting sets of multiple cash flows as quickly as possible. As a result, it normally consists of two sets of variables or *cells*, one for the cash flows, and one to hold a set of frequency counts for the cash flows, so that we can tell it we've got seven $1,500 cash flows in a row instead of having to type in $1,500 seven times.

Using the frequency counts to reduce the number of inputs is handy, but you have to be careful. These frequency counts are only good for embedded annuities of identical cash flows, so you have to ensure that you don't mistake something for an annuity when it's not.

Also, using the frequency counts will usually affect the way that the calculator is counting time periods. As an example, let's talk about how we would go and put the set of cash flows shown in Figure 10-1 into a CF worksheet.

To designate putting a value into a particular cash flow cell in this worksheet, we'll put the value and the cell identifier, such as CF0, CF1, and so forth; we'll do the same for the frequency cells, using $F1$, $F2$, and so forth, to identify which CF cell the frequency cell goes with.

NOTE *In most calculators, CF0 is treated as a unique value with an unalterable frequency of 1; we're going to make the same assumption, here, too, so there will never be a listing shown for F0.*

For this sample timeline, our inputs would be:

−$800	[CF0]		
$150	[CF1]	1	[$F1$]
$200	[CF2]	1	[$F2$]
$0	[CF3]	1	[$F3$]
$150	[CF4]	3	[$F4$]
$75	[CF5]	2	[$F5$]

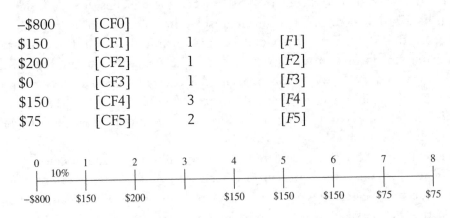

FIGURE 10-1 · Sample project timeline for CF worksheet.

There are a couple of things of importance to observe about this example:

1. Note that we had to manually enter a value of $0 for CF3; if we hadn't, the calculator wouldn't have known about it, and would have assumed that CF4 came one period after CF2.

2. Once we make use of the frequency cell for one cash flow, all of the numbering on any subsequent cash flows that we put into the calculator is going to be messed up, at least from our point of view. For instance, the first $75 isn't what *we* would call "CF5," is it? We'd call it "CF7" because it comes at time period 7; but calculators usually think of CF5 as "the fifth *set* of cash flows," so we'll just have to try and do the same if we use the frequency cells.

Net Present Value

Actually, we already know how to calculate the NPV statistic; in fact, we've used a very similar approach in developing our pricing equations for bonds and stocks. However, even though the mechanics of calculating the NPV statistic explained below are very similar to the mathematics performed in finding a bond or stock price, there is one very important intuitive difference in what we're doing and the assumptions underlying it. We'll discuss that difference after we've covered the rule itself.

The NPV statistic is simply the sum of all the cash flows' present values. To calculate it, we would start with an equation very similar to the one we started with when we were discussing the present value of a constantly growing perpetuity in the last chapter, but if we can't count on the cash flows being related by a constant growth rate it doesn't simplify very much:

$$NPV = \frac{CF_0}{(1+r)^0} + \frac{CF_1}{(1+r)^1} + \cdots + \frac{CF_T}{(1+r)^T}$$
$$= \sum_{i=0}^{T} \frac{CF_i}{(1+r)^i}$$

One slight difference between this formula and the one for the constant-growth perpetuity is that this one starts with a cash flow at time 0, where the other started at time 1. We'll discuss why this difference exists in the next section.

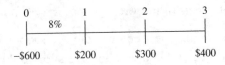

FIGURE 10-2 · Sample project cash flows.

To illustrate computation of the NPV statistic, as well as most of the other decision statistics in this chapter, we'll use the set of cash flows shown in Figure 10-2. For this project, the NPV statistic would be equal to:

$$NPV = \sum_{i=0}^{T} \frac{CF_i}{(1+r)^i}$$
$$= \frac{-\$600}{(1.08)^0} + \frac{\$200}{(1.08)^1} + \frac{\$300}{(1.08)^2} + \frac{\$400}{(1.08)^3}$$
$$= -\$600 + \$185.1952 + \$257.2016 + \$317.5329$$
$$= \$159.92$$

Or, using our shorthand notation, this problem would be solved on a calculator by first entering the following into the CF worksheet:

-$600   [CF0]
$200   [CF1]   1   [F1]
$300   [CF2]   1   [F2]
$400   [CF3]   1   [F3]

Then, on the NPV worksheet, you would simply need to enter the interest rate and solve for the NPV:

8%   [r]
[CPT]   [NPV] = $159.92

For the NPV decision rule, the benchmark to which we compare this statistic is always zero: projects with an NPV > 0 should be accepted, while those with an NPV < 0 should be rejected. (We're indifferent to those with an NPV exactly equal to 0.)

Since our sample project has an NPV of $159.92 > 0, we should accept the project.

The Intuition behind NPV

If we take the entire NPV decision rule, both the calculation of the statistic and the acceptance criterion, we can express the rule as:

$$\text{Accept the project IF:}\qquad NPV = \sum_{i=0}^{T} \frac{CF_i}{(1+r)^i} > 0$$

If we then group the cash flows according to their signs, this can be rewritten as:

$$\sum_{\forall CF_i < 0} \frac{CF_i}{(1+r)^i} + \sum_{\forall CF_i >= 0} \frac{CF_i}{(1+r)^i} > 0$$

where $\forall$ is the mathematical symbol denoting "for all." This makes the first term equal to the present value of all the cash outflows, and the second term equal to the present value of all the cash inflows. Rearranging this, we get our first insight into exactly what the NPV decision rule is doing when it accepts a project:

$$\sum_{\forall CF_i >= 0} \frac{CF_i}{(1+r)^i} > \sum_{\forall CF_i < 0} \frac{CF_i}{(1+r)^i}$$

By choosing to accept projects when NPV > 0, the decision rule is actually choosing projects where the present value of the cash inflows is greater than the present value of the project outflows, or, put more simply, *it's accepting projects that are worth more than they cost.*

We can also refine this intuition to get an even deeper understanding of what's going on. It's not just that the project makes more money than the *initial* cost; by making this comparison on the present values of the cash flows instead of their face values, NPV is determining worth versus cost on a basis which could be stated as *over and above the cost to borrow the money to do the project to start with.*

When students first start calculating NPV, they often miss this deeper meaning, and when they get a rather small NPV, such as the value of $159.92, they seem to want to struggle with the question of whether $159.92 is "worth it," in the sense of whether it will cover the opportunity cost of using the $600 of necessary capital for this project. The point, of course, is that the $159.92 is above and beyond the recovery of that opportunity cost, so, yes, it's worth it.

As we go through the rest of the decision rules, keep in mind that, though they may be using different metrics or variables, they're all seeking to ask this same type of deeper question.

Payback

The payback decision rule is one of the easiest to calculate, primarily because it completely ignores the time value of money; this ease of use also makes it one of the most widely used decision rules, too.

To calculate the statistic, we simply have to keep track of the cumulative cash flow as we go from period to period, identifying the period in which the cumulative cash flow reaches zero; that is, the period in which the initial investment (the cash outflow at time 0) is repaid.

If we didn't need to be very precise about computing this statistic, we could simply keep a running total:

Year 0:   −$600
Year 1:   −$600 + $200 = −$400
                    ("Nope, the sum isn't nonnegative yet: better keep going.")
Year 2:   −$400 + $300 = −$100
                    ("Still negative: keep going.")
Year 3:   −$100 + $400 = $300

This would make it pretty easy to say that payback occurs sometime in year 3. However, we do tend to value precision in these decision statistics, so we need to try and determine *exactly* when the project would reach payback as precisely as possible.

To do this, we're going to need to make some sort of assumption about how the cash flows arrive within a year: if we assume that they arrive *linearly*, so that a yearly total cash flow of $400 implies that $200 would arrive after six months, and that $100 would arrive every three months, and so forth, then we can use a process called *linear interpolation*.

In order to use linear interpolation, it helps if you construct a table such as that shown in Figure 10-3; in fact, you're probably going to want to model your table *exactly* like this so that the final answer can be calculated using a certain memory device, which, though it might seem silly, won't seem so silly on an exam.

Period	CF	Cumulative CF
0	−$600	−$600
1	$200	−$400
2	$300	−$100
3	$400	$300

FIGURE 10-3 · Sample table for calculating payback.

Period	CF	Cumulative CF
0	−$600	−$600
1	$200	−$400
2	$300	−$100
3	$400	$300

FIGURE 10-4 · Identification of payback range.

Notice that the far-right column consists of the running totals we calculated above; one thing to note about this column is that, once the cumulative CF goes from negative to positive, you can stop calculating it. Then draw a line between the last row where cumulative CF was negative and the first row it was positive, as shown in Figure 10-4.

Now, here's where constructing the table consistently will pay off. If you circle the left-most number above the line, the middle number below the line, and the right-most number above the line, making an inverted triangle as shown in Figure 10-5, then the *absolute values* of these numbers (i.e., ignore the negative sign) are the inputs you need for the following equation.

$$\text{Payback} = \frac{\text{last period with negative}}{\text{cumulative CF}} + \frac{\text{CF needed in next period}}{\text{CF earned in next period}}$$

In this formula, the time period becomes the last period with negative cumulative CF, the absolute value of the last negative cumulative CF (i.e., the right-most number above the line) becomes the CF needed in next period, and the incremental CF for the next year (i.e., the number below the line) becomes the denominator of the equation, the CF earned in next period:

$$\text{Payback} = 2 + \frac{100}{400} = 2.25$$

Of course, if you are lucky enough to have one of the few calculators that will compute payback for you, all you have to do, once you've entered the cash flows, is:

[CPT]   [Payback] = 2.25

Period	CF	Cumulative CF
0	−$600	−$600
1	$200	−$400
2	$300	$100
3	$400	$300

FIGURE 10-5 · Identification of formula inputs for payback.

One of the frequent criticisms of the payback rule is that there is no objective benchmark for it. Ideally, it should be set based upon some external-to-the-project constraint on how long the necessary funds are available, but, in practice, the benchmark is often simply set to some arbitrarily low number and left there.

Once the maximum allowable payback is set, we should accept projects where the computed payback statistic is less than the maximum allowable payback, and reject projects where the computed statistic is greater. So, for example, if this firm had set a maximum allowable payback of 2.4 years, we would accept the project based upon payback.

Discounted Payback

The methodology for computing discounted payback is almost identical to that of payback, except that we use cumulative *present values* instead of the cumulative cash flows to calculate when payback is achieved, as shown in Figure 10-6.

In Figure 10-6, the third column, the one entitled "PV of CF," consists of the present value at time 0 of each respective cash flow. Note that these are calculated *one at a time*, so we can't use the NPV worksheet on a calculator to get all of these values in one step. Instead, we have to calculate the PV of each cash flow separately.

Once we have the individual PV of each cash flow, we then keep track of the cumulative PV as we go from period to period, once again looking for the point where the cumulative amount goes from negative to positive. In this simple example, it happens to occur during the third year again, just like payback did; but it won't always be the case that payback and discounted payback occur during the same period, so don't expect it.

Also, as before, we want to form the same inverted triangle that we saw with payback; however, as shown in Figure 10-7, this time it will be a little skewed, because we now have four columns instead of three. Make sure you select the

Period	CF	PV of CF	Cumulative CF
0	−$600	−$600.00	−$600.00
1	$200	$185.19	−$414.81
2	$300	$257.20	−$157.61
3	$400	$317.53	$159.92

FIGURE 10-6 · Sample table for calculating discounted payback.

Period	CF	PV of CF	Cumulative CF
0	−$600	−$600.00	−$600.00
1	$200	$185.19	−$414.81
②	$300	$257.20	−$157.61
3	$400	$317.53	$159.92

FIGURE 10-7 • Identification of formula inputs for discounted payback.

number below the line from the PV of CF column and not from the CF column!

Once you've identified the inputs using the inverted triangle, the actual calculation of the discounted payback statistic is identical to that of the payback statistic:

$$\text{Discounted payback} = 2 + \frac{157.61}{317.53} = 2.4964$$

Now, before we rush to compare this statistic to the maximum allowable payback for the company of 2.4 quoted before, we need to think about this for a minute: notice that the computed statistic here, 2.4964, is larger than the "regular" payback we computed, 2.25. In fact, for any project that you can calculate these two statistics for, discounted payback will *always* be greater than regular payback.

This is because these two decision rules really only make sense if you use them on projects with what are called *normal* cash flows; normal, in this case, indicates that all the negative cash flows are at time 0, and that all the future cash flows are positive, as shown in Figure 10-8.

So, when we go from regular payback to computing discounted payback, which group of cash flows will tend to have its face value reduced when we take present values, the cash flow at time 0, or the ones in the future? The ones in the future.

The point here is that, because we're dealing with normal cash flows, the positive values shrink when we take their present values, but the negative value, being at time 0, doesn't.

FIGURE 10-8 • Signs of normal cash flows.

Should we be surprised that it's going to take longer to offset a same-sized negative cash flow if we make the positive cash flows smaller? Not really, but if that's the case, then we probably shouldn't be using the same benchmark for both regular payback and discounted payback either.

Unfortunately, there's no systematic way to convert the maximum allowable payback benchmark into a maximum allowable discounted payback value; once again, we're forced to use a number that is highly subjective.

For instance, if this firm's maximum allowable statistic had been set to, say, five years, this project would be accepted by discounted payback; if the benchmark had been lower than 2.4964, the project would have been rejected.

A Comparison of the Intuitions in Payback and Discounted Payback

By using TVM, discounted payback is basically asking the question, "How long will it be before the project earns back not only the initial investment, but also the interest we would have to pay in order to borrow the money to do that project?" That is, discounted payback asks how long it will take to earn back both the *capital invested* in a project and the *required rate of return* on that invested capital.

On the other hand, regular payback completely ignores TVM and disregards any measure of interest, so it is asking, "How long will it take to earn back just the initial investment, without any interest?"

Average Accounting Return (AAR)

The *Average Accounting Return* (AAR) decision rule claims to compare the rate of return earned by a project with the cost of capital, but it doesn't do a very good job of it. To see why, let's look at the formula for the statistic:

$$AAR = \frac{\text{average net income}}{\text{average book value of assets}}$$

Though at first glance this *does* look like it will give us a percentage rate of return, it suffers from several critical flaws.

First, as we've already discussed, net income does not do a good job of measuring cash inflows; second, the average book value of assets doesn't necessarily do a very good job of measuring the amount of capital invested in the firm, either, primarily because of the effects of depreciation (which we'll discuss in more detail later in the book).

Once calculated, this statistic is normally compared to the firm's or the project's *cost of capital*, the average rate of return necessary to pay back the project's capital providers. If the rate earned, the AAR, is greater than the cost of capital, you accept; if it's less, you reject.

One of the only good things about this statistic is that it *does* try to express the inflows to the project in the form of an interest rate; for several reasons that we'll discuss later, this is often a good idea. However, while the idea of using a ratio here is good, the implementation is seriously flawed. There are several better ways of coming up with the rate of return expected to be earned by a project, including the *Internal Rate of Return* (IRR), which we'll cover next.

Internal Rate of Return (IRR)

The IRR succeeds at being what the AAR attempts to be. To compute this more appropriate rate of return, we set the NPV problem up, putting in the cash flows and the time periods, but setting the NPV itself to zero, and then we solve for the rate that will make this formula work. In the case of our sample project from Figure 10-2, the equation would look like this:

$$NPV = \sum_{i=0}^{T} \frac{CF_i}{(1+r)^i}$$

$$0 = \frac{-\$600}{(1.0r)^0} + \frac{\$200}{(1.0r)^1} + \frac{\$300}{(1.0r)^2} + \frac{\$400}{(1.0r)^3}$$

While it is theoretically possible to solve this equation for r, we really don't want to go there. This is one of the problems where you virtually *have* to use the calculator. Assuming that you've still got the cash flows typed in from when we solved for NPV, all you have to do is compute the IRR:

[CPT]   [IRR] = 20.6140%

The benchmark for the IRR rule is always the cost of capital, r, and the rule itself says to accept the project if IRR > r, reject if IRR < r. Since r for this project is only 8 percent, it should be accepted.

The Intuition behind IRR

The IRR decision rule, accept the project if IRR > r, is really saying to accept the project if the *expected* rate of return is greater than the *required* rate of return.

Up until this chapter, we've been using these two phrases interchangeably; that's because, for stock, bonds, and any other type of financial asset that trades in a relatively liquid financial market, we've been dealing with a competitive environment, one where it makes sense to assume that we're not going to be able to earn any "extra" return above and beyond what's appropriate for the amount of risk we're bearing.

In this chapter, we're no longer dealing with financial assets, but with real assets, such as pieces of land and production lines. These types of assets don't necessarily trade in perfectly competitive markets; instead, they trade in markets where it is possible for an individual or a firm to gain at least some amount of monopoly power.

This idea goes back to the discussion that we had in Chapter 1 concerning the primary difference between the formulas for financial assets such as stocks and bonds, and the equations we're using in this chapter to value projects. The formulas we used to value stocks and bonds had "=" signs because those assets trade in near-perfectly competitive markets, where what you get is (approximately, at least) equal to what you paid for it; here, we are dealing with situations where the name of the game is to choose projects that are worth more than you pay for them. That's why all of these capital budgeting rules use ">" and "<" signs.

So, when dealing with projects, we have to expect that there will be two different rates of return running around; the best way to think of them is as the *expected* rate of return (IRR) and the *required* rate of return (r).

Problems with IRR

Internal Rate of Return (IRR) provides us with the return on a project in the form of an interest rate. This is valuable for several reasons: first, banks and other lenders habitually quote the cost of capital in the form of a rate, so having the rate we expect to earn from the project quoted in the same manner allows for easy comparison; second, many people are more comfortable with rates of return than with dollar figures, particularly if they don't understand the point we made earlier in this chapter about NPV measuring dollars of return above and beyond the cost of capital.

However, there are some pitfalls associated with using an interest rate, too. Primarily, these stem from the fact that, while interest rates are great at measuring "bang per buck invested," they don't measure *how many* bucks are being invested. More formally, this is described as a problem concerning differences in scale between projects, and it comes into play when we start thinking about using these decision rules to choose between two or more *mutually exclusive* projects (i.e., between projects where we can do one or the other, but not both).

So far we've been focusing on using the decision rules in this chapter to make a go/no-go decision on one project at a time; to do so, we've basically been using a two-step process:

1. Compute the statistic.
2. Compare the statistic to the appropriate benchmark.

If we want to expand this process to encompass choosing between multiple projects, we're going to have to add an additional step in the middle:

1. Compute the statistic for each project.
2. Have a "run-off" between projects, choosing the one with the best statistic.
3. Compare the statistic of the winning project to the appropriate benchmark.

Net Present Value (NPV) has no problem with this expanded three-step process, and if we use NPV to choose between multiple mutually exclusive projects, it will consistently pick the best one of the bunch.

However, IRR, or any other statistic constructed as a rate of return, will have problems choosing between projects, and may sometimes choose a project as the "winner" at step 2, above, which no logical person would ever pick.

This discrepancy between the two types of decision rules is due to how they use the cost of capital, r. NPV and other similar statistics use r in calculating their own statistic at step 1, above, so when they reach the runoff at step 2 the results of that runoff will incorporate r. IRR and the other rate-denominated statistics do *not* use r in the calculation of their statistic, but as their benchmark, so r is not incorporated in the runoff decision at step 2.

To see what kind of problems this can create, consider a computer choosing between two projects: Project A has an IRR of 10 percent and an NPV of $100; Project B has an IRR of 9 percent and an NPV of $1,000,000,000,000,000. At step 2, NPV would choose project B, but IRR would choose Project A.

Can this problem with IRR be fixed? No, because it's part of the tradeoff inherent in using a rate-based statistic. If you want the benefits, you have to bear this cost.

Internal Rate of Return (IRR) also has a couple of other problems. For one, it implicitly assumes that any cash inflows will be reinvested in another project that will earn the IRR; NPV, on the other hand, assumes that cash inflows will be reinvested at the cost of capital, r.

Which assumption is more reasonable? *Net Present Value's* (NPV's), because one way to "make" the cost of capital is to pay back your capital investors. Also, because IRR's assumption doesn't make sense: assuming that this project beat out a bunch of other projects at step 2, it must have had the highest possible IRR among all the alternatives, right? But, now that the cash flows are starting to come in, we find another project with the same highest possible rate of return? Wow, what a coincidence!

Another problem affecting IRR arises if the cash flows are not normal; in general, a set of cash flows can (but not "must"—more on that later) have as many possible IRR statistics as there are changes in sign in the cash flows.

To understand what causes a single set of cash flows to have multiple IRRs, we'll make use of a visual tool called an NPV *profile*, which is simply a chart of a project's NPV as a function of r. For the sample project we've been using so far, the NPV profile is shown in Figure 10-9.

In this graph, the project's IRR of 20.6140 percent that we computed above can be seen to be the intercept of the NPV profile with the x axis; or, as we defined it, as the interest rate which causes the NPV to equal zero.

This NPV profile will only have one single such intersection with the x axis because, with normal cash flows, increasing r will always decrease NPV. (The two cases of $r = 0\%$ and $r = 8\%$ that we discussed in our coverage of discounted payback also illustrate this point, and can be seen graphically here.)

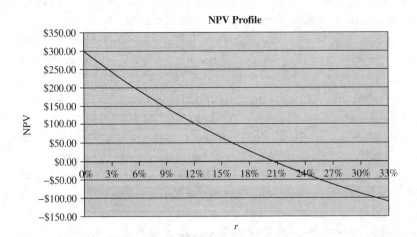

FIGURE 10-9 · NPV profile for sample project.

FIGURE 10-10 · Sample project with nonnormal cash flows.

On the other hand, if we have a set of cash flows with multiple changes in sign, the NPV profile may not be monotonically decreasing. For example, consider the project cash flows shown in Figure 10-10.

The NPV profile of this project can be seen in Figure 10-11.

The multiple changes in sign of the cash flows in this project cause the NPV profile to change directions multiple times. As we can see here, it causes the NPV profile to cross over the *x* axis at least twice, so there are at least two interest rates where NPV = 0, one at 4.96 percent and another at 28.71 percent. (There may be more, but once you figure out that there are more than one, it's a moot point.)

So, if we wanted to use the IRR decision rule, which of these two numbers would we use as this project's statistic? Both are equally valid, so the correct answer is, "neither." Regardless of which one you chose, there would be a range of *r* that would give you a wrong answer if you used the IRR rule.

Luckily, both the problem concerning IRR's inappropriate reinvestment rate assumption and the one just discussed, concerning the potential of multiple IRRs with nonnormal cash flows, can be fixed by using a slightly modified version of IRR.

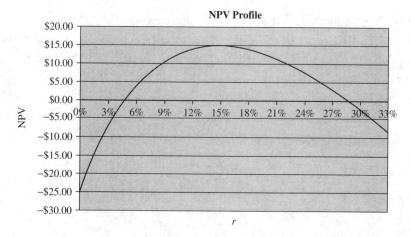

FIGURE 10-11 · NPV profile for project with nonnormal cash flows.

Modified IRR (MIRR)

Before we proceed with our discussion of this decision rule, we should point out that the name is a little misleading. *Modified IRR* (MIRR) uses the same methodology as IRR, it just uses it on a *modified* set of cash flows. Namely, we correct the faulty reinvestment rate assumption of IRR by first using r to move any negative cash flows to the front of the project timeline, and any positive cash flows to the end of the project timeline.

For example, if we go back to our sample project from Figure 10-2, the only negative cash flows are already at the beginning, so all we have to do is move all the positive cash flows to period 8. Using the FV formula for the relevant cash flows, we would get a total time 8 value of:

$$FV = \$200 \times (1.08)^2 + \$300 \times (1.08) + \$400$$
$$= \$957.28$$

(Some of the newest financial calculators have the ability to find the total future value of the cash flows in the CF worksheet; but, if you use this, note that you will have to replace any negative cash flows with zeros, first.)

This transforms our timeline into the one shown in Figure 10-12. We can now calculate the IRR of the transformed set of cash flows:

−$800	[CF0]		
$0	[CF1]	2	[F1]
$957.28	[CF2]	1	[F2]
[CPT]	[IRR] = 16.8501%		

There are a couple of things to note about this statistic.

First, the MIRR decision rule uses the same benchmark as the IRR rule, r. Since 16.8501 percent is greater than 8 percent, MIRR says that this is a good project and should be accepted.

Second, note that the MIRR statistic is less than the IRR statistic, which will always be the case if IRR is greater than r. To the extent that we were worried

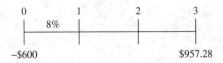

FIGURE 10-12 · Modified cash flows of sample project.

that IRR might have been too high because of the unreasonable reinvestment rate assumption, the MIRR being lower than the IRR will help reduce that concern.

Lastly, notice how many cash flows we had after we modified them—two. Using MIRR, we will *always* wind up with two cash flows, one negative and one positive, before we find the rate of return. And, if there are only two cash flows, there can be, at most, only one change in sign. So, even though we only explicitly fixed IRR's reinvestment rate function, the way we went about it will always result in only one MIRR, no matter how many potential IRRs are being caused by nonnormal cash flows.

Profitability Index (PI)

Another decision rule using a rate of return as a statistic, the PI, simply takes the NPV of a project and converts it into a percentage rate. The mathematics of doing so are fairly simple, but there are actually two competing methodologies that both go by the name "PI."

In one methodology, the most common, and which we'll designate as approach "A," the statistic is computed by taking NPV and dividing it by the project's initial investment:

$$PI_A = \frac{NPV}{CF_0}$$

Since all this does is scale NPV, it will have the same benchmark as NPV, with the decision rule—if $PI_A > 0$, accept; if $PI_A < 0$, reject.

However, the most common alternative to this approach, which we'll designate as approach "B," divides the present value of all future cash flows by the initial investment. This is the same as calculating:

$$PI_B = \frac{NPV + CF_0}{CF_0}$$

A little algebra shows that this can be rearranged as:

$$PI_B = \frac{NPV}{CF_0} + \frac{CF_0}{CF_0}$$
$$= \frac{NPV}{CF_0} + 1$$
$$= PI_A + 1$$

So, the benchmark of this version will be 1, with the decision rule being, if $PI_B > 1$, accept; if $PI_B < 1$, reject.

In both cases, PI will always make the same accept/reject decision as NPV. Also, we should never use r as a benchmark for PI, because PI is still measuring return above and beyond r, the same way NPV does.

Repeated Projects: Equivalent Annual Cost

At times, you will need to compare the costs of benefits of two alternatives, both of which involve a choice that will be repeated, time after time. In such a situation, it's not really the two alternatives that you need to choose between, but two *infinite streams* of those alternatives.

For example, suppose you are considering two alternative machines for your production process: machine A costs $50,000, will last three years, and will have after-tax operating costs of $15,000 per year; machine B costs $80,000, but will last five years and has operating costs of only $10,000 per year. Also, let's suppose that the appropriate interest rate for valuing these two machines is 10 percent, and that either machine would be used until it's worthless (i.e., that there will be no salvage values involved).

It is tempting to compute the NPVs of one machine A and one machine B, the cash flows for which are shown below in Figure 10-13 and Figure 10-14, respectively.

If we do compute these NPVs, we will get $NPV_A = -\$87,302.78$ and $NPV_B = -\$117,907.87$. Notice that both the NPVs are negative; normally, that would lead us to reject both projects, but not in this case. When faced with choices such as the one we're analyzing here, we're usually not dealing with an entire project's cash flows; the inherent assumption is that the NPV for making the product or providing the service is, overall, positive, and that we're just trying to decide the cheapest way to support that overall decision. So, rather than choosing the project with the *highest positive* NPV, we're going to be looking to choose the part of a project with the *least negative* NPV.

Looking at these two NPVs, you might be thinking of choosing machine A. However, making a decision now would be a mistake, because the two machines

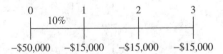

FIGURE 10-13 • Cash flows for one machine A.

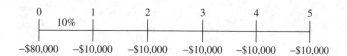

FIGURE 10-14 • Cash flows for one machine B.

are not otherwise equivalent: Machine A will only support three years worth of production, while machine B will support five years. In order to choose between them, we really need to convert these NPVs to cost figures for a common length of time; typically, we choose to convert to an annual basis by calculating the *Equivalent Annual Cost* (EAC) for each project.

The first step in calculating the EAC is to compute the NPV, which we've already done. Next, we use that NPV as the present value of an annuity for each machine, computing the EAC as the payment amount which would give us that same NPV while keeping T equal to the machine's expected life. In our example, machine A's EAC would be computed as:

3	[T]
10%	[r]
–$87,302.78	[PVA]
[CPT]	[PMT] = –$35,105.74

and machine B's EAC would be computed as:

5	[T]
10%	[r]
–$117,907.87	[PVA]
[CPT]	[PMT] = –$31,103.80

Based on these cost figures, which are expressed in terms of the same length of time, machine B costs less on an annual basis than machine A.

Notice that in computing the annuity payments for each machine, we use that machine's usable life as T. Effectively, we're taking each machine's NPV and "smoothing it out" (i.e., converting it to an annuity of equal payments per year) over the life of that machine.

QUIZ

1. Suppose you are examining a project with the cash flows shown below. What is the maximum number of IRRs that this set of cash flows can have?

Period	0	1	2	3	4	5
Cash Flows	-300	400	-400	-300	300	400

   A. 1
   B. 2
   C. 3
   D. 4

2. Which of the following capital budgeting decision rules is the best choice for selecting projects if used alone?

   A. Discounted payback
   B. IRR
   C. MIRR
   D. NPV

3. Which of the following capital budgeting decision rules does *not* use the cost of capital, *r*, in the calculation of its statistic?

   A. Discounted payback
   B. MIRR
   C. NPV
   D. IRR

4. Which of the following problems with IRR is *not* corrected by MIRR?

   A. Faulty reinvestment rate assumption
   B. Multiple possible values for the decision statistic when cash flows are not normal
   C. Does not measure "bucks invested"
   D. Does not use TVM at all

Please use the following information to answer the next six questions.

Your company is evaluating a new project. You estimate that the required rate of return for the project should be 13 percent, and you have estimated the project's cash flows to be:

Year	0	1	2	3	4	5
Cash Flow	-$150,000	$74,000	$60,000	$80,000	$60,000	$30,000

5. **What will this project's payback be?**
   A. 2.20 years
   B. 3.16 years
   C. 3.54 years
   D. 3.65 years

6. **What will this project's discounted payback be?**
   A. 2.06 years
   B. 2.68 years
   C. 3.40 years
   D. 3.65 years

7. **What will this project's NPV be?**
   A. $29,409
   B. $38,258
   C. $47,108
   D. $71,001

8. **What will this project's IRR be?**
   A. 25.45%
   B. 28.13%
   C. 30.42%
   D. 32.98%

9. **What will this project's MIRR be?**
   A. 15.88%
   B. 18.33%
   C. 22.11%
   D. 25.37%

10. **Using the second version of the profitability index formulas discussed earlier, what will this project's profitability index be?**
    A. 1.26
    B. 1.31
    C. 1.39
    D. 1.47

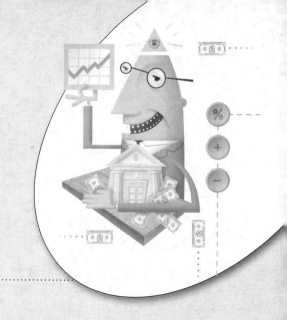

Part IV

Where Do Interest Rates Come From? Risk, Return, and the Cost of Capital

chapter **11**

Measuring Risk and Return

CHAPTER OBJECTIVES

At the end of this chapter, the reader should be able to:

- Calculate the arithmetic and geometric averages of a series of returns
- Calculate the historic standard deviation of a series of returns
- Calculate the expected return and standard deviation in returns across expected states of nature
- Calculate a portfolio average return and standard deviation

One of the fundamental assumptions of finance is that there is a positive relationship between the perceived risk of any investment and the expected rate of return that a rational person would require to get them to invest in it. We've touched upon this assumption previously as we were constructing the stock and bond pricing formulas and the capital-budgeting decision rules for project evaluation, but we've never really covered why we believe this is so, or what the implications are of such a relationship.

In this chapter, we're going to take a first stab at measuring asset risk and return using two commonly calculated statistical measures, the *average* and the *standard deviation*, to measure the expected return and the risk of an investment.

There are two basic approaches to calculating the average and standard deviation of an investment's returns; we can either measure the average and standard deviation of the returns that the investment has had during some past period, and then use them as a proxy of what we think is going to happen in the future; or we can try to explicitly predict everything that might happen in the future and then use the average and standard deviation of those possibilities to summarize them. Let's go over each approach first, and then we'll discuss under what circumstances each might be appropriate.

Using the Past to Predict the Future: Computing the Average and Standard Deviation of Historic Returns

In many cases, the simplest and most straightforward way to predict the future return and risk (or the tradeoff between the two) for an investment is to assume that they're going to look a lot like they did in the past. But "the past" covers a lot of territory, and, unless we're going to assume that the very latest individual historic observation is the best estimate of the future that we can come up with, we're going to need some way to summarize and incorporate multiple observations of risk or return. Such summarization is exactly what statistics are intended for, so we're going to use the average statistic to measure the "usual" level of return in the past.

Actually, there are two versions of average return that play important parts in finance: the *arithmetic* and *geometric averages*. The arithmetic average is the simple average that we all learned about in basic statistics—the mean; the geometric average is intuitively tied to the concept of compound interest discussed in basic finance texts.

For example, suppose that you are told that an investment of $1,000 earned a 100 percent return one year, and that the proceeds (i.e., principal and interest) were reinvested in the same asset the next year, earning a 50 percent return and resulting in a cash value at the end of the two years of $3,000. The arithmetic average return would be equal to (1.00 + 0.50)/2 = 0.75, or 75 percent, while the geometric average return would be equal to the annual rate of return, which, if earned each of the two years and compounded on an annual basis, would cause the $1,000 investment to grow to the same $3,000 ending value. Or, put mathematically, the geometric average rate of return across this two-year period would be the solution of the following equation:

$$[\$1,000 \times (1+1.00)] \times (1+0.50) = \$1,000 \times (1+gmean)^2$$

If we solve this equation for *gmean*, we get 73.2051 percent.

Why the difference between the two averages? Because the two methods for computing these averages are making different implicit assumptions about the *holding periods* we're interested in, and therefore different assumptions about compounding periods.

When you calculate the arithmetic average, you are averaging two one-year returns to get the average one-year holding period return; when you solve the preceding equation for the geometric mean, you are solving for the annual rate of return which, if earned and compounded annually for a two-year holding period, will yield you the same ending value as the original, given interest rates if the interest from the first year can be compounded in the second year.

Given that this chapter deals with predicting the future from the past, which of the two types of average do you think we want to calculate? If you notice that the equation we used to solve for the geometric mean looks remarkably like the FV formula for the future value of a lump sum, the fact that we use TVM so much in finance might mislead you into thinking that the geometric average is always the one that we're going to want, but the answer is actually a little more complicated than that.

The version of the average that we need will be based on the relationship between the length of time over which returns are computed and the length of time that we intend to own the security in question, called the *expected holding period*.

If, for example, we had a set of historic *annual* returns and we were trying to estimate the expected future return under the assumption that we would hold the stock for one year, then we'd want to estimate the arithmetic average.

However, if we were intending to hold the stock for several years and wanted to express the expected return as an annual rate, which would be subject to compounding during that multiyear holding period, we'd want to estimate the geometric average.

This distinction can get a little confusing, so let's use the following rule for right now: unless otherwise directed, let's assume that when we're asked to calculate an average, we're in a situation where the expected holding period is "not long," compared to the return calculation periods, implying that we need an arithmetic average.

Of course, we also need a statistic to summarize the risk of returns. As a starting point, we're going to use the standard deviation statistic because it measures variability in returns around the average, which would seem to be logically related to the concept of risk or uncertainty.

If you've already had statistics, you can probably guess what's coming next, and you're probably asking, "OK, so *which* standard deviation do we use, population or sample?" Good question! But, you can probably figure the answer out yourself with a hint: the *population* of returns on, say, XYZ stock would have to include all the returns on that stock that have ever happened in the past or *will ever happen in the future*. Given that the future hasn't happened yet, any set of XYZ returns that we gather will have to be a subset, or sample, of XYZ's return population.

So, to summarize, when we have a set of historic returns that we're going to use either to describe what has happened in the past or to predict what we can expect to happen in the future, we're going to want to calculate the arithmetic average and the sample standard deviation.

The formula for the arithmetic average is:

$$\text{Arithmetic average} = \overline{R} = \sum_{t=1}^{T} \frac{R_t}{T}$$

and the formula for the sample standard deviation is:

$$S_x = \sqrt{\frac{\sum_{t=1}^{T}(R_t - \overline{R})^2}{(T-1)}}$$

For example, let's suppose we were analyzing the stock of Walter Industries Incorporated (WLT), which had earned the annual returns shown in Table 11-1 during the last five years. What was the arithmetic average and sample standard deviation during this period?

TABLE 11-1	Historic Returns for Walters Industries Incorporated as of June 1st of Years Indicated

Year Ending December 31	Return (%)
2009	256.44
2008	−55.54
2007	49.14
2006	−9.99
2005	81.35

The average would be:

$$\overline{R} = \sum_{t=1}^{T} \frac{R_t}{T}$$

$$= \frac{2.5644 - 0.5554 + 0.4914 - 0.0999 + 0.8135}{5}$$

$$= 0.6428, \text{ or } 64.28\%$$

and the standard deviation would be:

$$S_x = \sqrt{\frac{\sum_{t=1}^{T}(R_t - \overline{R})^2}{(T-1)}}$$

$$= \sqrt{\frac{\begin{array}{l}(2.5644 - 0.6428)^2 + (-0.5554 - 0.6428)^2 \\ +(0.4914 - 0.6428)^2 + (-0.0999 - 0.6428)^2 \\ +(0.8135 - 0.6428)^2\end{array}}{5-1}}$$

$$= 1.1971, \text{ or } 119.71\%$$

Explicit Guessing: Calculating the Expected Return and Standard Deviation across Expected States of Nature

In some cases, we can't use historic returns to predict the future, either because they simply don't exist or because there's not enough of them to provide a reasonable sample size. Also, even if an adequate number of historic observations do exist, we might feel that there's been some underlying, fundamental shift in the company's operations that make those historic observations unrepresentative of what we might expect in the future.

In such cases, there is another way to come up with expected returns—guess. Of course, it's best if you make an *educated* guess, and one of the common ways to construct an educated guess is to forecast company performance as a function of some observable and predictable macroeconomic variable. Though it's possible to model the expected values of the macroeconomic variable (and, hence, the resulting company returns) as having a continuous distribution, the usual approach is to divide the possible macroeconomic values into a discrete set of likely "states of nature," along with the expected returns and probabilities for each state.

For example, suppose we have determined that our company's expected return is positively related to the state of the economy, that we've researched the likely states of the economy and their probabilities, and that we've figured out what return we can expect to earn in each economic state, as shown in Table 11-2.

When using data like these, based on the probabilities of various expected states of nature occurring in the future, the formulas we need for calculating the expected return or standard deviation of these numbers are:

$$E(R) = \sum_{i=1}^{n} p_i R_i$$

and

$$\sigma = \sqrt{\sum_{i=1}^{n} p_i [R_i - E(R)]^2}$$

where $E(R)$ = weighted average expected return across states of nature
n = number of states of nature
p_i = probability of the ith state of nature
R_i = return to the stock the ith state of nature
σ = population standard deviation across states of nature

TABLE 11-2 Sample Distribution of States of Nature and Expected Returns

State of the Economy	Probability	Company Return (%)
Boom	.15	25
Expansion	.30	18
Steady	.30	8
Contraction	.20	−5
Recession	.05	−20

So, using these equations, our expected return can be calculated as:

$$E(R) = \sum_{i=1}^{n} p_i R_i$$

$$= (0.15 \times 25\%) + (0.30 \times 18\%) + (0.30 \times 8\%)$$
$$+ (0.20 \times -5\%) + (0.05 \times -20\%)$$
$$= 0.0955, \text{ or } 9.55\%$$

And our standard deviation can be calculated as:

$$\sigma = \sqrt{\sum_{i=1}^{n} p_i [R_i - E(R)]^2}$$

$$= \sqrt{\begin{matrix} 0.15 \times (25\% - 9.55\%)^2 + 0.30 \times (18\% - 9.55\%)^2 + \\ 0.30 \times (8\% - 9.55\%)^2 + 0.20 \times (-5\% - 9.55\%)^2 + \\ 0.05 \times (-20\% - 9.55\%)^2 \end{matrix}}$$

$$= 0.1200, \text{ or } 12.00\%$$

Note that, unlike in the previous section, we are calculating the *population* standard deviation. Why? Well, to put it simply, as long as we're guessing what might happen in the next period, we might as well guess everything that could happen, right? That is also why the probabilities in such problems should always add up to one, or 100 percent.

Choosing Which Method to Use for Average and Standard Deviation

As we've seen, the methodology for calculating the expected future return to a security and the likely deviation around that expectation varies according to whether we can use the past to predict the future. If we can, then we calculate the simple mean and the sample standard deviation using historic returns and use these as proxies for what we expect to happen in the future; if we can't, then we have to explicitly forecast a distribution of expected returns and their associated probabilities, taking the expected value of this distribution as our expected return.

Portfolio Averages and Standard Deviations

Whichever method we choose for computing the average and standard deviation, that same approach can be extended to portfolios of stocks and other investments.

The most direct way to do this starts with computing what the portfolio returns would have been in each historic period (if we're using historical data), or what they may be in each future state of nature (if we're using explicit guesses concerning the future), and then treating this new asset, the portfolio, the same as we would any individual stock in computing its returns.

For example, let's suppose that we're considering investing 40 percent of our money in Stock S and 60 percent in stock T, the expected returns for different states of nature are shown below in Table 11-3. To calculate the expected return and standard deviation to our prospective portfolio *across states of nature*, we would first need to calculate what the portfolio would earn in each state of nature, as shown in Table 11-4. Once we've got these possible returns to the portfolio for each state of nature, calculating the expected return and standard deviation across states of nature is the same as it would be for an individual stock:

$$E(R) = \sum_{i=1}^{n} p_i R_i$$
$$= (0.25 \times 15.2\%) + (0.60 \times 11.6\%) + (0.15 \times 2.8\%)$$
$$= 0.1118, \text{ or } 11.18\%$$

$$\sigma = \sqrt{\sum_{i=1}^{n} p_i [R_i - E(R)]^2}$$
$$= \sqrt{\begin{array}{l} 0.25 \times (15.2\% - 11.18\%)^2 + 0.60 \times (11.6\% - 11.18\%)^2 \\ + 0.15 \times (2.8\% - 11.18\%)^2 \end{array}}$$
$$= 0.0383, \text{ or } 3.83\%$$

Using this approach to come up with an expected portfolio return and standard deviation based on historic returns to the individual stocks comprising the portfolio would be equally straightforward.

TABLE 11-3 Expected Returns to Stocks S and T

State of the Economy	Probability	Company S Return (%)	Company T Return (%)
Good	.25	20	12
Indifferent	.60	14	10
Bad	.15	−5	8

TABLE 11-4 Portfolio Returns in Each State of Nature

State of the Economy	Probability	Company S Return (%)	Company T Return (%)	Portfolio Return
Good	.25	20	12	$(.4 \times 20\%) + (.6 \times 12\%) = 15.2\%$
Indifferent	.60	14	10	$(.4 \times 14\%) + (.6 \times 10\%) = 11.6\%$
Bad	.15	−5	8	$(.4 \times -5\%) + (.6 \times 8\%) = 2.8\%$

There are mathematical formulas which use the correlations or covariances between the individual components of a portfolio to compute the expected return and standard deviation of the portfolio. They manage to do so without needing to go through calculating the individual portfolio returns for each historic observation or for each future state of nature. But, except for the rather trivial case of a two-asset portfolio, these formulas get quite involved and complicated, and really should only be done with matrix math, which is a little beyond the scope of this text.

QUIZ

1. Which of the following statistics is really the same thing as the effective periodic interest rate that we've discussed in earlier chapters?

   A. Population standard deviation
   B. Sample standard deviation
   C. Arithmetic average
   D. Geometric average

2. When using historic data to predict the future, we should use:

   A. The arithmetic average and the population standard deviation
   B. The arithmetic average and the sample standard deviation
   C. The geometric average and the sample standard deviation
   D. The geometric average and the population standard deviation

3. When using explicit forecasts of future returns, we should use:

   A. The arithmetic average and the population standard deviation
   B. The arithmetic average and the sample standard deviation
   C. The geometric average and the sample standard deviation
   D. The geometric average and the population standard deviation

4. If we choose to calculate and use an arithmetic average as our predictor of future expected returns, we are implicitly assuming that:

   A. The expected holding period is long compared to the return calculation period
   B. The expected holding period is not long compared to the return calculation period
   C. The expected holding period is one year or less
   D. The expected holding period is one year or more

5. Suppose that you are told that an investment of $500 earned returns of 17 percent, 32 percent, and 8 percent during each of the last three years, and that the proceeds (i.e., principal and interest) were reinvested in the same asset every year. What was the geometric average return during this three-year period?

   A. 16.76%
   B. 18.59%
   C. 19.00%
   D. 42.68%

6. Continuing the previous problem, what was the arithmetic average return during this three-year period?

   A. 16.76%
   B. 18.59%
   C. 19.00%
   D. 42.68%

Use the following information about the returns of PDL Corp. to answer the next two problems:

Year	Return
2007	37.34%
2008	−23.67%
2009	12.45%
2010	17.87%
2011	−8.08%

7. **What was the arithmetic average return to PDL during this period?**
   A. 6.32%
   B. 6.45%
   C. 7.18%
   D. 7.78%

8. **What was the standard deviation in returns to PDL during this period?**
   A. 22.04%
   B. 23.64%
   C. 24.67%
   D. 26.84%

Use the following information about the expected future returns of IAD Corp. to answer the next two problems:

State of the Economy	Probability	Company Return
Boom	.30	15%
Average	.40	6%
Bust	.30	−6%

9. **What is the expected return to IAD next year?**
   A. 4.30%
   B. 4.80%
   C. 5.10%
   D. 5.90%

10. **What is the standard deviation for IAD's expected return?**
   A. 8.17%
   B. 8.35%
   C. 8.58%
   D. 8.96%

chapter 12

Calculating Beta

At the end of this chapter, the reader should be able to:

- Explain how diversification will mitigate unsystematic risk
- Calculate beta for an individual asset
- Compute portfolio betas

The standard deviation statistics that we've used so far do a fine job of measuring the risk of a stock, bond, or project when it's held by itself. However, once you start holding such an asset as part of a well-diversified portfolio, there's a pretty good chance that at least some of the unique volatility in that asset's returns is going to be "canceled out" by similar, but offsetting, volatility in other parts of the portfolio. (This is the concept that your finance textbook refers to as *diversification*.) This means that we need a new measure of risk, one that calculates how much of the volatility is left when the security is held in a well-diversified portfolio.

The volatility that is left is caused by risks that all securities face, called *systematic* or *nonidiosyncratic* risks. The statistic of choice for measuring this type of risk is called *beta*.

Those of you who have taken a class in statistics might recognize that beta is another name sometimes used for the slope coefficient that you get when you run a linear regression and, sure enough, *this* beta is calculated by running a regression of "excess" returns (defined below) on the stock or asset against the excess returns on a large, well-diversified portfolio.

Beta Estimation Methodology

Under a set of assumptions too complex to go into here, the relationship between the expected returns on a particular asset i and the expected returns of a large, well-diversified investment portfolio, called the market portfolio, can be written as:

$$E(R_i) = R_f + \beta_i [E(R_M) - R_f]$$

where $E(R_i)$ = expected return on asset i
R_f = risk-free rate
β_i = sensitivity of security i's returns to those of the market risk premium, $[E(R_m) - R_f]$
$E(R_M)$ = expected return on the market portfolio

This is the famous *Capital Asset Pricing Model* (CAPM), and we'll cover its usage in more depth in the next chapter; for now, just notice that this formula is expressed in terms of expectations concerning the future. In this chapter, we're just going to discuss how past data can be used to forecast the expected value for β_i.

If this relationship is restated in terms of past (realized) returns, the expectation operators can be dropped and, with a little rearrangement, we can get a linear regression model that can be used to estimate β_i.

$$[R_{it} - R_{ft}] = \alpha_i + \beta_i[R_{Mt} - R_{ft}] + \varepsilon_i$$

where R_{it} = return on security i during time period t
R_{ft} = risk-free rate during time period t
α_i = estimated intercept of the regression
R_{Mt} = return on the market portfolio during time period t
ε_i = an error term, theoretically equal to zero

You'll often hear $[R_{it} - R_{ft}]$ and $[R_{Mt} - R_{ft}]$ referred to as *excess* returns, meaning that these are the returns to the security and to the market portfolio above and beyond the risk-free rate. Accordingly, we'll refer to this regression model as the *excess returns* model.

You'll sometimes see the following alternate equation used in a finance text:

$$R_{it} = \alpha_i + \beta_i R_{Mt} + \varepsilon_i$$

If someone is using this equation instead of the excess returns model, they're assuming that the risk-free rate is constant during the estimation period, which allows them to "cancel out" all the instances of R_{ft}. While appealing, this assumption is really only valid for very short estimation periods, and using it when it's not appropriate will insert error into your beta estimate, so we won't be using this equation.

Choosing and Gathering the Necessary Data

When gathering data to be used in the excess return model, the first question we have to ask ourselves is, "How far back do we want to go?" Remember that we are trying to estimate the *past* relationship (i.e., beta) with the hope that it will predict the *future* relationship, so we have to juggle two opposite effects when choosing the length of our estimation period: increasing the sample size by including "older" observations will increase the statistical validity of our estimated beta, but it will also decrease the applicability of that estimate if the relationship has changed over time.

Unfortunately, there is no single "correct" choice of the optimal tradeoff between these two effects: for some firms, going back more than a single year will be too far, but for other firms the optimal estimation period can be upward of nine years. In addition, the "correct" choice of estimation period for a firm also changes over time as the firm or the economy goes through cyclical changes; the estimation period you used last year to successfully predict this year's beta for firm ABC might not work as well when predicting next year's beta.

As a compromise, many professional beta providers have chosen to standardize their beta estimation periods, choosing a period of between two and five years and then using that common estimation period to calculate all the betas they report. For example, Bloomberg calculates betas using a two-year estimation period, Morningstar reports betas estimated on three years' worth of data, and Yahoo! reports betas estimated using five years of data.

One thing that all of the professional beta providers do agree on, though, is two to five annual observations is not an acceptable sample size. So, how do they get around this problem? They use monthly, or in some cases, even weekly returns, which increases the sample sizes while keeping the observations relatively recent.

So, for our example below, we really *should* use an estimation period of five years of monthly observations (giving us a sample size of 60); we'll stick to shorter estimation periods, however, for expositional purposes.

We also have to decide what market index we're going to use as a proxy for the market portfolio. Ideally, we would like to choose an index that contains all possible investment securities, including not only stocks and bonds but also real estate, gold bullion, collectible art, and so forth. Unfortunately, such broad-based indices just aren't available in the real world, so we're forced to choose from a number of stock and bond indices. By far the most popular such choice is the S&P 500 (ticker symbol $\wedge SPX$), and that's the one we'll use as our proxy for the market portfolio.

We're also going to need a proxy for the risk-free rate. In line with our assumption in the previous chapter concerning a "not long" holding period, we will use a short-term U.S. treasury bond.

Calculating the Beta

Even though it would be much easier to perform the regression for beta using Excel, most of you are unlikely to have access to a computer for your exams. Luckily, most financial calculators also include at least some statistical analysis functions, which can be used to perform the regression for us.

Similar to the set of CF worksheet/NPV worksheet that we noted previously, these calculators normally require that you input the data for the statistical analysis into one worksheet, which we'll refer to as the DATA worksheet, and then go to another, which we'll call the STAT worksheet, to view the outputs of the statistical analysis.

Let's assume that we've gone and carefully collected information on the returns to stock *S*, the returns to the S&P 500, and the short-term T-bond for the last five years, and used this information to construct the excess return data shown in Table 12-1.

When we put this in the DATA worksheet, we have to be very careful to make sure that we enter the stock's excess returns as the "*Y*" variable and the market portfolio's excess returns as the "*X*" variable:

[X1]	1.65%	[Y1]	4.74%
[X2]	5.00%	[Y2]	15.88%
[X3]	0.64%	[Y3]	2.90%
[X4]	5.42%	[Y4]	2.77%
[X5]	−1.27%	[Y5]	−9.05%

Once we've got this data entered, we should be able to go to the STAT worksheet and have it compute for us:

[CPT]   [Beta] = 2.3110

This value for beta implies that this stock tends to move in the same direction as the market in response to systematic events, but to a greater (approximately 2.31×) extent.

If, instead, we had gotten a beta *less* than 1, it would have implied that the stock's returns tend to move in the same direction as the market's, but to a lesser extent.

Finally, while it is theoretically possible for a stock to have a negative beta, such cases don't tend to occur very often in the real world.

TABLE 12-1 Historic Excess Returns

Observation	Stock Excess Returns (%)	Market Excess Returns (%)
1	4.74	1.65
2	15.88	5.00
3	2.90	0.64
4	2.77	5.42
5	−9.05	−1.27

Portfolio Betas

Unlike the case with the standard deviation of a portfolio, where directly computing the standard deviation without calculating the individual portfolio returns for each historic period or in each future state of nature would require extensive information concerning the correlations or covariances of the components' returns, calculating the beta of a portfolio is very simple. All we have to do is to take a weighted average of the betas of the individual components, where the weights are the proportions of our wealth invested in each asset.

For example, let's suppose that we've invested 35 percent of our money in stock D, which has a beta of 1.3, and the remaining 65 percent of our money in stock E, which has a beta of 1.5. Then our portfolio beta would simply be:

$$\beta_{portfolio} = (0.35 \times 1.3) + (0.65 \times 1.5)$$
$$= 1.43$$

QUIZ

1. **Beta measures:**
   A. Idiosyncratic risk
   B. Systematic risk
   C. Stock-specific risk
   D. Total risk

2. **In the linear equation used to calculate beta, it is the:**
   A. Intercept
   B. Slope
   C. *X* variable
   D. *Y* variable

3. **The most common choice for the appropriate estimation sampling period to use when estimating beta is to choose:**
   A. 5 years of yearly data
   B. 5 years of monthly data
   C. 10 years of monthly data
   D. 10 years of yearly data

4. **The most common proxy for the hypothetical market portfolio in the calculation of beta is:**
   A. The Dow Jones Industrial Average
   B. The Russell 1000
   C. The S&P 500
   D. The Wilshire 5000

5. **A calculated beta statistic of 0.80 would imply that:**
   A. The stock tends to move against the market, but to a greater extent.
   B. The stock tends to move against the market, but to a lesser extent.
   C. The stock tends to move with the market, but to a greater extent.
   D. The stock tends to move with the market, but to a lesser extent.

6. **A calculated beta statistic of −0.30 would imply that:**
   A. The stock tends to move against the market, but to a greater extent.
   B. The stock tends to move against the market, but to a lesser extent.
   C. The stock tends to move with the market, but to a greater extent.
   D. The stock tends to move with the market, but to a lesser extent.

7. Use the following historic excess returns to XYZ Corp. and the market to compute XYZ's beta:

Observation	Stock Excess Returns	Market Excess Returns
1	4.82%	1.73%
2	−15.81%	−5.08%
3	2.98%	0.71%
4	2.85%	5.50%
5	−8.97%	−1.19%

A. −0.30
B. 0.23
C. 2.02
D. 3.84

8. Use the following historic excess returns to ABC Corp. and the market to compute ABC's beta:

Observation	Stock Excess Returns	Market Excess Returns
1	−5.14%	1.79%
2	12.95%	1.62%
3	−0.49%	1.13%
4	−13.17%	5.09%
5	9.49%	8.10%

A. −0.30
B. 0.23
C. 2.30
D. 3.84

9. Use the following historic excess returns to IMY Corp. and the market to compute IMY's beta:

Observation	Stock Excess Returns	Market Excess Returns
1	9.20%	0.84%
2	-1.22%	1.70%
3	36.07%	-2.74%
4	-17.73%	-6.03%
5	39.56%	5.71%

A. -0.30
B. 0.23
C. 3.08
D. 3.84

10. Which of the following beta values is least likely to occur in reality?
A. -0.30
B. 0.23
C. 2.30
D. 3.84

chapter 13

Analyzing the Security Market Line

CHAPTER OBJECTIVES

At the end of this chapter, the reader should be able to:

- Explain how to estimate the intercept of the security market line
- Calculate the slope of the security market line
- Adjust beta to allow for mean reversion
- Estimate expected return using the security market line

Even though we referred to the equation for the *Capital Asset Pricing Model* (CAPM) in the last chapter, we didn't go into much detail concerning it. That's because we were in a sort of "Which came first—the chicken or the egg?" situation. You use a reworked version of the CAPM to solve for beta, but then you use beta as an input to the CAPM, and so forth. As with the chicken and the egg problem, one of them had to come first, so we chose to cover calculating beta first.

In this chapter, we're going to talk about what the CAPM is and where it comes from, but mostly we're going to talk about what goes into using it; how the assumptions that we talked about in the previous chapter influence our choice of input variables, and how varying those assumptions will affect our results.

The Relationship between the Security Market Line and the CAPM Equation

The CAPM formula (shown once again for reference) is the linear equation describing a theoretical relationship between the expected risk of security *i* and the expected risk of the market portfolio, *M*. The line that this equation is describing is called the *Security Market Line* (SML).

$$E(R_i) = R_f + \beta_i[E(R_M) - R_f]$$

This equation seems to have the typical "$Y = a + b \times X$" format that we expect from a linear equation, but the ordering of its variables is misleading: β_i is *not* the slope, it's the "X" variable. The slope is actually the entire portion within the brackets, $[E(R_M) - R_f]$, usually called the "market risk premium."

Perhaps a better way to think of the market risk premium is as the *market price* of one unit of risk. If, for example, the current risk-free rate is 4 percent and the average expected return on a well-diversified market portfolio is 11 percent, then the "going price" of one unit of systematic, nondiversifiable risk is (11% − 4%) = 7%. A security with twice as much systematic risk (i.e., $\beta_i = 2$) will command twice as much risk premium as the market portfolio, while one with a beta of 0.5 would only be expected to yield $0.5 \times 7\% = 3.5\%$ above and beyond the risk-free rate.

So, if we want to calculate the expected return for a security using the SML, we need to make sure that we know how to come up with the three parts of the right-hand side of the CAPM equation: the intercept, R_f; the slope, $[E(R_M) - R_f]$; and the independent variable, β_i.

Since we've already calculated a sample beta in the last chapter, let's continue the example and take a look at what additional data we need to calculate the stock's expected return.

Estimating the Intercept of the SML

As per our discussion in the previous chapter concerning expected holding period of the security being examined, we will assume that we are calculating expected return in a situation where our expected holding period is "not long." Once again, this will imply that we should use a short-term U.S. government bond, and we'll choose the three-month T-bill rate for the sake of consistency.

However, unlike when we were calculating beta in the previous chapter, we don't want a historic rate; instead, we want to use a "forward-looking" rate, the currently prevailing yield on these T-bills. These rates are available from a variety of sources on the web and are currently running at around 3.0 percent.

Estimating the Slope of the SML

The easiest (and most common) approach to estimating the expected market risk premium, $[E(R_M) - R_f]$, is to simply calculate the average historic excess return to the market portfolio and assume that this value will persist, on average, into the future. To construct this average, observations are usually taken from the year 1926 onward, resulting in averages on the order of 8 to 9 percent.

Up until the last few years, this approach worked fairly well, but lately both academics and practitioners are starting to question whether, in this case, what we've seen in the past is really representative of what we can expect in the future. If you don't want to use the past to predict the future, then there are two basic methods you can use to come up with an expected future market risk premium:

1. You can survey investors, using the average of their responses as an estimate of the forward-looking market risk premium.

2. You can "back out" the implied forward-looking market risk premium from current prices or other market information.

The first approach is fairly easy to implement, as the Federal Reserve Bank of Philadelphia already conducts a survey of professional forecasters concerning a variety of macroeconomic variables. Once a year, during the first quarterly survey, the data gathered includes forecasts of the anticipated returns to the S&P 500 and Treasury securities. As of the writing of this book, the pertinent section of the report stated:

> The forecasters see the S&P 500 returning 7.00 percent per year, up from 6.50 percent, and 10-year Treasuries returning 4.95 percent, up from 4.85 percent. The forecasters continue to expect that three-month Treasury bills will return 3.0 percent per year over the next 10 years.

Implicitly, the forecasters are anticipating a market risk premium over the next 10 years of only 7.0% − 3.0% = 4.0%. To be conservative, we'll use this figure.

(To access the reports of these surveys, go to http://www.philadelphiafed .org/research-and-data/real-time-center/survey-of-professional-forecasters/ and click on the link for the most recent first quarter report.)

Estimating the *X* Variable, Beta

Remember that the methodology for estimating beta that we discussed in the last chapter measures the sensitivity of the stock's excess returns to those of the market portfolio in the past. Assuming that we're primarily concerned with estimating the value of this relationship in the future, we have to address the question of how well the past predicts the future for betas.

The answer is, "not too well." Over the life cycle of the firm, both its business and financial risk will change, so we would expect the beta, which can be linked to these factors, to change as well. In light of this, many practitioners take the beta from the historical regression and adjust it to more accurately reflect what they expect to see in the future before they use it.

There are two basic approaches to making this adjustment:

1. The simplest approach, and the one used quite often in practice, is to assume that future betas will move back toward 1. This approach is based on re-search showing that betas are "mean reverting" (statistical-speak for "they usually *do* move back toward one"). Most of the users of this approach adjust the beta through the use of a simple weighted average of the calcu-lated regression beta and the beta of the market, 1:

$$\beta_{adjusted} = \left(\frac{2}{3} \times \beta_{regression} \right) + \left(\frac{1}{3} \times 1 \right)$$

For example, using this equation with the calculated regression beta for our sample stock in the previous chapter will give us an adjusted beta of $(2/3 \times 2.3110) + (1/3) = 1.8740$. Most beta providers use equations similar to this one, with small differences in the weights assigned to the regression beta and the market beta (i.e., 1).

2. A more involved approach is to use some observable characteristics of the firm or its industry, along with a cross-sectional analysis of how those characteristics contribute to risk, to either adjust (or completely replace) the regression beta with a function of those firm-specific factors. This approach is less widely used, and the firms that do use it tend to be a little reticent about discussing the exact functional form that they use.

Given that its usage is so widespread among practitioners (and so prevalent in finance textbooks), we will tend to use the first approach.

Bringing It All Together

Using our "best practice" estimates of the components of the SML that we've just developed, we can solve for the expected return to our sample stock as:

$$E(R_i) = R_f + \beta_i[E(R_M) - R_f]$$
$$E(R_i) = 3.0\% + 1.8740[4.0\%] = 10.496\%$$

To summarize, our choices for inputs in this chapter, where we've once again been assuming a relatively short holding period, were:

- R_f: The current yield on three-month T-bills.
- $[E(R_M) - R_f]$: The implicit expected market risk premium from the Philadelphia Federal Reserve's latest quarterly *Survey of Professional Forecasters*.
- β_i: The adjusted beta, calculated using our regression beta from the previous chapter and the adjustment equation detailed earlier.

Of these three choices, the only one that is likely to be at odds with your textbook is the second one, concerning the expected market risk premium. Most textbooks advocate using a historic average of the past excess return to the market as a proxy for the future expected market risk premium, and if you use that approach with an assumed 8 percent market risk premium, then our stock's expected return would be:

$$E(R_i) = 3.00\% + 1.8740(8\%) = 17.992\%$$

This represents a large difference from our initial estimate, so which one is right? Well, right now, the experts are still undecided, so it's probably best to stick with the one your textbook (or your professor) advocates.

In the next chapter, we'll discuss how to use the CAPM equation as part of the calculation of a firm's or a project's cost of capital. As we'll see, the assumptions that we've been making concerning a short holding period may no longer be appropriate, and changing those assumptions may also require changes to our inputs for the CAPM.

QUIZ

1. When we use beta in the linear equation of the security market line, it is the:
   A. X variable
   B. Y variable
   C. Intercept
   D. Slope

2. Which part of the CAPM is best thought of as the "market price of risk"?
   A. R_f
   B. β_i
   C. $E(R_i)$
   D. $[E(R_M) - R_f]$

3. As of the writing of this book, conservative forecasters were anticipating a market risk premium over the next 10 years closest to:
   A. 3%
   B. 4%
   C. 5%
   D. 6%

4. If betas truly are mean reverting, we would expect them to move back toward:
   A. −1
   B. 0
   C. 1
   D. +∞

5. Assume that you have used regression to calculate the beta for a stock you are considering purchasing, and have gotten a value of 1.3. If you wanted to use the adjustment procedure outlined in this chapter, what would be your adjusted beta?
   A. 1.13
   B. 1.20
   C. 1.47
   D. 1.56

6. Assume that you have used regression to calculate the beta for a stock you are considering purchasing, and have gotten a value of 0.7. If you wanted to use the adjustment procedure outlined in this chapter, what would be your adjusted beta?
   A. 0.27
   B. 0.40
   C. 0.60
   D. 0.80

7. Using the CAPM, what would be the expected rate of return for a stock with a beta of 1.4 when the risk-free rate is 4 percent and the expected market risk premium is 5 percent?

   A. 5.3%

   B. 8.6%

   C. 10.4%

   D. 11.0%

8. Using the CAPM, what would be the expected rate of return for a stock with a beta of 0.6 when the risk-free rate is 3 percent and the expected return to the market is 9 percent?

   A. 6.6%

   B. 8.4%

   C. 10.2%

   D. 11.5%

9. Assume that the expected rate of return for a stock with a beta of 1.3 is 12 percent and that the risk-free rate is 4 percent. What is the expected market risk premium?

   A. 6.15%

   B. 7.27%

   C. 10.48%

   D. 11.27%

10. Assume that the expected rate of return for a stock with a beta of 0.7 is 11.7 percent and that the expected return to the market is 14 percent. What must the risk-free rate be?

   A. 2.50%

   B. 3.25%

   C. 4.40%

   D. 6.33%

chapter 14

The Weighted Average Cost of Capital

CHAPTER OBJECTIVES

At the end of this chapter, the reader should be able to:

- Calculate the component cost of equity
- Calculate the component cost of preferred stock
- Calculate the component cost of debt
- Compute the weighted average cost of capital

If firms were all-equity financed, then calculating the cost of capital would be as simple as applying one of the approaches we've already covered, though with some changes in the necessary assumptions underlying the pertinent formulas. However, when firms use multiple sources of capital, including not only equity but also debt and preferred stock, with possibly multiple classes of each, determining the cost of capital gets more complicated and a *Weighted Average Cost of Capital* (WACC) must be determined.

Finance textbooks cover the difference between calculating the WACC for the firm or for a particular project; of the two, calculating the WACC for a project when that project will be in a different line of business than the existing firm will usually require the most data collection and calculation, so we will focus on that situation in this chapter.

Specifically, let's assume that we're analyzing a project for a utility company who has developed a technology for delivering movies and other streaming video over power lines. They want to go into the video rental business, and would like to fund the expansion with a capital structure of 50 percent debt, 15 percent preferred stock, and 35 percent common equity. Let's also assume that the firm's marginal tax rate for the project would be 35 percent.

Let's see how we would go about calculating the appropriate WACC.

The WACC Formula

The formula for the WACC is:

$$\text{WACC} = \frac{E}{V} \times R_E + \frac{P}{V} \times R_P + \frac{D}{V} \times R_D \times (1 - T_C)$$

where E, P, D = market values of equity, preferred stock, and debt in the capital structure of the firm or project

$V = E + P + D$, the total market value of all capital in the firm or project

R_E, R_P = after-tax costs of equity and preferred stock, respectively

R_D = *before-tax* cost of debt

T_C = firm's marginal tax rate

At this point in most finance textbooks, the authors usually explain that, other than the weights themselves, all of the "component costs" of this formula are calculated using formulas that have been developed earlier in the text. That is also correct here. We'll be using equations for each of these parts that will look very similar to ones we've created before, though we *are* going to have to designate the returns generated by those equations a little differently than we've done in the past. Since we've never really used all these formulas at the same time before, calling all the rates of return r wasn't really a problem before now; but, now that we are going to be using all these different formulas at the same time, we'll use the R_E, R_P, and R_D variables from the preceding equation to help us keep track of the component costs as we create them.

We also need to realize that, even though the formulas we'll be using to compute these components will basically be the same ones used to value stocks and bonds in previous chapters, the *inputs* to these formulas are going to be slightly different, primarily due to a necessary shift in our assumption concerning expected holding periods.

In calculating the equivalents of the component costs in the previous chapters, we could have done so from the perspective of a potential investor with a long-expected holding-period or a short-expected holding-period. We chose the latter approach primarily to agree with the treatment in corresponding corporate finance textbooks, but now we have to switch gears: the WACC is calculated by firms, presumably for projects (or, in the case of the whole firm or a division, groups of projects) that usually *will* last a relatively long length of time. As we'll see below, this will have implications for each of the component costs.

Calculating the Component Cost of Equity, R_E

To calculate the cost of equity, we have two choices: we can either use the nonconstant-growth stock valuation model or we can use the CAPM. If we use the CAPM, we are going to need to change some of our choices or sources of inputs due to the change in our assumption concerning holding-periods:

1. For the risk-free rate, we should use the current yield on a long-term U.S. government bond, for which we'll choose the 10-year T-bond. As of the writing of this book, the yield on 10-year T-bonds was 3.28 percent.

2. For the expected market risk premium, we should use the *geometric* average historic excess return to the S&P 500, which current studies put at approximately 6 percent.

3. For beta, we need to make sure that we use an appropriate proxy for the new project's beta, not for the firm as it exists today. Let's assume that the utility company's beta is 0.964, but that we've researched the leading firms in the deliver-it-to-your-doorstep portion of the video rental industry (such as Netflix and similar firms) and determined that they have an average beta of about 2.1. That's the estimate for beta that we should use.

Bringing these three estimates together, we can calculate the component cost of equity using the CAPM:

$$R_E = R_f + \beta_i[E(R_M) - R_f]$$
$$= 3.28\% + 2.1[6\%]$$
$$= 15.88\%$$

Calculating the Component Cost of Preferred Stock, R_P

Unlike with common stock, it is usually deemed appropriate to use the firm's existing costs for both preferred stock and debt. Both of these will be obligations of the firm in general, and not specifically of the new project.

Preferred stock receives a constant dividend, so it's valued as a simple perpetuity:

$$PV_{\text{preferred stock}} = \frac{D}{R_P}$$

To solve this equation for R_P, all we have to do is cross-multiply:

$$R_P = \frac{D}{PV_{\text{preferred stock}}}$$

Suppose that our utility company had outstanding preferred stock which carried a $5 per year dividend that was selling for $87, then R_P would be equal to:

$$R_P = \frac{\$5}{\$87} = 0.0575, \text{ or } 5.75\%$$

Calculating the Before-Tax Cost of Debt, R_D

For the cost of debt, we'd like to use the *Yield to Maturity* (YTM) on bonds of the company that are as close as possible to the 10-year maturity assumed earlier. Suppose that the utility company has 10-year, annual coupon bonds carrying an 11 percent coupon rate that is selling for $1,175; what would be the YTM?

Using our calculator notation, this would be equal to:

10	[T]
$1175	[PV]
$110	[C]
$1000	[FV]
[CPT]	[r] = 8.35%

This computed YTM will be our before-tax cost of debt, R_D.

Calculating the WACC

Once we've got the component costs, it's a simple matter to calculate the WACC using the formula:

$$\text{WACC} = \frac{E}{V} \times R_E + \frac{P}{V} \times R_P + \frac{D}{V} \times R_D \times (1 - T_C)$$
$$= (0.35 \times 15.88\%) + (0.15 \times 5.75\%) + [0.5 \times 8.35\% \times (1 - 0.35)]$$
$$= 9.13\%$$

This will be the interest rate that should be used as r in capital-budgeting decision rules for this project.

A Note on Nominal versus Effective Rates

So far in this book, we've tried to be pretty good about using effective rates in our calculations, and, in the example problem we solved in this chapter, the question of nominal vs. effective rates was a moot point because it was assumed that the company's stock, preferred stock, and bonds would all have annual cash flows.

In reality, of course, this will not be the case: stocks tend to pay dividends quarterly, while bonds tend to pay coupons semiannually. If we're going to be combining these two different types of nominal rates in a WACC and then using it as the r in the capital-budgeting decision rules, which are largely based on the TVM formulas, then we really need to convert these nominal rates to effective annual rates, right?

Well, theoretically, yes; but, in actuality, any error induced by using nominal rates in the WACC equation tends to be fairly small, so even practitioners tend to use the nominal annual rates for the WACC. That's also the practice we'll follow.

QUIZ

1. Which of the following represents the lowest possible value of a firm's WACC?
   A. R_E
   B. R_P
   C. R_D
   D. $R_D \times (1 - T_C)$

2. Assuming that a firm uses at least some debt, which of the following expressions must be correct?
   A. $R_E > WACC > R_D \times (1 - T_C)$
   B. $R_D \times (1 - T_C) > R_E > WACC$
   C. $WACC > R_E > R_D \times (1 - T_C)$
   D. $R_D \times (1 - T_C) > WACC > R_E$

3. A firm that refuses to use debt in its capital structure even though it is capable of doing so will:
   A. Have too low a WACC
   B. Incorrectly calculate prospective project NPVs as being too high
   C. Reject more projects than if it used debt
   D. Always face a positive tax bill

4. Assume that you are buying a share of preferred stock that pays an annual dividend of $5 per share for $87. What will R_P be?
   A. 5.75%
   B. 8.05%
   C. 9.10%
   D. 9.85%

5. Suppose a company has seven-year, semiannual coupon bonds carrying an 8 percent coupon rate that are selling for $1,200. What would be the before-tax cost of debt on these bonds if the appropriate tax rate is 35 percent?
   A. 1.79%
   B. 2.31%
   C. 3.59%
   D. 4.62%

6. Suppose a company has five-year, semiannual coupon bonds carrying a 9 percent coupon rate that are selling for $1,200. What would be the after-tax cost of debt on these bonds if the appropriate tax rate is 35 percent?
   A. 2.24%
   B. 2.92%
   C. 3.59%
   D. 4.49%

7. Given the following information, what is WBM Corporation's WACC?

   Common Stock: 1 million shares outstanding, $45 per share, $1 par value, beta = 1.3

   Bonds: 10,000 bonds outstanding, $1,000 face value each, 8 percent annual coupon, 22 years to maturity, market price = $1,101.23 per bond

   Market risk premium = 8.6 percent, risk-free rate = 4.5 percent, marginal tax rate = 34 percent

   A. 7.89%
   B. 9.90%
   C. 12.19%
   D. 13.52%

8. Suppose a firm has 19 million shares of common stock outstanding with a par value of $1.00 per share. The current market price per share is $18.35. The firm has outstanding debt with a par value of $114.5 million selling at 92 percent of par. What capital structure weight would you use for debt when calculating the firm's WACC?

   A. 0.15
   B. 0.23
   C. 0.54
   D. 0.77

9. When calculating WACC, if we wanted to abide by common practice, we would:
   A. Always use effective rates
   B. Always use nominal rates
   C. Use nominal rates on bonds only
   D. Use nominal rates on stock only

10. Which of the following is *not* a valid reason that two firms might have different WACCs when they evaluate the same project?
    A. They might have different target capital structures.
    B. They might have different costs of debt.
    C. They might have different tax rates.
    D. They might have different betas for their existing operations.

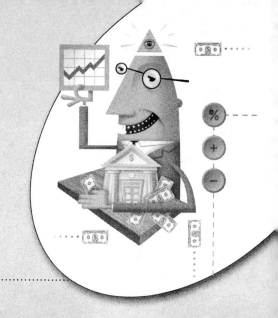

Part V

Advanced Topics in Corporate Finance

Estimating Future Cash Flows

CHAPTER OBJECTIVES

At the end of this chapter, the reader should be able to:

- Calculate operating cash flow
- Compute net capital spending
- Estimate changes in net working capital
- Compute depreciation for assets using both straight-line and Modified Accelerated Cost Recovery System methodologies

The process of estimating future cash flows is one part of a methodology called *pro forma* analysis. In *pro forma* analysis, the analyst tries to estimate what may happen in the future if certain actions are taken today, so it's also sometimes simply referred to as a "What if?" analysis.

There are a number of different rationales for performing a *pro forma* analysis: for example, the CFO of a firm might want to analyze what will happen to the firm's balance sheet if more equity is issued, or the accounting department might wish to assess the impact of a proposed change in the tax laws. In this chapter, we're going to focus on *pro forma* analyses of potential projects, where the "What if?" question we're asking will be, "What will be the impact on the firm's total cash flows if we do this project?"

Sample Project

As a working example, let's suppose that we're continuing the analysis of an entry into the online video rental business by the existing utility company that we discussed in the last chapter. We've already been told that the firm's marginal tax rate for the project would be 35 percent, so let's suppose that we've also gathered the following information.

The company estimates that adding the new project will require an immediate investment of $1.5 million, and they have forecasted the expected revenues shown in Table 15-1. To be conservative, the company is assuming only a five-year project life, and they feel that their revenue estimates are on the low side.

Variable costs are expected to run 38 percent of sales each year and fixed costs are expected to be $170,000 per year, while *Net Working Capital* (NWC) requirements at the beginning of each year are expected to be approximately 15 percent of the projected sales during the coming year.

The fixed assets fall into the *Modified Accelerated Cost Recovery System* (MACRS) five-year class and are expected to be sold for $150,000 at the end of the five-year project.

TABLE 15-1 Sample Project Revenues

Year	1	2	3	4	5
Revenues	$500,000	$1,000,000	$1,500,000	$1,200,000	$800,000

Calculating Total Cash Flow: The Formula

The formula that we'll be using to estimate total cash flow will be the same one we used in Chapter 3 to calculate *Cash Flow From Assets* (CFFA):

$$\begin{aligned} \text{Total cash flow} = \ &\text{operating cash flow} \\ &- \text{net capital spending} \\ &- \text{changes in NWC} \end{aligned}$$

However, in Chapter 3, we were using this formula on items taken from *existing* financial statements to track what had happened; in this chapter, we will be using it on *pro forma* statements that we construct to try to predict what will happen. As a result, while we were, more or less, just recipients of financial statement items in Chapter 3, here we will need to go into more discussion concerning how some of the critical numbers were formed and the assumptions underlying them.

Guiding Principles for Calculating Total Cash Flow

There are several rules of thumb that we need to abide by when calculating a project's total cash flows:

Only count incremental cash flows, but count ALL incremental cash flows. Incremental cash flows are those arising *from* the project, but not necessarily cash flows *of* the project. To see the difference, consider that, if our utility company does decide to add this project, it could conceivably prompt the company's existing customers to use more electricity (presumably, because now they'll be using their TVs more). This would cause the revenues, and the costs, of the company's existing lines of business to increase, and is an example of online video provision and electricity being *complementary goods*. The changes to the company's existing financial statements because of adding a complementary (or a substitutionary) good should be taken into account.

DO count opportunity costs. If a project is going to use an existing asset of the firm, or an existing employee of the firm, it should be charged a cost. In the case of an employee, the charge should obviously be equal to the employee's total benefit package (or a prorated portion, if the employee will still be partially employed on an existing line of business); in the case of an asset, the usual approach is to charge the project that the company could get by selling the asset.

DO NOT count sunk costs. If a charge has already been paid, or if the company has committed to pay charges regardless of whether or not they will proceed with the project, then those charges should not be charged to the project. Obvious examples include *Research and Development* (R&D) costs that have already been incurred, any costs associated with performing the analysis of the project, and so forth.

DO NOT include the costs of financing. In capital-budgeting analysis, we try to keep the question of whether to accept a project separate from the question of how to finance it, so as not to muddy the waters. Along those lines, we need to take great care to ensure that our *pro forma* statements do not include any charges for stock dividends, or interest, or principal repayments on debt.

Calculating Depreciation

The U.S. government's *Internal Revenue Service* (IRS) allows businesses to recover the cost of income-producing property through deductions from taxable income for asset depreciation. There are several allowable approaches to calculating these deductions, with the most popular being the MACRS and *Straight-Line* (SL) depreciation. The IRS provides precalculated percentage tables for several varieties of each approach in their *Publication 946: How to Depreciate Property*.

The amount of straight-line depreciation per year of life of the asset is fairly easy to calculate:

$$\text{Yearly depreciation} = \frac{\text{depreciation basis} - \text{salvage value}}{N}$$

The depreciation amounts for MACRS depreciation, on the other hand, are the result of a variety of formulas, so it's probably best to just look up the appropriate percentages for each year from the tables provided by the IRS. A copy of the entire table for MACRS is provided in Appendix A of this book, but the relevant section for our project has been reproduced here in Table 15-2.

As you can see, even though the asset is depreciated via the "5-year class," the percentages extend across a *six-year* period. This feature is common to all MACRS depreciation figures. If an asset falls into the N year class, it will always be depreciated over $N + 1$ years.

TABLE 15-2 MACRS Depreciation for 5-Year Class Life	
Year	Class 5 (%)
1	20.00
2	32.00
3	19.20
4	11.52
5	11.52
6	5.76

This is due to the *half-year convention*, an operating assumption of the IRS that directs that all property placed in service during a given year is assumed to be placed in service at the *midpoint* of that year. By implication, five years of "asset life" will extend over six calendar years of the firm, and so forth.

To convert these percentages into dollar depreciation amounts, we simply multiply the percentage for each year by the *depreciable basis* of the asset, which is normally the purchase price plus shipping and installation costs.

For our project, the purchase price of $1,500,000 for the required new assets would give us the depreciation amounts shown in Table 15-3.

Notice that the sixth year of depreciation, equal to 5.76 percent of the depreciable basis, or $86,400, is not taken. Since at any time, the remaining depreciation yet to be taken on an asset is its book value, this will be the book value of the assets when they are sold at the end of the project. As we'll see later, this number will be important for tax purposes.

TABLE 15-3 Depreciation for Sample Project	
Year	Depreciation
1	$300,000
2	$480,000
3	$288,000
4	$172,800
5	$172,800

Operating Cash Flow (OCF)

We had a formula in Chapter 3 for calculating OCF:

$$OCF = EBIT + depreciation - taxes$$

This formula is still valid, but there is an alternative way of computing OCF that might prove a little easier to use, particularly if we have to worry about the effect of complementary goods or something like that.

That alternative way basically consists of creating a net income statement, through one where we skip interest being paid out of EBIT, and then adding back depreciation, as shown in Figure 15-1.

Net Capital Spending

To compute net capital spending, we just have to address any additions to or subtractions from fixed assets, and then calculate the after-tax effect of that change.

For example, in our sample project we will purchase fixed assets at time 0 and sell them at time 5; the purchase at time 0 will require a cash outflow of $1.5 million, with no immediate tax effect (the delayed tax effect, depreciation, is handled in the OCF calculation, so we don't have to worry about it here), but the sale of the asset at time 5 will require a bit more calculation.

Whenever a firm sells an asset for its book value, there is no tax effect, and the entire amount received can be treated as a cash inflow. However, if the asset is sold for other than book value, there *will* be a tax effect, with the exact impact being determined by whether the asset is being sold for more than or less than book value.

Year	0	1	2	3	4	5
Sales	$0	$500,000	$1,000,000	$1,500,000	$1,200,000	$800,000
– Variable costs	$0	–$190,000	–$380,000	–$570,000	–$456,000	–$304,000
– Fixed costs	$0	–$170,000	–$170,000	–$170,000	–$170,000	–$170,000
– Depreciation	$0	–$300,000	–$480,000	–$288,000	–$172,800	–$172,800
EBIT	$0	–$160,000	–$30,000	$472,000	$401,200	$153,200
– Taxes	$0	$56,000	$10,500	–$165,200	–$140,420	–$53,620
Net income	$0	–$104,000	–$19,500	$306,800	$260,780	$99,580
+ depreciation	$0	$300,000	$480,000	$288,000	$172,800	$172,800
OCF	$0	$196,000	$460,500	$594,800	$433,580	$272,380

FIGURE 15-1 · OCF calculation for sample project.

Most finance textbooks will present you with two separate formulas for handling the tax impact of an asset sale, one for each case. However, these two "different" formulas are actually just two special cases of one underlying formula, which is:

$$\text{After-tax cash flow from the sale of an asset} = BV + (MV - BV) \times (1 - T_C)$$

where MV = price received for the assets
       BV = book value of the asset(s) at the time of sale
      T_C = firm's marginal tax rate

We were told that the fixed assets will be sold for $150,000 at the end of our project, and we've already determined that the ending book value will be $86,400, so the after-tax cash flow from this sale will be [$86,400 + ($150,000 − $86,400) × (1 − 0.35)] = $127,740.

Our net cash flow winds up being less than the sale price, because when we sell the asset for more than book value, we have to pay taxes on the difference.

Note that this formula would also handle the situation of selling an asset for *less* than book value equally well, as long as we consistently enter the values. In that situation, the cash flow would be greater than the selling price, as we would get a tax credit based on the difference between book value and the selling price.

Changes in NWC

In order to calculate the changes in NWC, we first have to calculate the *levels* each year.

There are several ways to determine the level of required NWC each year during the life of the project, and, in many problems, the exact methodology used won't be revealed to you; the problem will simply state that the project will require that the firm take on some given amount of NWC at the beginning of the project.

Now, handling such a situation is very easy, and only requires two steps:

1. Take that starting *level* and make it the change at time 0. This makes sense because you actually have no NWC in the project before it starts, so, to get NWC up to that "starting" level, you have to add that much.

2. Secondly, you simply *reduce* NWC by that much at the end of the project (i.e., take the negative of the level, because you'll be bringing it back down to zero when the project terminates).

The second step makes perfect sense. Whenever a project ends, you will sell off inventory, collect on accounts receivable, pay on accounts payable, and so forth, until NWC *does* become zero.

The first step makes sense, too, but only with respect to the rather weak assumption being made; namely, that NWC will stay constant during the life of the project. A more reasonable assumption would take into account that, since NWC "supports" revenues, it should *vary* with revenues, too.

In real life, there are good reasons to suspect that the association between incremental revenue to a project and incremental NWC won't be linear; for example, when you take a class on what's commonly called *operations* or *production management*, you will study inventory control models where, if sales increase, inventory needs only go up by the square root of the changes in sales. However, assuming a linear relation between sales and NWC, as is done in our sample problem when we're told that NWC will be 15 percent of next year's revenues, is probably a lot closer to reality than the usual assumption of a fixed amount of NWC throughout the project, regardless of any year-to-year changes in revenues.

Having said that, why does it make sense to calculate each period's NWC requirements as a function of the *next* period's revenues? Well, remember that balance sheet items, such as NWC is composed of, are expressed as a value *at* a particular point of time, while income statement items are expressed as flow variables that occur *over* a period of time. This means that, for any given income statement, there are actually *two* different "snapshots" (i.e., balance sheets) provided for the period of time that the income statement covers, one at the beginning, and one at the end. If we want NWC to *lead* a year's revenues (and we do), then the NWC needs to be available when the period covered by the income statement starts.

For example, when do the first year's sales actually start happening, at time 1 or at time 0? They start happening at time 0, so we need to have the NWC already in place and ready to go at time 0 to support the sales that show up on the year 1 income statement.

For our sample project, this means that the necessary levels of NWC will be as shown in Figure 15-2.

	Year 0	Year 1	Year 2	Year 3	Year 4	Year 5
Estimated unit sales		500,000	1,000,000	1,500,000	1,200,000	800,000
Yearly levels of NWC	$ 75,000.00	$ 150,000.00	$ 225,000.00	$ 180,000.00	$ 120,000.00	$ -

FIGURE 15-2 • NWC levels for sample project.

	Year 0	Year 1	Year 2	Year 3	Year 4	Year 5
Estimated unit sales		500,000	1,000,000	1,500,000	1,200,000	800,000
Yearly levels of NWC	$ 75,000.00	$ 150,000.00	$ 225,000.00	$ 180,000.00	$ 120,000.00	$ -
Changes in NWC	$ 75,000.00	$ 75,000.00	$ 75,000.00	–$ 45,000.00	–$ 60,000.00	–$ 120,000.00

FIGURE 15-3 • NWC changes for sample project.

Notice that by setting the level of NWC equal to a percentage of the next year's sales this way, the level is automatically brought back down to $0 at the end of the project, because 15 percent of year 6 sales (which don't exist) will be zero.

Once we have the levels, the changes can be calculated simply by taking the level in each year and subtracting the level in the previous year, with the results as shown in Figure 15-3.

As a quick check, note that the sum of the row of changes should *always* be equal to zero; we start the project with zero NWC, and we end it with zero NWC, so all of the changes have to cancel out.

Bringing It All Together: Total Cash Flow

Once you have the three components of total cash flow calculated, calculating total cash flow is a cinch, as shown in Figure 15-4.

These total cash flow numbers are the cash flows you would use for valuing this project using the capital-budgeting decision rules covered earlier. For example, if we use these cash flows, along with the project WACC of 9.13 percent computed in the previous chapter, this project's NPV would be $35,886.53, indicating that the project should be accepted.

	Year 0	Year 1	Year 2	Year 3	Year 4	Year 5
OCF	$0	$196,000	$460,500	$594,800	$433,580	$272,380
–ΔNWC	–$75,000	–$75,000	–$75,000	$45,000	$60,000	$120,000
–ΔFA	–$1,500,000	$0	$0	$0	$0	$127,740
Total cash flow	–$1,575,000	$121,000	$385,500	$639,800	$493,580	$520,120

FIGURE 15-4 • Total cash flow calculation for sample project.

QUIZ

1. A new project introducing a new product that is complementary to a firm's existing products would cause:

   A. Both incremental revenues and incremental costs to be lower than if the new product was being introduced in isolation (i.e., by a firm that did not have existing products)

   B. Both incremental revenues and incremental costs to be higher than if the new product was being introduced in isolation

   C. Incremental revenues to be higher and incremental costs to be lower than if the new product was being introduced in isolation

   D. Incremental revenues to be lower and incremental costs to be higher than if the new product was being introduced in isolation

2. Which of the following charges should *not* be counted against a new project when analyzing it for capital budgeting reasons?

   A. Future R&D costs necessary to "tweak" the product after it is introduced

   B. A portion of the salary of the manager assigned to oversee the new project

   C. The use of a previously existing asset of the firm

   D. Interest on debt used to finance the project

3. Assume that Alma Mater College is evaluating the benefits of offering an associate's degree in business (which it currently does not offer). If it does, it anticipates that some of its students who would have chosen to pursue a bachelor's degree in business will choose the new program instead. Therefore, yearly revenues in the evaluation should be calculated as the total tuition from the associate's degree students *minus* the lost tuition from the bachelor's degree–seeking business students that it will no longer teach. This discussion illustrates the concept of:

   A. The associate's degree program including a sunk cost

   B. The associate's degree program including an opportunity cost

   C. The associate's degree program being complementary to the existing under-graduate program

   D. The associate's degree program being a partial substitute for the existing under-graduate program

   Please use the following information to answer the next three questions.

   Your company, Dawgs 'R' Us, is evaluating a new project involving the purchase of a new oven to bake your hot dog buns. If purchased, the new oven will replace your existing oven, which was purchased seven years ago for a total installed price of $1,000,000.

Depreciation on the old oven has been being computed on a straight-line basis over its expected life of 15 years to an ending book value of $100,000, even though you expect it to be worthless at the end of that 15-year period. The new oven will cost $1,500,000 and will fall into the MACRS five-year class for depreciation purposes. If you purchase it, it is expected to last for eight years, at the end of which you expect to be able to sell it for $100,000. (Note that both of the ovens, old and new, therefore have an effective remaining life of eight years at the time of your analysis.) If you do purchase the new oven, you estimate that you can sell the old one for its current book value at the same time.

The advantages of the new oven are twofold: not only do you expect it to reduce the before-tax costs on your current baking operations by $75,000 per year, but you will also be able to produce new types of buns. The sales of the new buns are expected to be $200,000 per year throughout the eight-year life of the new oven, while associated costs of the new buns are expected to be only $80,000 per year.

Since the new oven will allow you to sell these new products, you anticipate that NWC will have to increase by $20,000 immediately upon purchase of the new oven. It will then remain at that increased level throughout the life of the new oven to sustain the new, higher level of operations.

Your company uses a required rate of return of 12 percent for such projects, and your incremental tax rate is 34 percent.

In the questions below, assume that you are evaluating both the oven replacement and the sale of the new buns together (i.e., as a single project), since you can't sell the new buns without the new oven.

4. **What will be the net cash flow at time 0 for this project?**
   A. −$940,000
   B. −$1,370,000
   C. −$1,416,667
   D. −$1,393,333

5. **What will be the incremental depreciation attributable to this replacement project in year 3?**
   A. $124,000
   B. $198,333
   C. $228,000
   D. $334,000

6. **What will be your company's incremental gross profit (i.e., revenues minus cost of goods sold, not including depreciation) from this project in year 4?**
   A. $195,000
   B. $200,000
   C. $205,000
   D. $210,000

7. Suppose your firm is considering a new project. The firm is currently projecting taxable income from current projects to be in excess of $1,000,000, and the project under consideration will require investment in fixed assets of approximately $10,000 and will last five years. Which of the following expensing/depreciation plans for these new assets, everything else about the project held constant, would result in the highest NPV for the project? (You may assume that all choices are valid for the company.)

A. Using MACRS 3-year class life depreciation
B. Using MACRS 7-year class life depreciation
C. Using straight-line depreciation over the life of the project
D. Expensing the assets in the first year of the project

8. You have been asked by the president of your company to evaluate the proposed acquisition of a new special-purpose truck for $60,000. The truck falls into the MACRS 3-year class, and it will be sold after three years for $20,000. Use of the truck will require an increase in net working capital (spare parts inventory) of $2,000. The truck will have no effect on revenues, but it is expected to save the firm $20,000 per year in before-tax operating costs, mainly labor. The firm's marginal tax rate is 40 percent. If the appropriate cost of capital is 10 percent, what is the NPV of buying the new truck?

A. −$562
B. −$320
C. $320
D. $562

Please use the following information to answer the next two questions.

You are evaluating a project for The Kieran Club golf club, guaranteed to correct that nasty slice. You estimate the sales price of The Kieran to be $400 per unit and sales volume to be 1,000 units in year 1; 1,500 units in year 2; and 1,325 units in year 3. The project has a three-year life. Variable costs amount to $225 per unit, and fixed costs are $100,000 per year. The project requires an initial investment of $210,000 in assets, which will be depreciated straight-line to zero over the three-year project life. The actual market value of these assets at the end of year 3 is expected to be $35,000. NWC requirements at the beginning of each year will be approximately 20 percent of the projected sales during the coming year. The tax rate is 34 percent, and the required return on the project is 10 percent.

9. What change in NWC occurs at the end of year 1?

A. There is a $40,000 decrease in NWC.
B. There is a $20,000 increase in NWC.
C. There is a $20,000 decrease in NWC.
D. There is a $40,000 increase in NWC.

10. What is the operating cash flow for the project in year 2?

A. $26,400
B. $68,200
C. $97,075
D. $131,050

chapter 16

Scenario Analysis and Sensitivity Analysis

CHAPTER OBJECTIVES

At the end of this chapter, the reader should be able to:

- Explain the difference between scenario analysis and sensitivity analysis
- Perform a scenario analysis
- Perform a sensitivity analysis

Up until now, when we've talked about estimating the future cash flows of a project or an investment, we've implicitly been using the expected values, or the average values we expect to occur, for our inputs. Using these "point estimates" resulted in one output in our calculations; for example, one expected cash flow for a particular period, or one *Net Present Value* (NPV) statistic for a project.

But many of these inputs are subject to a great deal of uncertainty, and sometimes we'd like to know how that uncertainty in the inputs translates into uncertainty in the output(s). The two procedures we use for measuring this are referred to as *scenario analysis* and *sensitivity analysis*. Both procedures basically involve doing an operation over and over again with different values for the input(s) and seeing how the output(s) change, but scenario analysis makes the assumption that there are underlying correlations or relationships between the independent variables, requiring that multiple inputs be changed in tandem, while sensitivity analysis assumes that the inputs are independent.

Sample Project

Let's continue the project analysis from the previous chapter, but now let's allow for some uncertainty concerning some of the project cash flows.

Specifically, while we took projected revenues to be a single set of estimates, one per year, in the previous chapter, let's now assume that our friendly neighborhood macroeconomist has determined that online video rental is likely to be a function of global oil prices (presumably because if gas is high, more people are likely to rent online), and he has been kind enough to predict our potential revenues and fixed costs (assuming that these are the only two inputs for our project that are affected by oil prices) under several different scenarios concerning oil prices:

Year	1	2	3	4	5
Revenues if Oil Cheap	$300,000	$700,000	$1,100,000	$900,000	$600,000
Fixed Costs if Oil Cheap	$155,000	$155,000	$155,000	$155,000	$155,000
Revenues if Oil Average	$500,000	$1,000,000	$1,500,000	$1,200,000	$800,000
Fixed Costs if Oil Average	$170,000	$170,000	$170,000	$170,000	$170,000
Revenues if Oil Expensive	$550,000	$1,100,000	$1,600,000	$1,100,000	$700,000
Fixed Costs if Oil Expensive	$190,000	$190,000	$185,000	$185,000	$180,000

There are a couple of things to note about these different scenarios:

1. Remember that fixed cost isn't necessarily fixed across time, it's fixed across possible levels of revenue during a particular year in a particular scenario; therefore, it's perfectly understandable for fixed costs to vary across scenarios, or even across years within a particular scenario. For example, if oil prices are high, then the initial fixed costs are much more expensive ($190,000) than they would be with average oil prices, but this difference in fixed prices between the two scenarios actually goes down in the later years of the project. This is perfectly feasible because, if oil prices are high, then the firm might seek an alternative provider of the portion of their fixed costs that are affected by oil prices, but it will take time for the firm to "shift gears" that way. For example, perhaps the firm will switch partially to solar power if oil prices are high, but the switch may take a couple of years to happen.

2. Notice that high oil prices do not increase projected revenues above the average case for all years: it actually decreases them in later years. Again, this is perfectly feasible because, if the market for online video rental is more lucrative due to high oil prices, then it is possible that competitors might choose to enter earlier than they would under the average oil price scenario.

Finally, let's also assume that, due to an increased perception of the amount of risk we're subject to by our potential lenders, our WACC for this project has increased to 9.40 percent.

Scenario Analysis

The objective of scenario analysis is to examine how an output variable (or variables) of interest will change as we go from scenario to scenario. Since we're performing scenario analysis on a project valuation, let's assume that we're interested in what will happen to the NPV, *Internal Rate of Return* (IRR), and *Modified IRR* (MIRR) statistics in each scenario.

Under our original scenario from the last chapter, which we're now calling the *average oil prices* scenario, our total cash flows and these three decision rule statistics will be as shown in Figure 16-1.

The cash flows and decision statistics under the other two scenarios, *cheap oil prices* and *expensive oil prices*, are shown in Figure 16-2 and Figure 16-3, respectively.

	Year 0	Year 1	Year 2	Year 3	Year 4	Year 5
Estimated sales		$ 500,000	$ 1,000,000	$ 1,500,000	$ 1,200,000	$ 800,000
Yearly levels of NWC	$ 75,000.00	$ 150,000.00	$ 225,000.00	$ 180,000.00	$ 120,000.00	$ -
Changes in NWC	$ 75,000.00	$ 75,000.00	$ 75,000.00	-$ 45,000.00	-$ 60,000.00	-$ 120,000.00

Year	0	1	2	3	4	5
Sales	$0	$500,000	$1,000,000	$1,500,000	$1,200,000	$800,000
– Variable costs	$0	–$190,000	–$380,000	–$570,000	–$456,000	–$304,000
– Fixed costs	$0	–$170,000	–$170,000	–$170,000	–$170,000	–$170,000
– Depreciation	$0	–$300,000	–$480,000	$288,000	–$172,800	–$172,800
EBIT	$0	–$160,000	–$30,000	$472,000	$401,200	$153,200
– Taxes	$0	$56,000	$10,500	–$165,200	–$140,420	–$53,620
Net income	$0	–$104,000	–$19,500	$306,800	$260,780	$99,580
+ depreciation	$0	$300,000	$480,000	$288,000	$172,800	$172,800
OCF	$0	$196,000	$460,500	$594,800	$433,580	$272,380
– ΔNWC	–$75,000	–$75,000	–$75,000	$45,000	$60,000	$120,000
– ΔFA	–$1,500,000	$0	$0	$0	$0	$127,740
Total cash flow	–$1,575,000	$121,000	$385,500	$639,800	$493,580	$520,120

NPV (@ $r = 9.40\%$)	$ 22,832.20
IRR	9.88%
MIRR	9.72%

FIGURE 16-1 · Cash flows and decision statistics with average oil prices.

For ease of reference, the inputs we changed in each scenario, as well as the values for the decision rule statistics we're interested in, are shown in Table 16-1.

As you can see, there are two levels of effect imposed by varying the inputs: the direct impact of the changes in revenues and fixed costs, and the indirect effects stemming from those direct changes, such as the resulting adjustments in both the levels and changes to *Net Working Capital* (NWC).

	Year 0	Year 1	Year 2	Year 3	Year 4	Year 5
Estimated sales		$ 300,000	$ 700,000	$ 1,100,000	$ 900,000	$ 600,000
Yearly levels of NWC	$ 45,000.00	$ 105,000.00	$ 165,000.00	$ 135,000.00	$ 90,000.00	$ -
Changes in NWC	$ 45,000.00	$ 60,000.00	$ 60,000.00	-$ 30,000.00	-$ 45,000.00	-$ 90,000.00

Year	0	1	2	3	4	5
Sales	$0	$300,000	$700,000	$1,100,000	$900,000	$600,000
– Variable costs	$0	–$114,000	–$266,000	–$418,000	–$342,000	–$228,000
– Fixed costs	$0	–$155,000	–$155,000	–$155,000	–$155,000	–$155,000
– Depreciation	$0	–$300,000	–$480,000	–$228,000	–$172,800	–$172,800
EBIT	$0	–$269,000	–$201,000	$239,000	$230,200	$44,200
– Taxes	$0	$94,150	$70,350	–$83,650	–$80,570	–$15,470
Net income	$0	–$174,850	–$130,650	$155,350	$149,630	$28,730
+ depreciation	$0	$300,000	$480,000	$288,000	$172,800	$172,800
OCF	$0	$125,150	$349,350	$443,350	$322,430	$201,530
– ΔNWC	–$45,000	–$60,000	–$60,000	$30,000	$45,000	$90,000
– ΔFA	–$1,500,000	$0	$0	$0	$0	$127,740
Total cash flow	–$1,545,000	$65,150	$289,350	$473,350	$367,430	$419,270

NPV (@ $r = 9.40\%$)	–$ 358,105.07
IRR	1.27%
MIRR	3.78%

FIGURE 16-2 · Cash flows and decision statistics with cheap oil prices.

	Year 0	Year 1	Year 2	Year 3	Year 4	Year 5
Estimated sales		$ 550,000	$ 1,100,000	$ 1,600,000	$ 1,100,000	$ 700,000
Yearly levels of NWC	$ 82,500.00	$ 165,000.00	$ 240,000.00	$ 165,000.00	$ 105,000.00	$ -
Changes in NWC	$ 82,500.00	$ 82,500.00	$ 75,000.00	-$ 75,000.00	-$ 60,000.00	-$ 105,000.00

Year	0	1	2	3	4	5
Sales	$0	$550,000	$1,100,000	$1,600,000	$1,100,000	$700,000
− Variable costs	$0	−$209,000	−$418,000	−$608,000	−$418,000	−$266,000
− Fixed costs	$0	−$190,000	−$190,000	−$185,000	−$185,000	−$180,000
− Depreciation	$0	−$300,000	−$480,000	−$288,000	−$172,800	−$172,800
EBIT	$0	−$149,000	$12,000	$519,000	$324,200	$81,200
− Taxes	$0	$52,150	−$4,200	−$181,650	−$113,470	−$28,420
Net income	$0	−$96,850	$7,800	$337,350	$210,730	$52,780
+ depreciation	$0	$300,000	$480,000	$288,000	$172,800	$172,800
OCF	$0	$203,150	$487,800	$625,350	$383,530	$225,580
−ΔNWC	−$82,500	−$82,500	−$75,000	$75,000	$60,000	$105,000
−ΔFA	−$1,500,000	$0	$0	$0	$0	$127,740
Total cash flow	−$1,582,500	$120,650	$412,800	$700,350	$443,530	$458,320

NPV (@ r = 9.40%) $ 9,689.36
IRR 9.61%
MIRR 9.53%

FIGURE 16-3 · Cash flows and decision statistics with expensive oil prices.

Looking at Figure 16-2, we see that low oil prices will cause the project to be unacceptable, no matter which decision rule statistic we use. Intuitively, this is probably what we should have expected to happen. *Net Present Value* (NPV) was positive in the average oil price scenario, but not really all that large, so the

TABLE 16-1 Scenario Summary

Input or Output	Average Oil Prices	Cheap Oil Prices	Expensive Oil Prices
Revenues1	$500,000	$300,000	$550,000
Revenues2	$1,000,000	$700,000	$1,100,000
Revenues3	$1,500,000	$1,100,000	$1,600,000
Revenues4	$1,200,000	$900,000	$1,100,000
Revenues5	$800,000	$600,000	$700,000
FixedCost1	$170,000	$155,000	$190,000
FixedCost2	$170,000	$155,000	$190,000
FixedCost3	$170,000	$155,000	$185,000
FixedCost4	$170,000	$155,000	$185,000
FixedCost5	$170,000	$155,000	$180,000
NPV	$22,832.20	−$358,105.07	$9,689.36
IRR	9.88%	1.27%	9.61%
MIRR	9.72%	3.78%	9.53%

reduction in demand for online video rental arising from low oil prices is apparently large enough that it more than offsets the relatively slight decrease in fixed costs.

On the other hand, the impact of expensive oil prices shown in Figure 16-3 is sort of surprising. While demand and revenues go up, as we would expect, the offsetting increase in both fixed costs and the required levels of NWC actually winds up driving the NPV of the projects down. But, that's why we're performing the scenario analysis, right? To see what might happen.

In fact, if we know the relative probabilities of the various scenarios, we can even make this idea of "seeing what might happen" a little more formal. Specifically, the values of the decision rule statistics that we computed under each scenario can give us an idea of the possible *distributions* of the output statistic.

These distributions will be a function of the distributions of the inputs that we varied. For example, if the three sets of inputs were truly the only possible values for revenues and fixed costs, then the value for the decision statistics would have the same, noncontinuous distribution; on the other hand, if the three sets of inputs corresponded to particular points drawn from a continuous population of possible inputs, then the decision statistics would have a correspondingly continuous distribution, also.

The bottom line—depending upon how relatively likely the sets of inputs were, we could make inferences about the probability of achieving various values of the decision statistics.

Though we haven't made any specification about the distributions of the inputs (and won't, because performing such statistical inference is beyond the scope of this book), one thing is clear from even a cursory glance at our results: the average NPV, $22,832.20, might not be such a sure thing. It seems that either an increase or decrease in oil prices is likely to cause it to go down. How far and how fast are questions that would require further analysis.

Sensitivity Analysis

At first glance, sensitivity analysis appears very similar to scenario analysis; you take a set of inputs, vary them, and see what happens to a selected set of outputs. The difference, though, is that you vary the inputs *one at a time*, not because you think they're unlikely to vary together, but because you're interested in identify-ing the relative importance of each input.

In order to make any analysis of the inputs' relative importance meaningful, you have to vary them "equally." However, in this context, "equal" is a little hard to define. For instance, if you're talking about two dollar figures, say variable costs and fixed costs during the first year of our project, you might be tempted to move those two variables, independently of each other, up and down by $100 and see what happens; but, is it really fair to call a ±$100 price move from a starting value of $209,000 for variable costs the same as a ±$100 price move on a starting value of $190,000 for fixed costs? Probably not; plus, what do you do if the inputs you're analyzing aren't all in dollars?

Because of this, we normally take "equally" to mean "proportionately," vary-ing each input up and down by a certain percentage of its starting value and using that same percentage across all the inputs of interest. Many times, the percentage that is chosen is relatively small, on the order of 1 or 10 *basis points* (i.e., hundredths of a percent), in order to make the calculated sensitivity intui-tively closer to the idea of it measuring the "slope" or coefficient of the func-tional relationship between the input and output variable.

For example, let's suppose that, in addition to the possible variations in reve-nues and fixed costs identified by our macroeconomist friend, we're also inter-ested in whether our calculation of NPV is more sensitive to the assumption that NWC will be 15 percent of the following years' sales, or to the anticipated salvage value for the assets at the end of the project life, $150,000. Let's also assume that we choose to set our percentage of variance used to determine sensitivity to 10-basis points, or 0.1 percent. The *base case*, or starting point, of our analysis is identical to the *average oil prices* scenario depicted in Figure 16-1. The analyses to determine the effect on NPV of a 10-basis point decrease in NWC as a percent of sales, a 10-basis point increase in NWC as a percent of sales, a 10-basis point decrease in salvage value, and a 10-basis point increase in salvage value are shown in Figures 16-4 through 16-7, respectively, and the pertinent inputs and resulting NPV statistics are summarized in Table 16-2, along with an analysis of the per-centage deviation in NPV due to the ±10-basis point shifts in the respective input variables.

As you can see in the far-right column of Table 16-2, NPV seems to be more sensitive to changes in the assets' salvage value than to the percentage of sales used to determine NWC.

NWC as % of revenue	14.9850%					
Salvage value of assets	$ 150,000					

	Year 0	Year 1	Year 2	Year 3	Year 4	Year 5
Estimated sales		$ 500,000	$ 1,000,000	$ 1,500,000	$ 1,200,000	$ 800,000
Yearly levels of NWC	$ 74,925.00	$ 149,850.00	$ 224,775.00	$ 179,820.00	$ 119,880.00	$ -
Changes in NWC	$ 74,925.00	$ 74,925.00	$ 74,925.00	–$ 44,955.00	–$ 59,940.00	–$ 119,880.00

Year	0	1	2	3	4	5
Sales	$0	$500,000	$1,000,000	$1,500,000	$1,200,000	$800,000
– Variable costs	$0	–$190,000	–$380,000	–$570,000	–$456,000	–$304,000
– Fixed costs	$0	–$170,000	–$170,000	–$170,000	–$170,000	–$170,000
– Depreciation	$0	–$300,000	–$480,000	–$228,000	–$172,800	–$172,800
EBIT	$0	–$160,000	–$30,000	$472,000	$401,200	$153,200
– Taxes	$0	$56,000	$10,500	–$165,200	–$140,420	–$53,620
Net income	$0	–$104,000	–$19,500	$306,800	$260,780	$99,580
+ depreciation	$0	$300,000	$480,000	$288,000	$172,800	$172,800
OCF	$0	$196,000	$460,500	$594,800	$433,580	$272,380
–ΔNWC	–$74,925	–$74,925	–$74,925	$44,955	$59,940	$119,880
–ΔFA	–$1,500,000	$0	$0	$0	$0	$127,740
Total cash flow	–$1,574,925	$121,075	$385,575	$639,755	$493,520	$520,000

NPV (@ $r = 9.40\%$) $ 22,885.59

FIGURE 16-4 · Calculations for NWC as a % of sales to be 10-basis points *below* base case.

NWC as % of revenue	15.0150%					
Salvage value of assets	$ 150,000					

	Year 0	Year 1	Year 2	Year 3	Year 4	Year 5
Estimated sales		$ 500,000	$ 1,000,000	$ 1,500,000	$ 1,200,000	$ 800,000
Yearly levels of NWC	$ 75,075.00	$ 150,150.00	$ 225,225.00	$ 180,180.00	$ 120,120.00	$ -
Changes in NWC	$ 75,075.00	$ 75,075.00	$ 75,075.00	–$ 45,045.00	–$ 60,060.00	–$ 120,120.00

Year	0	1	2	3	4	5
Sales	$0	$500,000	$1,000,000	$1,500,000	$1,200,000	$800,000
– Variable costs	$0	–$190,000	–$380,000	–$570,000	–$456,000	–$304,000
– Fixed costs	$0	–$170,000	–$170,000	–$170,000	–$170,000	–$170,000
– Depreciation	$0	–$300,000	–$480,000	–$228,000	–$172,800	–$172,800
EBIT	$0	–$160,000	–$30,000	$472,000	$401,200	$153,200
– Taxes	$0	$56,000	$10,500	–$165,200	–$140,420	–$53,620
Net income	$0	–$104,000	–$19,500	$306,800	$260,780	$99,580
+ depreciation	$0	$300,000	$480,000	$288,000	$172,800	$172,800
OCF	$0	$196,000	$460,500	$594,800	$433,580	$272,380
–ΔNWC	–$75,075	–$75,075	–$75,075	$45,045	$60,060	$120,120
–ΔFA	–$1,500,000	$0	$0	$0	$0	$127,740
Total cash flow	–$1,575,075	$120,925	$385,425	$639,845	$493,640	$520,240

NPV (@ $r = 9.40\%$) $ 22,778.81

FIGURE 16-5 · Calculations for NWC as a % of sales to be 10-basis points *above* base case.

| NWC as % of revenue | 15.0000% |
| Salvage value of assets | $ 149,850 |

	Year 0	Year 1	Year 2	Year 3	Year 4	Year 5
Estimated sales		$ 500,000	$ 1,000,000	$ 1,500,000	$ 1,200,000	$ 800,000
Yearly levels of NWC	$ 75,000.00	$ 150,000.00	$ 225,000.00	$ 180,000.00	$ 120,000.00	$ -
Changes in NWC	$ 75,000.00	$ 75,000.00	$ 75,000.00	-$ 45,000.00	-$ 60,000.00	-$ 120,000.00

Year	0	1	2	3	4	5
Sales	$0	$500,000	$1,000,000	$1,500,000	$1,200,000	$800,000
– Variable costs	$0	–$190,000	–$380,000	–$570,000	–$456,000	–$304,000
– Fixed costs	$0	–$170,000	–$170,000	–$170,000	–$170,000	–$170,000
– Depreciation	$0	–$300,000	–$480,000	–$288,000	–$172,800	–$172,800
EBIT	$0	–$160,000	–$30,000	$472,000	$401,200	$153,200
– Taxes	$0	$56,000	$10,500	–$165,200	–$140,420	–$53,620
Net income	$0	–$104,000	–$19,500	$306,800	$260,780	$99,580
+ depreciation	$0	$300,000	$480,000	$288,000	$172,800	$172,800
OCF	$0	$196,000	$460,500	$594,800	$433,580	$272,380
–ΔNWC	–$75,000	–$75,000	–$75,000	$45,000	$60,000	$120,000
–ΔFA	–$1,500,000	$0	$0	$0	$0	$127,643
Total cash flow	–$1,575,000	$121,000	$385,500	$639,800	$493,580	$520,023

NPV (@ $r = 9.40\%$) $ 22,769.98

FIGURE 16-6 · Calculations for salvage value to be 10-basis points *below* base case.

| NWC as % of revenue | 15.0000% |
| Salvage value of assets | $ 150,150 |

	Year 0	Year 1	Year 2	Year 3	Year 4	Year 5
Estimated sales		$ 500,000	$ 1,000,000	$ 1,500,000	$ 1,200,000	$ 800,000
Yearly levels of NWC	$ 75,000.00	$ 150,000.00	$ 225,000.00	$ 180,000.00	$ 120,000.00	$ -
Changes in NWC	$ 75,000.00	$ 75,000.00	$ 75,000.00	-$ 45,000.00	-$ 60,000.00	-$ 120,000.00

Year	0	1	2	3	4	5
Sales	$0	$500,000	$1,000,000	$1,500,000	$1,200,000	$800,000
– Variable costs	$0	–$190,000	–$380,000	–$570,000	–$456,000	–$304,000
– Fixed costs	$0	–$170,000	–$170,000	–$170,000	–$170,000	–$170,000
– Depreciation	$0	–$300,000	–$480,000	–$228,000	–$172,800	–$172,800
EBIT	$0	–$160,000	–$30,000	$472,000	$401,200	$153,200
– Taxes	$0	$56,000	$10,500	–$165,200	–$140,420	–$53,620
Net income	$0	–$104,000	–$19,500	$306,800	$260,780	$99,580
+ depreciation	$0	$300,000	$480,000	$288,000	$172,800	$172,800
OCF	$0	$196,000	$460,500	$594,800	$433,580	$272,380
–ΔNWC	–$75,000	–$75,000	–$75,000	$45,000	$60,000	$120,000
–ΔFA	–$1,500,000	$0	$0	$0	$0	$127,838
Total cash flow	–$1,575,000	$121,000	$385,500	$639,800	$493,580	$520,218

NPV (@ $r = 9.40\%$) $ 22,894.42

FIGURE 16-7 · Calculations for salvage value to be 10-basis points *above* base case.

TABLE 16-2 Sensitivity Analysis

Variable and Change	Value	NPV	Percent Deviation from Base
NWC – 10–Basis Points	14.9850%	$22,885.59	0.2338%
NWC Base	15.0000%	$22,832.20	
NWC + 10–Basis Points	15.0150%	$22,778.81	–0.2338%
Salvage Value – 10–Basis Points	$149,850	$22,769.98	–0.2725%
Salvage Value Base	$150,000	$22,832.20	
Salvage Value + 10–Basis Points	$150,150	$22,894.42	0.2725%

When to Use Which

Scenario analysis is ideally suited for getting a feel of what may happen, and with what probabilities; sensitivity analysis, on the other hand, is not intended for modeling likely events at all. Instead, it is intended to assist an analyst in determining which variables matter the most, with an eye toward either improving an analysis by devoting resources to uncertainty resolution where they can do the most good, or to simply modeling the amount of remaining uncertainty.

Pro forma analysis, at its heart, is about guessing. Both of these tools help us to model the impact of that uncertainty of the decision-making process.

QUIZ

1. Which of the two procedures that we discussed in this chapter use the assumption that multiple uncertain inputs will move in tandem?
   A. Scenario analysis only
   B. Sensitivity analysis only
   C. Both procedures
   D. Neither procedure

2. Suppose you're performing sensitivity analysis on a variable expressed as a percentage; specifically, suppose the base value is 25 percent. What value would represent a 10-basis point decrease in this value?
   A. 22.5000
   B. 24.7500
   C. 24.9750
   D. 24.9975

3. Which of the following will be necessary for a scenario analysis to give us an idea of the distribution of the output of interest?
   A. We would need to have some idea of the probabilities of the various scenarios.
   B. We would need to have at least one scenario with a negative NPV.
   C. We would need the majority of the scenarios to have positive NPVs.
   D. We would need the base NPV to be the average of that distribution.

4. Using the sample project from this chapter, perform a sensitivity analysis (+/– 10 basis points) of r's effect on NPV, starting from its base value for this project of 9.40 percent. Which of the following statements is true?
   A. NPV for this project is indifferent to changes in r.
   B. NPV for this project is more sensitive to increases in r than to decreases.
   C. NPV for this project is more sensitive to decreases in r than to increases.
   D. NPV is equally sensitive to both increases and decreases in r.

5. Using the sample project from this chapter, perform a sensitivity analysis (+/- 10 basis points) of r's effect on IRR, starting from its base value for this project of 9.40 percent. Which of the following statements is true?
   A. IRR for this project is indifferent to changes in r.
   B. IRR for this project is more sensitive to increases in r than to decreases.
   C. IRR for this project is more sensitive to decreases in r than to increases.
   D. IRR is equally sensitive to both increases and decreases in r.

Please use the following information to answer the next five questions:

Your company is considering selling a newly developed portable video product, the jView. You have developed some forecasts for unit sales and selling price per unit, shown below. You also anticipate that selling the new product will require the purchase of $10 million in fixed assets, which will be depreciated under the MACRS five-year class life, and which you anticipate can be sold at the end of the project for $2,500,000. You also anticipate that the required level of NWC will be 20 percent of the following year's sales, that variable costs will run 40 percent of sales, that yearly fixed costs will be $2 million, that you will face a 34 percent marginal tax rate, and that sales of the jView will end after year 5. Assume that the appropriate rate of interest for projects such as this is 10 percent.

Year	1	2	3	4	5
Best Case Estimated Unit Sales	30,000	60,000	30,000	15,000	7500
Best Case Estimated Selling Price per Unit	$399.00	$299.00	$278.00	$250.00	$200.00
Worst Case Estimated Unit Sales	15,000	40,000	20,000	10,000	5000
Worst Case Estimated Selling Price per Unit	$350.00	$289.00	$265.00	$200.00	$150.00

6. What will be the NPV of this project under the best case assumptions?
   A. −$136,186
   B. $216,145
   C. $327,487
   D. $533,702

7. What will be the NPV of this project under the worst case assumptions?
   A. −$4,479,605
   B. −$2,532,739
   C. $2,532,739
   D. $4,479,605

Suppose that the best case is actually the scenario that you expect, and so you have decided to focus on it. Now, you'd like to determine whether your analysis is more sensitive to the assumption that NWC will run 20 percent of sales or to the assumption of a $2,500,000 salvage value for the fixed assets.

8. **What will be the effect on NPV of a 10-basis point decrease in salvage value?**

    A. It lowers NPV by 0.0474%.
    B. It raises NPV by 0.0474%.
    C. It lowers NPV by 0.4740%.
    D. It raises NPV by 0.4740%.

9. **What will be the effect on NPV of a 10-basis point increase in NWC requirements (i.e., to 19.98 percent)?**

    A. It lowers NPV by 0.2338%.
    B. It increases NPV by 0.2338%.
    C. It lowers NPV by 0.7338%.
    D. It increases NPV by 0.7338%.

10. **If you had additional time or resources to devote to refining one of these estimates, either NWC or salvage value, which one would you choose to address, and why?**

    A. Salvage value, because the change listed above is negative
    B. NWC, because the change listed above is positive
    C. Salvage value, because NPV is more sensitive to it
    D. NWC, because NPV is more sensitive to it

chapter 17

Option Valuation

At the end of this chapter, the reader should be able to:

- Explain option terminology
- Illustrate the values of options at expiration
- Value an option using the binomial option pricing model
- Value an option using the Black-Scholes option pricing model

Options are contracts that give the owner the right, but not the obligation, to buy or sell an underlying asset at a prenegotiated price. This means that the owner always has a choice, and that choice always has value; if it's in her or his best interest to *exercise* the option (i.e., to claim the right granted in the option contract), then they'll do so; but if exercising would cost money, then we assume that they'll walk away and leave the option unexercised.

As we'll see later, options do use *Time Value of Money* (TVM) principles; however, unlike the case in all of the previous chapters that we've discussed, the TVM formulas are not the major components of option valuation formulas. Instead, that honor goes to the *cumulative normal distribution*, which is used to reflect the probabilities of the option being worth something, and how much it will be worth if it is. However, before we look at the formulas used to price options, we first need to define quite a few terms used in discussing options, because they tend to have a language that's very different from the one used by TVM problems.

If you're familiar at all with options, you've probably heard about them in the context of options on shares of stock. There are options on other types of assets, but, as stock options tend to be most frequently discussed in finance classes, we're going to stop referring to the general "option on an asset," and start implicitly assuming that it's an option on a stock that we're discussing. The terminology below reflects that assumption.

Options: The Basics

There are two basic types of options, *calls* and *puts*:

- A call option gives the holder the right (but not the obligation) to *buy* a certain number of shares of stock at a particular price up until the expiration date, *T*.
- A put option gives the holder the right (but not the obligation) to *sell* a certain number of shares of stock at a particular price up until the expiration date.

When we talk about the buyer and the seller of an option contract, we have to be careful, because it's very easy to get confused. For example, suppose that we wanted to talk about the buyer of a put option; this person is buying the right to sell, so do we refer to them as the option buyer or as the stock seller?

To prevent this confusion, we use special terms to denote the buyer and seller of the option contract:

- The *long*—the buyer of an option.

- The *short*, or the *writer*—the seller of an option.

There are also special names for the terms of the option contract:

- That particular price at which the stock can be bought or sold is usually referred to as the *strike* or *exercise* price, and we'll denote it as E in our formulas.

- The price of the option itself at time t is usually called the *premium*, and is denoted either by C_t for a call or by P_t for a put.

Options also differ on whether they can or cannot be exercised early:

- An *American* option gives the holder the right to exercise *on or before* the expiration date.

- A *European* option gives the holder the right to exercise *only on* the expiration date.

We also would like to have concise terms to designate whether an option is worth exercising at a particular point in time, t. We could use mathematical terms involving the relationship between E and the current stock price, S_t, but it gets kind of awkward throwing around mathematical equations, plus the equations differ based on whether you're talking about a call or a put. So, to simplify discussing such things, we use the following phrases:

- *In the money*—immediately exercising would result in a positive payoff:

    - For a call, this means $S_t > E$, because you could buy the asset at E and sell it for S_t.

    - For a put, this means $E > S_t$, because you could buy the asset at S_t and sell it for E.

- *Out of the money*—immediately exercising would result in a negative payoff:

    - For a call, this means $E > S_t$.

    - For a put, this means $S_t > E$.

- *At the money*—immediately exercising would result in a payoff of 0:

    - For call or put, this means $E = S_t$.

Values of Options at Expiration

In general, the value of an option is a function of at least five variables:

1. The value of the underlying stock, S_t
2. The exercise price, E
3. The appropriate risk-free interest rate, R_F
4. The time until expiration, t
5. The standard deviation in the price of the underlying stock, s

In addition, there are often special circumstances that require the inclusion of additional variables, such as dividends being paid to the underlying stock prior to expiration of the option.

However, if we examine the option at expiration, when $t = 0$, then it, as well as r and s, no longer affect the value of the option. Doing so allows us to focus on the effect of the relationship between S_t and E, and one of the most popular tools for looking at this relationship is the *payoff diagram*, a graph which values an option or combination of options as a function of the underlying asset price as the option(s) approach maturity.

As an example, consider the payoff diagram shown in Figure 17-1. The owner of this call will make $1 for every dollar that S_t is above the $47 exercise price, but will choose not to exercise the call if S_t is at or below the $47 exercise price.

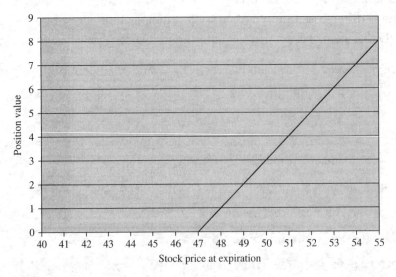

FIGURE 17-1 • Long call, $E = \$47$.

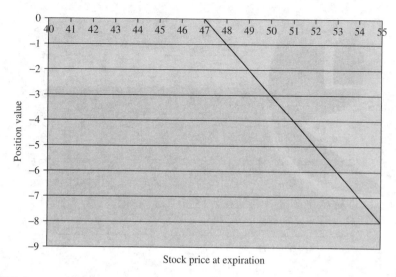

FIGURE 17-2 · Short call, E = $47.

The payoff diagram shown in Figure 17-1 is one of the four "basic" payoff diagrams; the other three are shown in Figures 17-2 through 17-4.

With different exercise prices, combinations of these four basic positions can be used to create just about any total position payoff you want. For example, suppose you simultaneously entered into a long call position at E = $45 (shown in

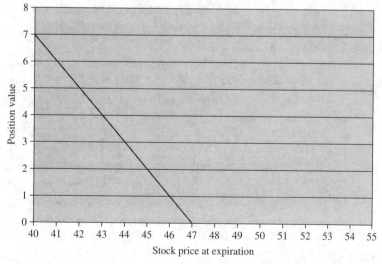

FIGURE 17-3 · Long put, E = $47.

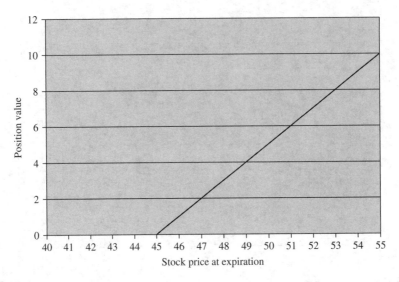

FIGURE 17-4 • Short put, *E* = $47.

(Figure 17-5) and a short call position with *E* = $50 (shown in Figure 17-6); your total position payoff, the sum of the two payoffs at any given *S_t*, would be as shown in Figure 17-7.

Why would anyone want to hold both of the positions simultaneously? Well, someone who thought that there was a good chance that the underlying stock

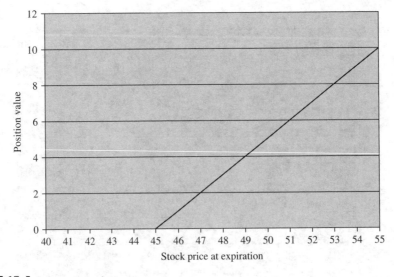

FIGURE 17-5 • Long call, *E* = $45.

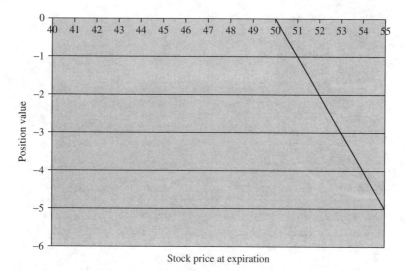

FIGURE 17-6 · Short call, $E = \$50$.

would be around $50, but who also thought that there wasn't much chance that it would be *substantially* above $50, would be able to partially subsidize their long position in the $45 call by writing the $50 call.

Likewise, you can usually back out which combination of the four basic positions was probably used to create one of these more complex positions by carefully looking at the direction and slope of the lines in the position. For example, consider the total position payoff shown in Figure 17-8. This payoff

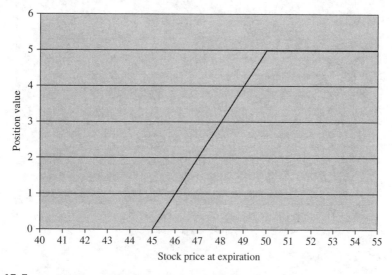

FIGURE 17-7 · Combined payoff of long call at $45 and short call at $50.

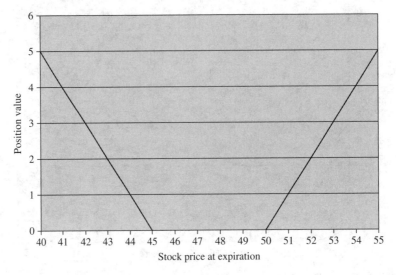

FIGURE 17-8 · Combined payoff of long put at $45 and long call at $50.

has two sloping lines, and it's pretty easy to see that the line sloping up on the left is the payoff to a long put at $45 (shown individually in Figure 17-9), while the line sloping up on the right is the payoff to a long call at $50 (shown individually in Figure 17-10).

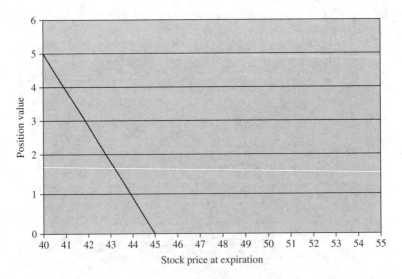

FIGURE 17-9 · Long put, $E = \$45$.

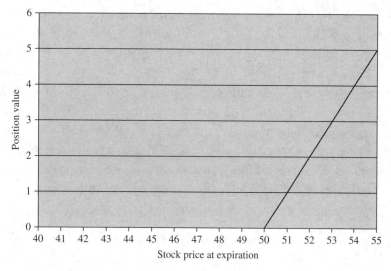

FIGURE 17-10 • Long call, $E = \$50$.

One interesting thing to note about payoff diagrams is that they do not include the price of the option, the option premium. This is because they are primarily intended to model the decision-making process of long option holders after they've already entered the position; at that point the premium they paid for the option is a sunk cost and will not enter into their decision to exercise their option(s) or not.

For example, suppose the position holder shown in Figure 17-8 above had paid $3 for the put and that the underlying stock price was $43 at expiration. Would he exercise the put? Yes, because even though his expected profit from buying and exercising the option would be the payoff from exercising, $(E - S_t)$ $- P_t = (\$45 - \$43) - \$3 = -\$1$, the profit if he doesn't exercise would be $-\$3$.

Valuing a Call Option before Expiration: The Binomial Option Pricing Model

As we allow ourselves to move back in time prior to the expiration of the option, we need to decide how we're going to handle measuring time, as that will affect the measurement and expression of the other variables. One choice is to break it into a lot of discrete but very small chunks, and that is the approach taken by the binomial option pricing model.

This model uses the fact that, under what is referred to as a *no-arbitrage assumption*, there will always exist a combination of positions in stocks, bonds, and borrowing or lending at the risk-free rate that will exactly replicate the pay-offs to an option, and which therefore must have the same value as that option.

In order to apply the binomial option pricing model, you must be able to specify the number of periods until maturity, the current price of the underlying stock, the possible changes in value of that stock price during each period between the current period and option expiration, the risk-free rate of interest, and the exercise price of the option. Once you have all this information, you can always follow the same series of steps to determine the current value of the option:

1. Figure out the possible values of the underlying stock at option expiration.

2. Using the formulas for an option payoff at expiration, calculate the possible values of the option at expiration. For a call, payoff at expiration will be equal to:

$$C_i = \max(S_{T,i} - E, 0)$$

where C_i = payoff to the option in state i
$\quad\quad S_{T,i}$ = value of the underlying stock at time T in state i
$\quad\quad E$ = exercise price of the call

3. Calculate the *state prices*, the prices that an investor would be willing to pay at the beginning of a period in order to ensure that he received a \$1 payoff if a particular "state" (used, loosely, in this discussion to stand for which underlying asset price prevails at option expiration) occurred, then use these prices to back out option values a single period before expiration and then, iteratively, to back out values for each previous time period all the way back to the current time.

If we define:
$\quad\quad u$ as the percentage change in stock price each period if it goes "up," and
$\quad\quad d$ as the percentage change in stock price each period if it goes "down," then we can solve for the state prices as:

$$q_u = \frac{R_F - d}{(1 + R_F)(u - d)}$$

$$q_d = \frac{u - R_F}{(1 + R_F)(u - d)}$$

where q_u is the price at the beginning of the period for locking in the right to receive $1 at the end of the period if the "up" state of the world occurs, and q_d is the price at the beginning of the period for locking in the right to receive $1 at the end of the period if the "down" state of the world occurs.

We can then use these state prices to price the call option at the beginning of that period as a weighted average of the state-contingent values that it might be worth at the end of the next period:

$$C = q_u \times V_u + q_d \times V_d$$

For example, let's suppose that we are trying to value a three-period call option on a stock that will either go up by 10 percent or down by 3 percent per period, that the exercise price of the option is $50, that the current stock price is only $45 per share, and that the going risk-free rate is 6 percent per period.

First, we need to figure out what the possible values of the underlying stock will be at maturity. For an N-period problem, there will always be $N + 1$ possible ending stock prices at time T, reached through all possible combinations of growing the stock price at either $(1 + u)$ or $(1 + d)$ during each of the periods until maturity.

Specifically in this problem, we can figure the possible stock prices at the time of option expiration as:

$$S_{T,uuu} = \$45 \times (1.10) \times (1.10) \times (1.10) = \$59.8950$$
$$S_{T,uud} = \$45 \times (1.10) \times (1.10) \times (0.97) = \$52.8165$$
$$S_{T,udd} = \$45 \times (1.10) \times (0.97) \times (0.97) = \$46.5746$$
$$S_{T,ddd} = \$45 \times (0.97) \times (0.97) \times (0.97) = \$41.0703$$

The paths that the stock price can follow over the next three periods to get from the current price of $45 to these four possible values are shown in Figure 17-11. Notice that, since the order of growing the stock price at either $(1 + u)$ or $(1 + d)$ doesn't matter, all equivalent *combinations* of u and d over the next three periods will result in the same stock price. For example, $59.895 is not only the value for $S_{T,uud}$, but also for $S_{T,udu}$ and $S_{T,duu}$, as well.

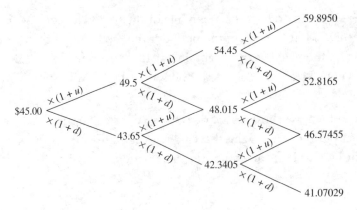

FIGURE 17-11 · Stock price path.

These prices, in turn, can be used to solve for the possible values of the option at expiration:

$$C_i = \max(S_{T,i} - E, 0)$$
$$C_{uuu} = \max(\$59.8950 - \$50, 0) = \$9.8950$$
$$C_{uud} = \max(\$52.8165 - \$50, 0) = \$2.8165$$
$$C_{udd} = \max(\$46.5746 - \$50, 0) = \$0$$
$$C_{ddd} = \max(\$41.0703 - \$50, 0) = \$0$$

And, calculating our state prices as:

$$q_u = \frac{R_F - d}{(1 + R_F)(u - d)} = \frac{0.06 - (-0.03)}{(1 + 0.06)[0.10 - (-0.03)]} = \$0.6531$$

$$q_d = \frac{u - R_F}{(1 + R_F)(u - d)} = \frac{0.10 - 0.06}{(1 + 0.06)[0.10 - (-0.03)]} = \$0.2903$$

we can use these state prices to back out, starting at time $T - 1$ and working backward, what the price of the option will be at each intermediate step.

For instance, the value of the call after two u movements, C_{uu}, will be equal to:

$$C_{uu} = q_u \times V_u + q_d \times V_d$$
$$= (0.6531 \times C_{uuu}) + (0.2903 \times C_{uud})$$
$$= (0.6531 \times \$9.8950) + (0.2903 \times \$2.8165)$$
$$= \$7.2801$$

The value of the call after one u and one d movement, C_{ud}, will be:

$$
\begin{aligned}
C_{ud} &= q_u \times V_u + q_d \times V_d \\
&= (0.6531 \times C_{udu}) + (0.2903 \times C_{udd}) \\
&= (0.6531 \times \$2.8165) + (0.2903 \times \$0) \\
&= \$1.8395
\end{aligned}
$$

and the value of the call after two d movements, C_{dd}, will be:

$$
\begin{aligned}
C_{dd} &= q_u \times V_u + q_d \times V_d \\
&= (0.6531 \times C_{ddu}) + (0.2903 \times C_{ddd}) \\
&= (0.6531 \times \$0) + (0.2903 \times \$0) \\
&= \$0
\end{aligned}
$$

Stepping back in time one more period, these three possible values of the call time at time 2 can be used, along with the state prices, to find the possible values of the option at the end of the first period, C_u and C_d:

$$
\begin{aligned}
C_u &= q_u \times V_u + q_d \times V_d \\
&= (0.6531 \times C_{uu}) + (0.2903 \times C_{ud}) \\
&= (0.6531 \times \$7.2801) + (0.2903 \times \$1.8395) \\
&= \$5.2886 \\
C_d &= q_u \times V_u + q_d \times V_d \\
&= (0.6531 \times C_{du}) + (0.2903 \times C_{dd}) \\
&= (0.6531 \times \$1.8395) + (0.2903 \times \$0) \\
&= \$1.2014
\end{aligned}
$$

And then, finally, these two possible values at time 1 can be used to value the option at the current time:

$$
\begin{aligned}
C_u &= q_u \times V_u + q_d \times V_d \\
&= (0.6531 \times C_u) + (0.2903 \times C_d) \\
&= (0.6531 \times \$5.2886) + (0.2903 \times \$1.2014) \\
&= \$3.8028
\end{aligned}
$$

Essentially, what we have done is to work our way down to the "tips" of the branches of the *binomial tree* shown in Figure 17-11 and then worked our way back, branch-by-branch, at each point converting the two possible values that might result from a branch into a value at the base of the branch. If we think of our first calculations above as forming the binomial tree in Figure 17-11 from left to right, then calculating the values of the option at each point as we've just done is equivalent to creating the binomial tree shown in Figure 17-12 *backward*, from right to left.

While it is possible to construct a separate methodology for valuing put options, it's not really necessary, as the existence of the put-call parity relationship, discussed briefly below, allows us to price an otherwise analogous put option once we have the value for the call option.

The big advantage the binomial model has over the Black-Scholes model, which we'll discuss next, is that it can be used to accurately price American options. This is because with the binomial model it's possible to check at every point in an option's life for the possibility that early exercise will make sense, either due to a pending dividend payment on the underlying stock in the case of a call option, or due to a put being so deeply in the money that there's no sense in waiting to exercise. When it seems to make sense that an option would be exercised early in a particular state at a particular point in the binomial tree, we can just replace the value of the option at that point with the *intrinsic value* at that point (i.e., the value if exercised). This value will then be used as we work our way back up the tree to get the value of the option at the current time.

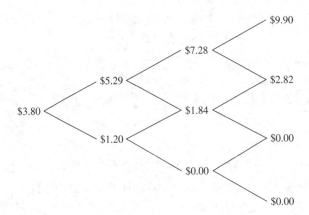

FIGURE 17-12 • Option price path.

Valuing a Call Option before Expiration:
The Black-Scholes Option Pricing Model

Though it is usually viewed by students as a totally separate approach to computing option values from the binomial option pricing model, it can be shown (under certain assumptions) that the Black-Scholes option pricing model is actually equivalent to a binomial model where the number of time periods increases to infinity and the length of each time period is infinitesimally short.

The formula varies based upon whether the option being priced is an American or European call; in line with the discussion found in your finance textbooks concerning why even an American option will usually be treated like a European option, we will cover only the European pricing formula here.

The Black-Scholes formula for a European call is:

$$C_e = S_t N(d_1) - Ee^{-rT} N(d_2)$$

where

$$d_1 = \frac{\ln\left(\frac{S_t}{E}\right) + \left(r + \frac{\sigma^2}{2}\right)T}{\sigma\sqrt{T}}$$

$$d_2 = d_1 - \sigma\sqrt{T}$$

and where S_t = price of the underlying stock today
$N(\ )$ = standard normal cumulative distribution function
r = nominal annual continuously compounded risk-free rate
σ = standard deviation of the rate of return on the underlying asset
T = length of time, expressed in years, until the option expires

Notice that we've been careful to try and keep this notation in line with what was used earlier with the binomial option pricing model, with one major exception—where we used R_F above to denote the effective periodic risk-free rate, here we're using r, the nominal annual continuously compounded risk-free rate. The continuous-time version of the PV formula for lump sums that we discussed in Chapter 5 is:

$$PV = \frac{FV}{e^{rT}} = FV \times e^{-rT}$$

and using this formula requires that the interest rate be expressed as a nominal annual rate that is to be continuously compounded.

If you'll look closely at the Black-Scholes formula listed above, you'll see that the latter half of the formula includes this continuous-time version of the PV formula, so the requirement that the interest rate be expressed in terms of a nominal annual rate to be continuously compounded holds for the Black-Scholes formula, too.

The easiest way to solve this formula is to first solve for d_1 and d_2. For example, suppose that we wish to value a call with a strike price of $44 on a stock that is currently selling for $42, when the call has six months until expiration, the current nominal annual continuously compounded interest rate is 3 percent, and the standard deviation in returns of the underlying stock is 70 percent. We first would solve for d_1 and d_2:

$$d_1 = \frac{\ln\left(\frac{S_t}{E}\right) + \left(r + \frac{\sigma^2}{2}\right)T}{\sigma\sqrt{T}}$$

$$= \frac{\ln\left(\frac{\$42}{\$44}\right) + \left(0.03 + \frac{(0.70)^2}{2}\right)0.5}{0.70\sqrt{0.5}}$$

$$= 0.1838$$

$$d_2 = d_1 - \sigma\sqrt{T}$$

$$= 0.1838 - 0.70\sqrt{0.5}$$

$$= -0.3112$$

These can then be inserted into the Black-Scholes formula itself, along with values for the standard normal cumulative distribution function taken from the table in Appendix B:

$$C_e = S_t N(d_1) - E e^{-rT} N(d_2)$$

$$= [\$42 \times N(0.1838)] - [\$44 \times e^{-0.03 \times .5} \times N(-0.3112)]$$

$$= [\$42 \times 0.5729] - [\$44 \times e^{-0.03 \times .5} \times 0.3778]$$

$$= \$7.6861$$

Put-Call Parity

Though it is possible to formulate dedicated pricing formulas for put options, and, given that there are actually situations where such dedicated put formulas will come in handy, much of the put valuation that takes place in the real world is accomplished through the use of the put-call parity formula, the classic version of which is usually stated as:

$$S + P = PV(E) + C$$

Like the binomial option pricing model, this formula is also based on a no-arbitrage argument, because the basic idea is that the portfolio position represented on the left-hand side of the "=" sign, long a share of stock and long a single put, has exactly the same payoffs as the portfolio position on the right-hand side, long a risk-free investment with a face value of E plus a long call position. When used to value a put in a discrete-time situation, such as when dealing with the binomial model discussed above, this algebraic expression is normally rearranged as:

$$P = PV(E) + C - S$$

and, when used in a continuous-time formulation, as:

$$P = E \times e^{-rT} + C - S$$

So, continuing our example from the previous section, if the option in question was a put instead of a call contract, we might very well find ourselves pricing it as if it were a call, and then using put-call parity to compute the value of the put:

$$
\begin{aligned}
P &= E \times e^{-rT} + C - S \\
&= (\$44 \times e^{-0.03 \times .5}) + \$7.6861 - \$42 \\
&= \$9.0310
\end{aligned}
$$

QUIZ

1. The person who buys an option giving him or her the right to sell shares in an underlying stock at a prespecified price would be said to have:

   A. A long call position
   B. A long put position
   C. A short call position
   D. A short put position

2. A call will be out of the money if:

   A. $S_t > E$
   B. $C_t > E$
   C. $S_t < E$
   D. $Ct < E$

3. The payoff diagram in Figure 17-13 represents what combination of positions?

   A. Long put at $45 and long put at $50
   B. Long put at $45 and short call at $50
   C. Short put at $45 and long put at $50
   D. Short put at $45 and short call at $50

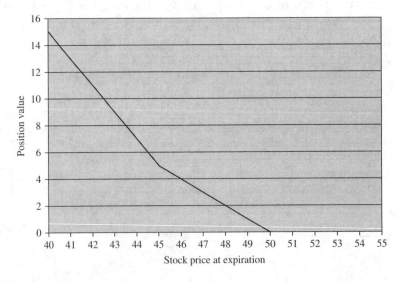

FIGURE 17-13 · Combined payoff diagram.

4. If someone had paid $5 for a call with $E = \$36$, and the stock was selling for $40 at termination of the call, what would be this person's profit on the call?

    A. −$1

    B. −$2

    C. $2

    D. $3

Please use the following information, along with the binomial option pricing model, to answer the next three questions.

Suppose that we are trying to value a three-period call option on a stock that will either go up by 7 percent or go down by 4 percent per period, that the exercise price of the option is $35, that the current stock price is only $35 per share, and that the going risk-free rate is 4 percent per period. Use the binomial option pricing model to answer the following questions:

5. What will be $S_{T,udu}$?

    A. $30.97

    B. $34.51

    C. $38.47

    D. $42.88

6. What will be C_{ud}?

    A. $0.00

    B. $2.43

    C. $4.44

    D. $6.42

7. What will be the value of the call today?

    A. $4.03

    B. $6.27

    C. $6.45

    D. $7.76

Please use the following information to solve the next three problems.

Suppose that we wish to value a call with a strike price of $32.50 on a stock that is currently selling for $35 when the call has nine months until expiration, the current nominal annual continuously compounded interest rate is 4 percent, and the standard deviation in returns of the underlying stock is 47 percent.

8. What will be the value of d_1?

    A. 0.3732
    B. 0.4593
    C. 0.4983
    D. 0.5652

9. What will be the value of the call?

    A. $2.37
    B. $3.87
    C. $4.27
    D. $7.27

10. Using put-call parity, what will be the value of an otherwise equivalent put in this situation?

    A. $2.31
    B. $3.81
    C. $4.21
    D. $7.21

Final Exam

1. What combination of two options would give you the total position pay-off shown in Figure FE-1? (You may assume that any sloped lines are at a 45-degree angle to the horizontal.)

   A. Short call ($E = 40$), long call ($E = 45$)

   B. Long put ($E = 45$), short call ($E = 40$)

   C. Long put ($E = 45$), short put ($E = 40$)

   D. Short put ($E = 40$), short call ($E = 45$)

2. If you buy a new condo for $200,000, financing the entire purchase price plus $10,000 in closing costs via a 360-month mortgage with an APR of 7 percent, how much total interest (to the nearest dollar) will you pay over the life of the loan if you take the full 30 years to pay it off?

   A. $139,006

   B. $292,969

   C. $344,726

   D. $2,678,400

3. Everything else held constant, and considering a group of options all written on the same underlying stock, which of the following sets of parameters would result in a put option with the highest value?

   A. $S = 40$, $E = 35$, Time until expiration = 0.25 years

   B. $S = 35$, $E = 40$, Time until expiration = 0.25 years

   C. $S = 40$, $E = 35$, Time until expiration = 0.50 years

   D. $S = 35$, $E = 40$, Time until expiration = 0.50 years

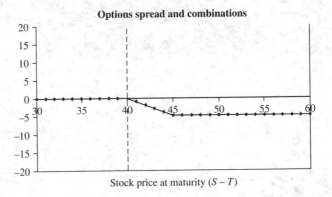

FIGURE FE-1 · Total position payoff.

4. You are evaluating a 20-year bond that carries a 6 percent coupon rate, has a current price of $1,234, and pays interest quarterly. How would this bond's *Yield to Maturity* (YTM) be quoted in the financial press?

A. 1.06%

B. 2.78%

C. 4.26%

D. 6.32%

5. You are contemplating buying stock in FMS Corp. FMS just paid a quarterly dividend of $1.00, and you expect future quarterly dividends to decline at a rate of 5 percent per quarter indefinitely. If the effective annual return on this stock is expected to be 10 percent, what price should it be selling for today?

A. $5.59

B. $11.88

C. $12.07

D. $12.82

6. In the Capital Asset Pricing Model formula, the expected return to the market portfolio, $E(R_M)$, represents the:

A. X variable

B. Y variable

C. Slope

D. None of the above

7. Suppose you have a $20,000 portfolio, which is equally invested in 10 different stocks and that the portfolio beta is 1.3. If you sell all your holdings in one of the stocks (which has a beta of 0.9) for $2,000 and use the proceeds to buy T-bills, what will be the new beta of your portfolio?

   A. 1.2100

   B. 1.2667

   C. 1.3444

   D. 1.4667

8. Given the probabilities of expected states of the economy shown here, and the expected returns to stocks A and B in those states, what is the standard deviation of a portfolio with weights of 40 percent in stock A and the remainder in stock B?

State	Probability	Return on A (%)	Return on B (%)
Boom	.25	15	−3
Normal	.55	10	4
Bust	.2	4	9

   A. 1.0029%

   B. 1.0474%

   C. 1.0527%

   D. 1.3004%

9. Stock W has an expected return of 12.4 percent and a beta of 1.8. If the expected market return is 10 percent, what is the risk-free rate?

   A. −5.6%

   B. 3.0%

   C. 5.6%

   D. 7.0%

10. Suppose that noncollege-graduates earn a salary of $25,000 per year in your hometown, and that salary will never change. If you go to college for four years, forgoing four years worth of that salary, but expect to work for 45 years until retirement after you graduate earning a different, higher, constant, "postcollege" salary, how much higher (per year, and to the closest dollar) must the "postcollege" salary be in order for the decision to

attend college to be the financially preferred one? (Assume that your cost of capital is 6 percent; that you would have worked until the exact same retirement age if you hadn't gone to college, and that all salaries are paid at the end of the year for simplicity.)

A. You must earn at least $2,273 more per year.

B. You must earn at least $7,076 more per year.

C. You must earn at least $9,328 more per year.

D. You must earn at least $32,269 more per year.

11. You are evaluating a project which will cost $3,000 and has an expected future cash flow of $700 per year, forever, if we start it immediately. If we wait one year to start the project, the cost will increase to $3,500 and the expected future cash flows will increase to $795 per year; if we wait two years to start the project, the cost will increase to $4,000 and the expected future cash flows will increase to $885 per year. If the required return is 10 percent, what should we do?

A. Reject the project

B. Begin the project immediately

C. Decide today to start the project in one year

D. Decide today to start the project in two years

12. First Strike Software has 7 percent coupon bonds on the market with 10 years to maturity. The bonds make semiannual payments and currently sell for 94 percent of par. What is the effective annual yield on First Strike's bonds?

A. 3.9191%

B. 7.8782%

C. 8.0334%

D. 9.0565%

13. KAD Enterprises, Inc., is growing quickly. Dividends are expected to grow at a 50 percent rate for the next year, at a 30 percent rate for the following year, and at a 15 percent rate for the year after that, with the growth rate falling off to a constant 5 percent per year thereafter. If the required rate

of return is 18 percent and the company just paid a $1.75 dividend, what is the current share price?

   A. $26.36

   B. $31.69

   C. $35.62

   D. $38.73

14. Imagine that you see an advertisement for Manic Wesley's Used Car Emporium that reads something like this: "$10,000 Instant Credit! Seven Years to Pay! Low, Low Monthly Payments: Only $231.99 per Month!" You're not exactly sure how these payments were computed, and somebody has spilled ink over the APR on the loan contract, so you ask the owner for clarification. Wesley explains that if you borrow $10,000 for seven years at 10 percent interest, in seven years you will owe $10,000 × (1.10)7 = $19,487.17.

Now, Wesley recognizes that coming up with $19,487.17 all at once might be a strain, so he lets you make "low, low monthly payments" of $19,487.17/84 = $231.99 per month, even though this is extra bookkeeping for him.

What is the Effective Annual Rate (EAR) on this loan?

   A. 1.8026%

   B. 10.0000%

   C. 21.6317%

   D. 23.9106%

15. What quoted rate, if compounded weekly, would give you an effective annual rate of 8.5 percent?

   A. 7.5817%

   B. 8.1644%

   C. 9.8763%

   D. 10.0032%

16. You have just arranged for a $157,000 mortgage to finance the purchase of a large tract of land. The mortgage has a 7.65 percent APR, and it calls for monthly payments over the next 20 years. However, the loan has a seven-year balloon payment, meaning that the remaining principal must

be paid off at the end of the seven-year period. How big will the balloon payment be?

A. $105,304

B. $117,290

C. $126,201

D. $136,624

17. You are evaluating a new cookie-baking oven. The CookieMunster costs $90,000, has a seven-year life, and has an annual Operating Cash Flow (OCF), after tax, of –$8,000 per year. If your discount rate is 12 percent, what is this machine's Equivalent Annual Cost (EAC)?

A. $27,720.60

B. $35,888.70

C. $45,910.76

D. $56,000.00

18. ABC, Inc., has a target debt-equity ratio of 0.4. Its before-tax cost of equity is 16 percent and its before-tax cost of debt is 8 percent. If the tax rate is 32 percent, what is ABC's WACC?

A. 10.3847%

B. 11.6723%

C. 12.9829%

D. 13.9935%

19. Assuming they have the same (positive) expected rate of return, which of the following investments should be cheapest?

A. One that promises to pay you $100 in five years

B. One that promises to pay you $200 in three years

C. One that promises to pay you $200 in five years

D. One that promises to pay you $100 in three years

20. Suppose you are considering an investment that grew by 32 percent across a five-year holding period. If you wanted to state this rate of return

as an effective annual rate (that is, with annual compounding), what would it be?

A. 5.71%

B. 6.40%

C. 7.27%

D. 36.67%

21. You are considering purchasing shares of Microsap's stock. These shares just paid a dividend of $2.00 per share, and dividends are expected to grow at a rate of 15 percent per year for the next three years, after which the growth rate is expected to fall off to a constant 8 percent per year thereafter. If the required rate of return for this stock is 14 percent, what would your expected capital gains yield be if you bought the stock today with the intention of selling it one year from now?

A. 7.52%

B. 8.00%

C. 8.66%

D. 15.00%

22. When using the formula for the present value of a constantly growing perpetuity, $P_0 = D_1/(r - g)$, what is the entire "set" of variables that have to exhibit temporal congruence with one another?

A. r and D_1

B. P_0 and D_1

C. P_0, r, and g

D. D_1, r, and g

23. Black Eyed Peas, Inc., has an issue of preferred stock outstanding that pays a dividend of $2.50 per quarter in perpetuity. If a dividend was just paid and the preferred stock is currently selling for $78 per share, what is the EAR for this investment?

A. 2.50%

B. 3.21%

C. 12.82%

D. 13.45%

24. If you wanted to start and own a business, which of the following forms of business organization would minimize both your personal liability for the firm's obligations and the total amount of taxes that your income from the business is subject to?

   A. A general partnership.

   B. A limited partnership, with yourself as one of the general partners.

   C. An S corporation.

   D. More than one of the above are correct.

25. Radakad, Inc., makes cassette tapes. Radakad just paid a $3 per share dividend, but future dividends are expected to decline at a rate of 15 percent per year indefinitely due to the shrinking market for cassette tapes. If the required rate of return on Radakad's stock is 13 percent, what is this stock worth today?

   A. $0.00

   B. $9.11

   C. $10.71

   D. $+\infty$

26. Assume that you buy a new car for $24,000, and that you finance $20,000 of the purchase price with a five-year (i.e., 60 monthly payments) loan, for which you are quoted an APR of 7.52 percent. What will be the EAR of this loan?

   A. 5.01%

   B. 6.27%

   C. 7.78%

   D. 58.80%

27. The primary goal of financial management should be to:

   A. Maximize the owner's equity account on the balance sheet.

   B. Maximize the number of shares of stock.

   C. Maximize firm profit.

   D. None of the above is correct.

28. How long will it take money to quadruple (i.e., increase by 300 percent) in an account earning an 8 percent EAR? (You may assume that interest is paid smoothly and continuously throughout the year, so answers in terms of fractional years, if necessary, are OK.)

   A. 8.00 years

   B. 9.01 years

   C. 18.01 years

   D. 50.00 years

29. Happy Days Medical Devices has a bond outstanding that has an 8 percent coupon rate and a market price of $912.35. If the bond matures in 15 years and interest is paid semiannually, what is the YTM?

   A. 4.54%

   B. 9.08%

   C. 9.29%

   D. 9.47%

30. Suppose that "Contract X" is an annuity due, specifying that the owner will receive 10 annual payments of $1,000 each, with the first payment occurring immediately upon the start of the contract. Now imagine a 30-year annuity of these contracts, where you will receive one Contract X that starts one year from today, another Contract X that starts two years from today, and so forth, out to the last Contract X, which will start 30 years from today. If the appropriate rate of return is 8 percent per year, how much would this annuity of Contract Xs be worth today?

   A. $11,257.78

   B. $75,540.64

   C. $81,583.89

   D. $96,574.04

Please use the following information to answer the next four questions.

Your company is evaluating a new project, and you've estimated that the cost of capital for the project will be 8 percent. Assume that you have also projected the following cash flows for the project:

Year	0	1	2	3	4	5	6
Cash Flow	−$25,700	$5000	$10,000	$0	$15,000	$8000	$4000

31. What will this project's discounted payback be?

   A. 2.82 years

   B. 3.27 years

   C. 4.27 years

   D. 4.60 years

32. What will this project's *Internal Rate of Return* (IRR) be?

   A. 13.28%

   B. 15.68%

   C. 19.66%

   D. 21.32%

33. What will this project's *Net Present Value* (NPV) be?

   A. $2,123.27

   B. $3,160.52

   C. $4,693.81

   D. $6,493.81

34. What will this project's *Profitability Index* (PI) be?

   A. 0.71

   B. 0.52

   C. 1.17

   D. 1.25

35. You are considering the following two mutually exclusive projects. If the cost of capital for both projects is 7 percent, which statement concerning capital-budgeting rules listed will be correct in this situation?

   NOTE *You may assume that any implicit reinvestment rate assumptions will NOT cause an incorrect choice.*

Time	Year 0	Year 1	Year 2	Year 3
Project A	–$567	$300	$400	$300
Project B	–$296	$500	$100	$ 50

A. Both NPV and IRR will choose the correct project(s).

B. Neither NPV nor IRR will choose the correct project(s).

C. NPV will choose the correct project(s), IRR will not.

D. IRR will choose the correct project(s), NPV will not.

36. You are looking at Jack's Shoes' accounting statements. Jack's Shoes has net income of $16,900 in 2010 and owes $8,650 in taxes for the year. The company repaid $4,200 in loan principal and $650 in loan interest during the year. No new funds were borrowed. The depreciation expense is $420. What is the operating cash flow for the year?

A. $17,970

B. $19,370

C. $20,670

D. $28,670

37. If the government were to change the tax laws so that all fixed asset purchases could be immediately expensed, this would cause all capital budgeting decisions involving the purchase of fixed assets to:

A. Experience an *increase* in NPV

B. Experience an *increase* in total project cash flow for all years of every project

C. Experience a *decrease* in total project cash flow for all years of every project

D. Experience a *decrease* in NPV

Use the following information to answer the next three questions.

The SCFE Co. wants to add an additional production line. To do this, the company must spend $200,000 to expand its current building, and purchase $1.0 million in new equipment. The company anticipates moving locations in five years, and it expects to sell its current building and the new equipment at that time. It estimates that the building expansion will add $80,000 to the price the building can be sold for, and that the equipment will have a market value of $290,000 at that time.

The new equipment falls into the MACRS 5-year class, and the building improvements fall into the "nonresidential real estate" MACRS category.

The new production line is expected to produce 100,000 units per year of a new product, which has a projected sales price of $7.75 per unit and a variable cost of $3.90 a unit. Introduction of the new product is expected to cause sales of existing products to decline by $89,000 per year and existing costs to decline by $49,000 per year. Fixed costs of the new line will be $142,000 annually, and the company expects NWC to increase by $1,800,000 when the new line is added.

The company requires a 15 percent rate of return on projects such as this, and faces a marginal tax rate of 34 percent.

38. **What will be the project's year 1 OCF?**
    A. $204,138.73
    B. $210,938.73
    C. $355,410.53
    D. $564,589.53

39. **What will be the project's net capital spending at the end of year 5?**
    A. –$388,948.76
    B. –$320,990.36
    C. $320,990.36
    D. $388,948.76

40. **What will be this project's change in NWC in year 5?**
    A. $0
    B. –$360,000
    C. –$1,800,000
    D. $1,800,000

41. You are trying to pick the least-expensive car for your new delivery service. You have two choices: the Scion xA, which will cost $14,000 to purchase and which will have OCF of –$1,200 annually throughout the vehicle's expected life of three years as a delivery vehicle; and the Toyota Prius, which will cost $20,000 to purchase and which will have OCF of –$650 annually throughout that vehicle's expected four-year life. Both cars will be worthless at the end of their life. If you intend to replace whichever type of car you choose with the same thing when its life runs

out, again and again out into the foreseeable future, and if your business has a cost of capital of 12 percent, which one should you choose?

A. The xA

B. The Prius

C. Neither, because they do not have positive NPVs

D. Either, because both have exactly the same EAC

Please use the following information to answer the next three questions.

You are considering investing in a stock that had the returns listed here over the past five years.

Year	2011	2010	2009	2008	2007
Return	8.00%	−13.6%	−10.45%	12.80%	−18.76%

42. What was the arithmetic average annual return during this period?

A. −0.22%

B. −1.14%

C. 3.10%

D. 8.69%

43. What was the geometric average annual return during this period?

A. −0.22%

B. −1.14%

C. 3.10%

D. 8.69%

44. What was the standard deviation in annual returns during this period?

A. 8.13%

B. 10.32%

C. 14.78%

D. 18.69%

45. How many possible PI may the set of cash flows shown here have?

Time	0	1	2	3	4	5
Cash Flow	−$1,000	−$200	$1,500	−$100	$2,000	−$200

    A. As many as 1

    B. As many as 2

    C. As many as 3

    D. As many as 4

46. Due to unforeseen circumstances, you have to take out a student loan for your senior year. Which one of the following loans should you choose?

    A. A loan with a nominal 10 percent interest rate with monthly compounding

    B. A loan with a nominal 10 percent interest rate with yearly compounding

    C. A loan with a nominal 9 percent interest rate with monthly compounding

    D. A loan with a nominal 9 percent interest rate with yearly compounding

47. An account was opened with $1,000 ten years ago. Today, the account balance is $1,700. If the account paid interest compounded monthly, how much interest on interest was earned?

    A. $155.04

    B. $168.20

    C. $531.80

    D. $544.96

48. Find the value at time 50 of the set of end-of-year cash flows shown, if the appropriate rate of return is 11 percent per year:

Year(s)	Cash Flow(s) Per Year
1 through 10	$25,000
11 through 79	$10,000
80 through 100	$15,000

A. $179,255

B. $1,255,000

C. $33,079,044

D. $6,106,191,094

49. On January 31st, 1985, Pontiac was running a series of ads urging consumers to "Buy a Grand Am for Under 10 Grand!" More specifically, they were selling such cars with an asking price of $9,995. Suppose that, taking into account current rebates, you could buy an equivalent new Grand Am on January 31st, 2010 for $20,989. What has been the yearly rate of growth in this car's price during this period?

A. 3.78%

B. 4.21%

C. 8.13%

D. 11.67%

50. *Jackson Heights Homes* (JHH) has an issue of preferred stock that is supposed to pay a $4 dividend every quarter; however, they have not paid the last 24 quarterly dividends, the latest of which was due today. These dividends are cumulative, and you have just learned that JHH will pay back all the skipped dividends one quarter from now and resume payment of the regularly scheduled dividend at the same time. If the EAR on this security is 10 percent, what should it sell for today?

A. $20.00

B. $60.00

C. $181.50

D. $259.62

51. Suppose that a Woodchuck logging machine can "chuck" (i.e., throw or hurl) 13 tons of wood an hour when freshly serviced, but that its performance decreases by 5 percent an hour until the next servicing. After a Woodchuck has been run for 12 hours since its previous servicing, how much wood can a Woodchuck chuck?

A. 7.02 tons per hour

B. 10.41 tons per hour

C. 13.00 tons per hour

D. 21.39 tons per hour

52. The firm's decision as to how to raise money is more formally referred to as:

   A. The capital-structure decision

   B. The capital-budgeting decision

   C. The dividend decision

   D. The financial-management decision

53. Suppose that a mutual fund has a five-year nominal rate of return of 50 percent. If this five-year rate was constructed from semiannual effective rates, what would be the equivalent EAR?

   A. 9.10%

   B. 10.25%

   C. 50.00%

   D. 61.05%

54. Cyclic, Inc., has announced that they intend to pay future dividends in a way so as to let them deal with seasonal fluctuations in the need for funds. They intend to pay dividends of $1, $2, $1, and $2 at the end of the first, second, third, and fourth quarters of each year, respectively, and intend on doing so forever. If the first quarter for this firm just started, and if the required rate of return on this stock is 13 percent per year, compounded quarterly, what should it sell for today?

   A. $45.91

   B. $75.69

   C. $87.69

   D. $90.60

55. A company wishes to raise $20,000,000 through the sale of a zero-coupon bond issue, in which the bonds will have a maturity of 10 years and a face value of $20,000 per bond. If the yield on these bonds will be equivalent to an APR of 6.3 percent with monthly compounding, how many of these bonds will the company have to sell to raise the full $20 million? (Round up to the next whole number.)

   A. 2000

   B. 1875

   C. 7028

   D. 67,873

56. JoeBook's common stock just paid a dividend of $0.57 per share, and dividends are expected to grow at a rate of 11 percent per year for the next two years, after which the growth rate is expected to fall off to a constant 5 percent per year thereafter. If the required rate of return for this stock is 12 percent, what would your expected capital gains yield be if you bought the stock today with the intention of selling it one year from now?

  A. 5.00%

  B. 5.36%

  C. 6.25%

  D. 6.67%

57. In a *Time Value of Money* (TVM) problem with all other variables held constant and where *Future Value* (FV) or *Payment* (PMT), as appropriate, are input as negative numbers, increasing N will:

  A. Increase the *Present Values* (PVs) of both a lump sum and annuity

  B. Decrease the PVs of both a lump sum and an annuity

  C. Increase the PV of a lump sum, but decrease the PV of an annuity

  D. Decrease the PV of a lump sum, but increase the PV of an annuity

58. Suppose you want to buy a house five years from today. You currently have $25,000 saved toward this purchase, but don't think you'll be able to save any more money, other than the interest that the $25,000 will earn between now and then, before you buy the house. Assuming that you will need to put down a 20 percent down payment and pay an additional 5 percent in closing costs to purchase a house, and that you can earn an APR of 4.80 percent on the $25,000 over the next five years, how much house can you buy? That is, what will be the maximum total purchase price that you will be able to afford?

  NOTE *Closing costs apply to the loan amount only, not to the entire purchase price.*

  A. $30,280

  B. $98,163

  C. $126,167

  D. $132,358

59. Suppose your company has just issued a $30 million bond with a sinking fund provision that calls for retiring a proportionate percentage of the bond during each year of the issue's 20-year life, so that 5 percent of the issue will be retired at the end of each year, immediately after that year's annual coupon payments have been made. If these bonds pay an annual coupon of 8 percent, how much interest (in $) will be paid during the third year of this issue's life? (Hint: think about the entire bond issue— what type of loan does it sound like?)

   A. $2,040,000

   B. $2,160,000

   C. $2,400,000

   D. $3,660,000

60. Suppose you are considering acquiring a house by assuming the remainder of the existing 30-year mortgage on the property. If there are 237 fixed monthly payments of $1,041.23 left to be paid, with the first payment being due exactly one month after you assume the loan, what price are you effectively paying for the house if your bank is quoting an APR of 6.25 percent on similar loans?

   A. $16,659

   B. $141,551

   C. $169,108

   D. $340,482

61. You've graduated and have been married for several years and your first child, Mary, has just been born. You want to start saving for Mary's college education. You will put the first of eighteen equal deposits into her college fund one year from now (on her first birthday). You anticipate that her tuition will run $35,000 per year for four years, with tuition for each year being due at the beginning of each year. Mary will start college exactly on her eighteenth birthday. If Mary's college fund will earn 8 percent interest per year, how much must you deposit each of those 18 years?

   A. $2,073

   B. $2,634

   C. $2,887

   D. $3,343

62. You want to buy a new Dodge Fandango SUV for $28,000 and plan on putting $2,000 down. If you finance the remainder for 72 months at an APR of 9 percent, what will your payments be?

    A. $307.98

    B. $389.76

    C. $468.66

    D. $498.07

63. You receive an offer for a new credit card offering an introductory APR of 8.5 percent for the first year. What is the corresponding EAR?

    A. 8.24%

    B. 8.50%

    C. 8.84%

    D. 8.97%

64. You have just bought a new condo for $125,000. If you financed 100 percent of the purchase price via a 30-year, 7.75 percent APR loan from your bank, what will be the total amount of interest paid during the first 12 monthly payments?

    A. $8,364.09

    B. $8,783.83

    C. $9,129.84

    D. $9,649.07

65. What maximum price would you be willing to pay for an annual coupon bond with 12 years remaining until maturity, an 8 percent coupon rate, and a YTM of 11 percent?

    A. $805.23

    B. $908.65

    C. $923.67

    D. $967.32

66. You are evaluating a project with the following cash flows. How many IRRs might there be?

Time	0	1	2	3	4	5	6
Cash Flow	−100	75	100	−35	70	100	−100

A. 4 or less

B. 4 exactly

C. 4 or more

D. 5 or less

67. There are two ways that stock can earn returns. These two ways are:

A. Through coupon payments and dividends

B. Through coupon payments and changes in price

C. Through changes in price and dividends

D. Through both direct and indirect payments

Use the following information to answer the next five questions.

Time	Cash Flow
0	−$750
1	$400
2	$300
3	$200
4	$400

Assume that the appropriate cost of capital for this project is 12 percent.

68. What is this project's payback period?

A. 2.00

B. 2.25

C. 2.50

D. 2.75

69. What is this project's discounted payback period?

A. 3.04

B. 3.24

C. 3.44

D. 3.64

70. What is this project's IRR?

    A. 25.67%

    B. 27.19%

    C. 28.76%

    D. 29.86%

71. What is this project's *Modified IRR* (MIRR)?

    A. 18.78%

    B. 19.65%

    C. 20.14%

    D. 21.37%

72. What is this project's NPV?

    A. $242.86

    B. $278.53

    C. $295.42

    D. $307.98

73. Assume that ABC Corp. just paid a dividend of $1 a share and that all future dividends are expected to grow at the rate of 9 percent per year. If the required rate of return for this stock is 15 percent, what should be the price today?

    A. $16.67

    B. $18.17

    C. $20.52

    D. $22.63

74. Assume that XYZ Corp. expects its next dividend to be $50, the two dividends following it to grow at a rate of 15 percent per year, and all subsequent dividends to grow at a rate of 10 percent per year. If the required rate of return for this stock is 18 percent, what should be the price of this stock today?

    A. $6.77

    B. $6.98

    C. $9.09

    D. $9.75

75. Suppose you pay $100 for a share of preferred stock that pays a dividend of $15 a year indefinitely. What is its nominal rate of return?

    A. 7.87%

    B. 10%

    C. 15%

    D. 17.87%

76. Which of the following statements is true?

    A. One of the benefits of incorporating your business is that you become entitled to receive unlimited liability.

    B. Sole proprietorships are subject to more regulations than corporations.

    C. Sole proprietorships do not have to pay corporate tax.

    D. All of the above are correct.

77. Holmes Aircraft recently announced an increase in its net income, yet its net cash flow declined relative to last year. Which of the following could explain this performance?

    A. The company's interest expense increased.

    B. The company's depreciation expense declined.

    C. The company's operating income declined.

    D. All of the statements above are correct.

78. Popsi Corporation's current ratio is 0.5, while Cake Company's current ratio is 1.5. Both firms want to "window dress" their coming end-of-year financial statements. As part of their window dressing strategy, each firm will double its current liabilities by adding short-term debt and placing the funds obtained in the cash account. Which of these statements best describes the actual results of these transactions?

    A. The transactions will have no effect on the current ratios.

    B. The current ratios of both firms will be increased.

    C. The current ratios of both firms will be decreased.

    D. Only Popsi Corporation's current ratio will be increased.

79. Which of the following statements is *incorrect*?

    A. The slope of the security market line is measured by beta.

    B. Two securities with the same stand-alone risk can have different betas.

    C. Company-specific risk can be diversified away.

    D. The market risk premium is affected by attitudes about risk.

80. Given the following returns on Stock J and "the market" during the last three years, what is the beta coefficient of Stock J? (Use linear regression.)

Year	Stock J	Market
1	−13.85%	−8.63%
2	22.90	12.37
3	35.15	19.37

    A. 0.80

    B. 1.25

    C. 1.50

    D. 1.75

81. It has been estimated that the new product just presented by your Research and Development (R&D) department will bring in net cash flows of $80,000 per year for four years. Marketing will begin immediately to sell this product. If these expectations are correct and your firm's discount rate is 12 percent, what is the approximate present value of this new product?

    A. $242,988

    B. $320,000

    C. $382,320

    D. $750,800

82. If you invest $200 each six months for the next six years (beginning six months from now) and these funds will earn 8 percent compounded semiannually, what will be the approximate value of this investment at the end of the six years?

    A. $1,100

    B. $2,254

    C. $3,005

    D. $4,127

83. Your bank has agreed to loan your firm $300,000. You will repay the loan in three years with one lump sum of $500,000 (covering both principal and interest). What is the implied interest rate on the loan?

   A. 10.00%

   B. 10.24%

   C. 10.76%

   D. 11.56%

84. A $1000 par bond with an 11 percent coupon rate has a YTM of 7 percent. If interest is paid annually and the bond has 11 years to maturity, what should be the price of this bond?

   A. $1,000

   B. $1,300

   C. $1,437

   D. None of the above is correct

85. John's Johns Inc. just paid a dividend of $2.00 per share on its common stock. Growth in this dividend is expected to be 10 percent for years one, two, and three, after which it is expected to be 2 percent to "infinity." If the required rate of return on this firm's common stock is 10 percent, what should be the current market value of this stock?

   A. $25.50

   B. $29.18

   C. $31.50

   D. $41.22

86. If a capital-budgeting project has a positive NPV, the IRR is

   A. Greater than the discount rate

   B. Less than the discount rate

   C. Equal to the discount rate

   D. A positive dollar value

87. Three years ago, Johnson Industrials purchased a piece of equipment for $685,000, which it is looking to replace. If the company just received a bid of $200,000 for this equipment, and it has been depreciating the equipment over a five-year period using straight-line depreciation, what will be the net cash proceeds from the sale if Johnson faces a marginal tax rate of 34 percent?

    A. $128,260

    B. $174,840

    C. $225,160

    D. $271,740

88. The person who sells an option giving another the right to buy shares in an underlying stock at a prespecified price would be said to have:

    A. A long call position

    B. A short call position

    C. A long put position

    D. A short put position

89. A call will be in the money if:

    A. $S_t > E$

    B. $S_t < E$

    C. $C_t > E$

    D. $C_t < E$

90. If someone had paid $3 for a put with $E = \$37$, and the stock was selling for $40 at termination of the put, what would be this person's profit on the put?

    A. –$3

    B. –$2

    C. $0

    D. $3

Please use the following information, along with the binomial option pricing model, to answer the next three questions.

Suppose that we are trying to value a three-period call option on a stock that will either go up by 6 percent or down by 3 percent per period, that the exercise price of the option is $30, that the current stock price is only $28 per share, and that the going risk-free rate is 4 percent per period. Use the binomial option pricing model to answer the following questions:

91. What will be $S_{T,udd}$?

    A. $25.56

    B. $27.93

    C. $30.52

    D. $33.35

    E. $38.47

    F. $42.88

92. What will be C_d?

    A. $0.00

    B. $0.29

    C. $0.39

    D. $2.04

93. What will be the value of the call today?

    A. $0.70

    B. $1.03

    C. $1.59

    D. $1.97

Please use the following information to solve the next three problems.

Suppose that we wish to value a call with a strike price of $35 on a stock that is currently selling for $32.50 when the call has nine months until expiration, the current nominal annual continuously compounded interest rate is 4 percent, and the standard deviation in returns of the underlying stock is 47 percent.

94. What will be the value of d_1?
    A. 0.0952
    B. 0.1265
    C. 0.2547
    D. 0.3119

95. What will be the value of the call?
    A. $2.37
    B. $3.87
    C. $4.66
    D. $5.47

96. Using put-call parity, what will be the value of an otherwise equivalent put in this situation?
    A. $2.31
    B. $3.81
    C. $4.21
    D. $6.12

97. If you had to choose one single capital-budgeting decision rule to use, it would probably be:
    A. Discounted payback
    B. IRR
    C. MIRR
    D. NPV

98. A beta of –0.3 would indicate that, on average, the stock tends to move:
    A. In the same direction as the market portfolio, but to a lesser extent
    B. In the same direction as the market portfolio, but to a greater extent
    C. In the opposite direction as the market portfolio, but to a lesser extent
    D. In the opposite direction as the market portfolio, but to a greater extent

99. Suppose that you are looking at two bonds, a 10-year bond and a 20-year bond, that are otherwise identical. If the YTM on these bonds goes up, then:

   A. The prices of both will go down, but the price of the 10-year bond will go down more.

   B. The prices of both will go down, but the price of the 20-year bond will go down more.

   C. The prices of both will go up, but the price of the 10-year bond will go up more.

   D. The prices of both will go up, but the price of the 20-year bond will go up more.

100. The firm's decision on how to go about paying back investors their money is more formally referred to as:

   A. The capital-structure decision

   B. The capital-budgeting decision

   C. The dividend decision

   D. The financial management decision

Answers to Quizzes and Final Exam

Chapter 1	Chapter 3	Chapter 5	Chapter 7
1. B	1. B	1. A	1. D
2. A	2. C	2. D	2. A
3. D	3. B	3. B	3. C
4. B	4. A	4. B	4. A
5. C	5. A	5. D	5. C
6. A	6. D	6. C	6. A
7. B	7. A	7. A	7. D
8. C	8. D	8. D	8. C
9. D	9. D	9. B	9. B
10. A	10. B	10. D	10. D

Chapter 2	Chapter 4	Chapter 6	Chapter 8
1. D	1. B	1. D	1. C
2. C	2. A	2. A	2. B
3. C	3. A	3. A	3. D
4. C	4. B	4. B	4. A
5. D	5. A	5. A	5. A
6. A	6. D	6. C	6. D
7. A	7. C	7. D	7. C
8. A	8. A	8. B	8. B
9. C	9. C	9. C	9. B
10. D	10. B	10. B	10. B

Chapter 9
1. C
2. B
3. B
4. A
5. B
6. D
7. A
8. A
9. B
10. D

Chapter 10
1. C
2. D
3. D
4. C
5. A
6. B
7. D
8. D
9. C
10. D

Chapter 11
1. D
2. B
3. A
4. B
5. B

6. C
7. C
8. B
9. C
10. A

Chapter 12
1. B
2. B
3. B
4. C
5. D
6. B
7. C
8. B
9. C
10. A

Chapter 13
1. A
2. D
3. B
4. C
5. B
6. D
7. D
8. A
9. A
10. D

Chapter 14
1. D
2. A
3. C
4. A
5. D
6. B
7. D
8. B
9. B
10. D

Chapter 15
1. B
2. D
3. D
4. A
5. C
6. A
7. D
8. A
9. D
10. D

Chapter 16
1. A
2. C
3. A
4. B
5. A

6. B
7. A
8. C
9. A
10. C

Chapter 17
1. B
2. C
3. A
4. A
5. C
6. B
7. A
8. B
9. D
10. B

Final Exam

1. A	21. C	41. A	61. D	81. A
2. C	22. D	42. A	62. C	82. C
3. D	23. D	43. C	63. C	83. A
4. C	24. C	44. A	64. D	84. B
5. D	25. B	45. A	65. A	85. C
6. D	26. C	46. D	66. A	86. A
7. A	27. D	47. B	67. C	87. C
8. B	28. C	48. C	68. B	88. B
9. D	29. B	49. B	69. A	89. A
10. B	30. C	50. D	70. B	90. A
11. C	31. C	51. A	71. C	91. B
12. C	32. B	52. A	72. A	92. B
13. A	33. D	53. B	73. B	93. C
14. D	34. D	54. A	74. A	94. A
15. B	35. C	55. B	75. C	95. C
16. C	36. A	56. B	76. C	96. D
17. A	37. A	57. D	77. B	97. D
18. C	38. A	58. D	78. D	98. C
19. A	39. B	59. B	79. A	99. B
20. A	40. C	60. B	80. D	100. C

appendix A

Depreciation Charts

Year	3%	5%	7%	10%	15%	20%	Real Estate Residential 27.5%	Nonresidential 31.5%	39%
1	33.33	20.00	14.29	10.00	5.00	3.750	3.485	3.0420	2.461
2	44.45	32.00	24.49	18.00	9.50	7.219	3.636	3.1750	2.564
3	14.81	19.20	17.49	14.40	8.55	6.677	3.636	3.1750	2.564
4	7.41	11.52	12.49	11.52	7.70	6.177	3.636	3.1750	2.564
5	0.00	11.52	8.93	9.22	6.93	5.713	3.636	3.1750	2.564
6	0.00	5.76	8.92	7.37	6.23	5.285	3.636	3.1750	2.564
7	0.00	0.00	8.93	6.55	5.90	4.888	3.636	3.1750	2.564
8	0.00	0.00	4.46	6.55	5.90	4.522	3.636	3.1750	2.564
9	0.00	0.00	0.00	6.56	5.91	4.462	3.636	3.1740	2.564
10	0.00	0.00	0.00	6.55	5.90	4.461	3.637	3.1750	2.564
11	0.00	0.00	0.00	3.28	5.91	4.462	3.636	3.1740	2.564
12	0.00	0.00	0.00	0.00	5.90	4.461	3.637	3.1750	2.564
13	0.00	0.00	0.00	0.00	5.91	4.462	3.636	3.1740	2.564
14	0.00	0.00	0.00	0.00	5.90	4.461	3.637	3.1750	2.564
15	0.00	0.00	0.00	0.00	5.91	4.462	3.636	3.1740	2.564
16	0.00	0.00	0.00	0.00	2.95	4.461	3.637	3.1750	2.564
17	0.00	0.00	0.00	0.00	0.00	4.462	3.636	3.1740	2.564
18	0.00	0.00	0.00	0.00	0.00	4.461	3.637	3.1750	2.564
19	0.00	0.00	0.00	0.00	0.00	4.462	3.636	3.1740	2.564
20	0.00	0.00	0.00	0.00	0.00	4.461	3.637	3.1750	2.564
21	0.00	0.00	0.00	0.00	0.00	2.231	3.636	3.1740	2.564
22	0.00	0.00	0.00	0.00	0.00	0.00	3.637	3.1750	2.564
23	0.00	0.00	0.00	0.00	0.00	0.00	3.636	3.1740	2.564
24	0.00	0.00	0.00	0.00	0.00	0.00	3.637	3.1750	2.564
25	0.00	0.00	0.00	0.00	0.00	0.00	3.636	3.1740	2.564
26	0.00	0.00	0.00	0.00	0.00	0.00	3.637	3.1750	2.564
27	0.00	0.00	0.00	0.00	0.00	0.00	3.636	3.1740	2.564
28	0.00	0.00	0.00	0.00	0.00	0.00	1.970	3.1750	2.564
29	0.00	0.00	0.00	0.00	0.00	0.00	0.00	3.1740	2.564
30	0.00	0.00	0.00	0.00	0.00	0.00	0.00	3.1750	2.564
31	0.00	0.00	0.00	0.00	0.00	0.00	0.00	3.1740	2.564
32	0.00	0.00	0.00	0.00	0.00	0.00	0.00	1.7200	2.564
33	0.00	0.00	0.00	0.00	0.00	0.00	0.00	0.00	2.564
34	0.00	0.00	0.00	0.00	0.00	0.00	0.00	0.00	2.564

| | Normal Recovery Period | | | | | | Real Estate | | |
| | | | | | | | Residential | Nonresidential | |
Year	3%	5%	7%	10%	15%	20%	27.5%	31.5%	39%
35	0.00	0.00	0.00	0.00	0.00	0.00	0.00	0.00	2.564
36	0.00	0.00	0.00	0.00	0.00	0.00	0.00	0.00	2.564
37	0.00	0.00	0.00	0.00	0.00	0.00	0.00	0.00	2.564
38	0.00	0.00	0.00	0.00	0.00	0.00	0.00	0.00	2.564
39	0.00	0.00	0.00	0.00	0.00	0.00	0.00	0.00	2.564
40	0.00	0.00	0.00	0.00	0.00	0.00	0.00	0.00	0.107
41	0.00	0.00	0.00	0.00	0.00	0.00	0.00	0.00	0.000

Values for the Standard Normal Cumulative Distribution Function

d	N(d)	d	N(d)	d	N(d)	d	N(d)	d	N(d)	d	N(d)
-3.00	0.0013	-2.00	0.0228	-1.00	0.1587	0.00	0.5	1.00	0.8413	2.00	0.9772
-2.99	0.0014	-1.99	0.0233	-0.99	0.1611	0.01	0.504	1.01	0.8438	2.01	0.9778
-2.98	0.0014	-1.98	0.0239	-0.98	0.1635	0.02	0.508	1.02	0.8461	2.02	0.9783
-2.97	0.0015	-1.97	0.0244	-0.97	0.166	0.03	0.512	1.03	0.8485	2.03	0.9788
-2.96	0.0015	-1.96	0.025	-0.96	0.1685	0.04	0.516	1.04	0.8508	2.04	0.9793
-2.95	0.0016	-1.95	0.0256	-0.95	0.1711	0.05	0.5199	1.05	0.8531	2.05	0.9798
-2.94	0.0016	-1.94	0.0262	-0.94	0.1736	0.06	0.5239	1.06	0.8554	2.06	0.9803
-2.93	0.0017	-1.93	0.0268	-0.93	0.1762	0.07	0.5279	1.07	0.8577	2.07	0.9808
-2.92	0.0018	-1.92	0.0274	-0.92	0.1788	0.08	0.5319	1.08	0.8599	2.08	0.9812
-2.91	0.0018	-1.91	0.0281	-0.91	0.1814	0.09	0.5359	1.09	0.8621	2.09	0.9817
-2.90	0.0019	-1.90	0.0287	-0.90	0.1841	0.10	0.5398	1.10	0.8643	2.10	0.9821
-2.89	0.0019	-1.89	0.0294	-0.89	0.1867	0.11	0.5438	1.11	0.8665	2.11	0.9826
-2.88	0.002	-1.88	0.0301	-0.88	0.1894	0.12	0.5478	1.12	0.8686	2.12	0.983
-2.87	0.0021	-1.87	0.0307	-0.87	0.1922	0.13	0.5517	1.13	0.8708	2.13	0.9834
-2.86	0.0021	-1.86	0.0314	-0.86	0.1949	0.14	0.5557	1.14	0.8729	2.14	0.9838
-2.85	0.0022	-1.85	0.0322	-0.85	0.1977	0.15	0.5596	1.15	0.8749	2.15	0.9842
-2.84	0.0023	-1.84	0.0329	-0.84	0.2005	0.16	0.5636	1.16	0.877	2.16	0.9846
-2.83	0.0023	-1.83	0.0336	-0.83	0.2033	0.17	0.5675	1.17	0.879	2.17	0.985
-2.82	0.0024	-1.82	0.0344	-0.82	0.2061	0.18	0.5714	1.18	0.881	2.18	0.9854
-2.81	0.0025	-1.81	0.0351	-0.81	0.209	0.19	0.5753	1.19	0.883	2.19	0.9857
-2.80	0.0026	-1.80	0.0359	-0.80	0.2119	0.20	0.5793	1.20	0.8849	2.20	0.9861
-2.79	0.0026	-1.79	0.0367	-0.79	0.2148	0.21	0.5832	1.21	0.8869	2.21	0.9864
-2.78	0.0027	-1.78	0.0375	-0.78	0.2177	0.22	0.5871	1.22	0.8888	2.22	0.9868
-2.77	0.0028	-1.77	0.0384	-0.77	0.2206	0.23	0.591	1.23	0.8907	2.23	0.9871
-2.76	0.0029	-1.76	0.0392	-0.76	0.2236	0.24	0.5948	1.24	0.8925	2.24	0.9875
-2.75	0.003	-1.75	0.0401	-0.75	0.2266	0.25	0.5987	1.25	0.8944	2.25	0.9878
-2.74	0.0031	-1.74	0.0409	-0.74	0.2296	0.26	0.6026	1.26	0.8962	2.26	0.9881
-2.73	0.0032	-1.73	0.0418	-0.73	0.2327	0.27	0.6064	1.27	0.898	2.27	0.9884
-2.72	0.0033	-1.72	0.0427	-0.72	0.2358	0.28	0.6103	1.28	0.8997	2.28	0.9887
-2.71	0.0034	-1.71	0.0436	-0.71	0.2389	0.29	0.6141	1.29	0.9015	2.29	0.989
-2.70	0.0035	-1.70	0.0446	-0.70	0.242	0.30	0.6179	1.30	0.9032	2.30	0.9893
-2.69	0.0036	-1.69	0.0455	-0.69	0.2451	0.31	0.6217	1.31	0.9049	2.31	0.9896
-2.68	0.0037	-1.68	0.0465	-0.68	0.2483	0.32	0.6255	1.32	0.9066	2.32	0.9898
-2.67	0.0038	-1.67	0.0475	-0.67	0.2514	0.33	0.6293	1.33	0.9082	2.33	0.9901
-2.66	0.0039	-1.66	0.0485	-0.66	0.2546	0.34	0.6331	1.34	0.9099	2.34	0.9904
-2.65	0.004	-1.65	0.0495	-0.65	0.2578	0.35	0.6368	1.35	0.9115	2.35	0.9906
-2.64	0.0041	-1.64	0.0505	-0.64	0.2611	0.36	0.6406	1.36	0.9131	2.36	0.9909
-2.63	0.0043	-1.63	0.0516	-0.63	0.2643	0.37	0.6443	1.37	0.9147	2.37	0.9911
-2.62	0.0044	-1.62	0.0526	-0.62	0.2676	0.38	0.648	1.38	0.9162	2.38	0.9913

d	N(d)	d	N(d)	d	N(d)	d	N(d)	d	N(d)	d	N(d)
−2.61	0.0045	−1.61	0.0537	−0.61	0.2709	0.39	0.6517	1.39	0.9177	2.39	0.9916
−2.60	0.0047	−1.60	0.0548	−0.60	0.2743	0.40	0.6554	1.40	0.9192	2.40	0.9918
−2.59	0.0048	−1.59	0.0559	−0.59	0.2776	0.41	0.6591	1.41	0.9207	2.41	0.992
−2.58	0.0049	−1.58	0.0571	−0.58	0.281	0.42	0.6628	1.42	0.9222	2.42	0.9922
−2.57	0.0051	−1.57	0.0582	−0.57	0.2843	0.43	0.6664	1.43	0.9236	2.43	0.9925
−2.56	0.0052	−1.56	0.0594	−0.56	0.2877	0.44	0.67	1.44	0.9251	2.44	0.9927
−2.55	0.0054	−1.55	0.0606	−0.55	0.2912	0.45	0.6736	1.45	0.9265	2.45	0.9929
−2.54	0.0055	−1.54	0.0618	−0.54	0.2946	0.46	0.6772	1.46	0.9279	2.46	0.9931
−2.53	0.0057	−1.53	0.063	−0.53	0.2981	0.47	0.6808	1.47	0.9292	2.47	0.9932
−2.52	0.0059	−1.52	0.0643	−0.52	0.3015	0.48	0.6844	1.48	0.9306	2.48	0.9934
−2.51	0.006	−1.51	0.0655	−0.51	0.305	0.49	0.6879	1.49	0.9319	2.49	0.9936
−2.50	0.0062	−1.50	0.0668	−0.50	0.3085	0.50	0.6915	1.50	0.9332	2.50	0.9938
−2.49	0.0064	−1.49	0.0681	−0.49	0.3121	0.51	0.695	1.51	0.9345	2.51	0.994
−2.48	0.0066	−1.48	0.0694	−0.48	0.3156	0.52	0.6985	1.52	0.9357	2.52	0.9941
−2.47	0.0068	−1.47	0.0708	−0.47	0.3192	0.53	0.7019	1.53	0.937	2.53	0.9943
−2.46	0.0069	−1.46	0.0721	−0.46	0.3228	0.54	0.7054	1.54	0.9382	2.54	0.9945
−2.45	0.0071	−1.45	0.0735	−0.45	0.3264	0.55	0.7088	1.55	0.9394	2.55	0.9946
−2.44	0.0073	−1.44	0.0749	−0.44	0.33	0.56	0.7123	1.56	0.9406	2.56	0.9948
−2.43	0.0075	−1.43	0.0764	−0.43	0.3336	0.57	0.7157	1.57	0.9418	2.57	0.9949
−2.42	0.0078	−1.42	0.0778	−0.42	0.3372	0.58	0.719	1.58	0.9429	2.58	0.9951
−2.41	0.008	−1.41	0.0793	−0.41	0.3409	0.59	0.7224	1.59	0.9441	2.59	0.9952
−2.40	0.0082	−1.40	0.0808	−0.40	0.3446	0.60	0.7257	1.60	0.9452	2.60	0.9953
−2.39	0.0084	−1.39	0.0823	−0.39	0.3483	0.61	0.7291	1.61	0.9463	2.61	0.9955
−2.38	0.0087	−1.38	0.0838	−0.38	0.352	0.62	0.7324	1.62	0.9474	2.62	0.9956
−2.37	0.0089	−1.37	0.0853	−0.37	0.3557	0.63	0.7357	1.63	0.9484	2.63	0.9957
−2.36	0.0091	−1.36	0.0869	−0.36	0.3594	0.64	0.7389	1.64	0.9495	2.64	0.9959
−2.35	0.0094	−1.35	0.0885	−0.35	0.3632	0.65	0.7422	1.65	0.9505	2.65	0.996
−2.34	0.0096	−1.34	0.0901	−0.34	0.3669	0.66	0.7454	1.66	0.9515	2.66	0.9961
−2.33	0.0099	−1.33	0.0918	−0.33	0.3707	0.67	0.7486	1.67	0.9525	2.67	0.9962
−2.32	0.0102	−1.32	0.0934	−0.32	0.3745	0.68	0.7517	1.68	0.9535	2.68	0.9963
−2.31	0.0104	−1.31	0.0951	−0.31	0.3783	0.69	0.7549	1.69	0.9545	2.69	0.9964
−2.30	0.0107	−1.30	0.0968	−0.30	0.3821	0.70	0.758	1.70	0.9554	2.70	0.9965
−2.29	0.011	−1.29	0.0985	−0.29	0.3859	0.71	0.7611	1.71	0.9564	2.71	0.9966
−2.28	0.0113	−1.28	0.1003	−0.28	0.3897	0.72	0.7642	1.72	0.9573	2.72	0.9967
−2.27	0.0116	−1.27	0.102	−0.27	0.3936	0.73	0.7673	1.73	0.9582	2.73	0.9968
−2.26	0.0119	−1.26	0.1038	−0.26	0.3974	0.74	0.7704	1.74	0.9591	2.74	0.9969
−2.25	0.0122	−1.25	0.1056	−0.25	0.4013	0.75	0.7734	1.75	0.9599	2.75	0.997
−2.24	0.0125	−1.24	0.1075	−0.24	0.4052	0.76	0.7764	1.76	0.9608	2.76	0.9971
−2.23	0.0129	−1.23	0.1093	−0.23	0.409	0.77	0.7794	1.77	0.9616	2.77	0.9972

d	N(d)	d	N(d)	d	N(d)	d	N(d)	d	N(d)	d	N(d)
−2.22	0.0132	−1.22	0.1112	−0.22	0.4129	0.78	0.7823	1.78	0.9625	2.78	0.9973
−2.21	0.0136	−1.21	0.1131	−0.21	0.4168	0.79	0.7852	1.79	0.9633	2.79	0.9974
−2.20	0.0139	−1.20	0.1151	−0.20	0.4207	0.80	0.7881	1.80	0.9641	2.80	0.9974
−2.19	0.0143	−1.19	0.117	−0.19	0.4247	0.81	0.791	1.81	0.9649	2.81	0.9975
−2.18	0.0146	−1.18	0.119	−0.18	0.4286	0.82	0.7939	1.82	0.9656	2.82	0.9976
−2.17	0.015	−1.17	0.121	−0.17	0.4325	0.83	0.7967	1.83	0.9664	2.83	0.9977
−2.16	0.0154	−1.16	0.123	−0.16	0.4364	0.84	0.7995	1.84	0.9671	2.84	0.9977
−2.15	0.0158	−1.15	0.1251	−0.15	0.4404	0.85	0.8023	1.85	0.9678	2.85	0.9978
−2.14	0.0162	−1.14	0.1271	−0.14	0.4443	0.86	0.8051	1.86	0.9686	2.86	0.9979
−2.13	0.0166	−1.13	0.1292	−0.13	0.4483	0.87	0.8078	1.87	0.9693	2.87	0.9979
−2.12	0.017	−1.12	0.1314	−0.12	0.4522	0.88	0.8106	1.88	0.9699	2.88	0.998
−2.11	0.0174	−1.11	0.1335	−0.11	0.4562	0.89	0.8133	1.89	0.9706	2.89	0.9981
−2.10	0.0179	−1.10	0.1357	−0.10	0.4602	0.90	0.8159	1.90	0.9713	2.90	0.9981
−2.09	0.0183	−1.09	0.1379	−0.09	0.4641	0.91	0.8186	1.91	0.9719	2.91	0.9982
−2.08	0.0188	−1.08	0.1401	−0.08	0.4681	0.92	0.8212	1.92	0.9726	2.92	0.9982
−2.07	0.0192	−1.07	0.1423	−0.07	0.4721	0.93	0.8238	1.93	0.9732	2.93	0.9983
−2.06	0.0197	−1.06	0.1446	−0.06	0.4761	0.94	0.8264	1.94	0.9738	2.94	0.9984
−2.05	0.0202	−1.05	0.1469	−0.05	0.4801	0.95	0.8289	1.95	0.9744	2.95	0.9984
−2.04	0.0207	−1.04	0.1492	−0.04	0.484	0.96	0.8315	1.96	0.975	2.96	0.9985
−2.03	0.0212	−1.03	0.1515	−0.03	0.488	0.97	0.834	1.97	0.9756	2.97	0.9985
−2.02	0.0217	−1.02	0.1539	−0.02	0.492	0.98	0.8365	1.98	0.9761	2.98	0.9986
−2.01	0.0222	−1.01	0.1562	−0.01	0.496	0.99	0.8389	1.99	0.9767	2.99	0.9986
−2.00	0.0228	−1.00	0.1587	0.00	0.5	1.00	0.8413	2.00	0.9772	3.00	0.9987

Index

Pages in **bold** indicate the pages on which questions are asked.

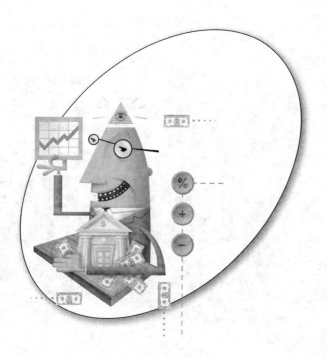

Financial Statements
DeMYSTiFieD

Hard stuff made easy™

Covers INCOME statements, BALANCE sheets, statement of STOCKHOLDERS' EQUITY, and statement of CASH FLOWS

Explains how to READ and INTERPRET financial statements accurately

Includes easy-to-understand explanations of PROFIT and LOSS

Complete with end-of-chapter QUIZZES and a FINAL EXAM

Bonita K. Kramer and Christie W. Johnson

All there is to know about financial statements— without the headache!

Contents

DeMYSTiFieD®

Hard stuff made easy

The DeMYSTiFieD series helps students master complex and difficult subjects. Each book is filled with chapter quizzes, final exams, and user friendly content. Whether you want to master Spanish or get an A in Chemistry, DeMYSTiFieD will untangle confusing subjects, and make the hard stuff understandable.

Intermediate Accounting DeMYSTiFieD
Geri B. Wink, CPA and Laurie Corradino
ISBN-13: 978-0-07173885-9 • $22.00

Investing DeMYSTiFieD, 2e
Paul J. Lim
ISBN-13: 978-0-07-174912-1 • $22.00

Corporate Finance DeMYSTiFieD , 2e
Troy A. Adair, Jr., Ph.D.
ISBN-13: 978-0-07-174907-7 • $22.00

Six Sigma DeMYSTiFieD, 2e
Paul Keller
ISBN-13: 978-0-07-174679-3 • $22.00

Learn more. **McGraw Hill** Do more.